Floating Vacations

River, Lake, and Ocean Adventures

MICHAEL WHITE

John Muir Publications
Santa Fe, New Mexico

John Muir Publications, P.O. Box 613, Santa Fe, NM 87504

First edition. First printing

Library of Congress Cataloging-in-Publication Data
White, Michael, 1940-
    Floating vacations : river, lake, and ocean adventures / Michael
White.—1st ed.
        p. cm.
    ISBN 0-945465-32-7
    1. Boats and boating.   2. Boat living.   I. Title.
    GV775.W54   1990   89-42942
    797.1—dc20   CIP

Distributed to the book trade by:

W. W. Norton & Company, Inc.
New York, New York

Front Cover Photos by Michael White, James Ulik, and Terry Conroy
Back Cover Photos (top to bottom) by Rick Friese, Santee Cooper Country, and
Michael White
Cover and Book Design by Susan Surprise
Map and Diagram Art by Janice St. Marie
Typography by Copygraphics, Inc., Santa Fe, N.M.
Printed by Banta

To Terry Ann Lane,
my First Mate

Contents

Part II: River Rafts and Canoes

Part III: Yachts

Introduction

A boat is like a magic carpet. On a boat, you can go places and do things that others only dream about. The spectacular North Woods are yours to explore the way the original explorers did, in a canoe. You experience the majestic Grand Canyon as a place to be—not just to look at—when riding a raft through it on the incredible whitewater of the Colorado River. The islands of the Caribbean become as accessible as your front yard when sailing among them on a yacht. Even the lakes and rivers near home offer adventure and new experiences when you cruise them on a houseboat. A boat lets you see the world in a new way, and it gives you a sense of freedom that landlubbers will never know.

People unfamiliar with boats seldom think about the possibility of taking a floating vacation. Most assume that boating experience is necessary. Not that many years ago, they would have been right—most boating vacations did require experience (or a lot of money).

But this is no longer true. Today, an incredible variety of boating vacations are available to people who have absolutely no prior experience. The fantasy can now become a reality.

The scope of this book is broad. We will look at boating vacations that range from primitive to luxurious—from "do-it-yourself" to full-service trips. The boats themselves vary from two-person portable canoes to magnificent yachts with full crews. These diverse vacations all have one thing in common: you do not need any boating experience to go on them.

Every boating vacation included in this book is professionally run by people trained and experienced in working with novice boaters. It is their business to see that you have a safe and enjoyable trip. They will provide you with instruction and equipment and assist you with the planning for trips you do on your own; on guided trips, they will take care of everything from running the boat to cooking meals. Most professionals agree that, even on the most demanding do-it-yourself trips, attitude is more important than experience. If a person is interested in learning and using new skills and is enthusiastic about the new adventure, he or she will do fine and have a great time. You can take a floating vacation even if your only knowledge of boats is that they float. That's what this book is all about: how even novices can turn "thinking about it" into doing it.

Although this book is written primarily for the beginner, it is also for the experienced boater who would like to expand his or her horizons. Even veteran boaters will probably find some new ideas and exciting alternatives here, some different ways to enjoy their love of boating. A vacation provides an excellent opportunity to try them out.

Most people think of a vacation as both an opportunity to see and do something different for a week or so and a chance to relax and escape from the pressures of work. Frequently, it is difficult to do both. All too often, a vacation that includes doing and seeing new things winds up being more hectic than life at home. Sometimes it hardly seems worth it. Yet it is true that the farther you can get from your usual life, the more of a vacation it is. The perfect vacation, then, would provide a chance to visit new places and do new things, plenty of time to relax, maybe a little adventure, and lots of memories to take home. This is what a floating vacation does.

Why is this "perfect vacation" not better known? Having been involved with recreational boating for many years—including five years in the Virgin Islands as the captain of *Esprit*, my own charter yacht—and having answered many questions about boating for people unfamiliar with it, I will venture a guess. Besides the mistaken belief that you need experience, there are several other common misconceptions about boating and boating vacations.

Let's clear the water. Boating vacations are not dangerous. It is highly unlikely you will get seasick, even in the open ocean and despite the fact that you did when you were eight years old and your dad took you fishing. You do not have to know how to swim. Sharks almost never attack people. Most boat trips are not physically demanding or that expensive.

The most serious danger involved in taking a boating vacation is that you could get hooked on boats. After years of cruising on houseboats, 25,000 miles at sea in sailing yachts, many miles on whitewater rivers in small boats ranging from inner tubes (I was young and foolish at the time) to the monstrous J-rigs used in the Grand Canyon—after more than ten years living on boats, I've still not had my fill. If someone says "boat," I'm ready to go. Beware—it could happen to you.

There are hundreds of places where boating vacations are available in North America or on islands easily accessible to the States. These are the vacations we will be looking at. The directories listed for each kind of vacation include more than 700 companies that provide tours, cruises, houseboat rentals, outfitting services, or expeditions. There is also a list of brokers you can use to book one of the several hundred independently operated charter yachts. This adds up to a lot of choices.

It is unlikely that you'll have a problem finding a vacation that meets your requirements. The problem will probably be how to choose among all the fantastic possibilities. For each type of vacation, we will look at the areas where it's available, the nature of the trip itself, and how to select the one that's best for you. After that, we will get into the "nuts and bolts" of planning and booking the trip and go through all the details you should know before leaving.

A Few Words about Words

To boating newcomers, boaters sometimes seem to be speaking a foreign language. Nautical terminology can be confusing, if not downright intimidating. Why don't boaters just say "the front of the boat" instead of letting you wander around trying to find a "bow"? But for many people, learning and using this new language is fun; it's part of the boating experience. I will use some of the more common ones (many of which are familiar even to non-boaters), putting the new word in quotes the first time it shows up and defining it in parentheses.

Remember, though, that it's OK to call the galley the kitchen if you want. It really makes no difference. The idea is to get out on the boat and have fun.

I
Houseboats

1 The Houseboat Experience

The captain eases back on the throttle and turns the wheel slightly. The fifty-foot boat glides closer to the tree-lined shore of the empty cove. A touch of reverse brings it to a stop as the anchor is dropped. He allows the boat to settle back and turns off the engine. The silence is broken by the shouts and splashes of the crew diving into the crystal-clear water of the cove. With a barely perceptible smile of satisfaction, the captain strolls out into the hot noonday sun of the foredeck. He has earned that feeling of satisfaction. You see, the captain's largest prior command was the family station wagon.

Over a quarter million people will take a houseboat vacation this summer. Many of them will have never been on a boat before they step aboard their vacation home. For a relatively small amount of money, they will be able to call their lives their own for a week, doing away with schedules, appointments, hotels, freeways, and most of the usual vacation problems that all too often leave us looking forward to getting back to work just to get some rest.

Instead, they will "park" their hotel room when and where they want and move it again when, and if, they feel like it. They will wake up each morning to the sounds of the birds and the water instead of car horns. There will be lazy days of exploring the remote areas of lakes and rivers and lying in the sun. Swimming, water skiing, wind surfing, fishing—any kind of water sport they want—will literally be at their doorstep. They'll have time to try new things, relax, and get to know their friends and family again. They will have found a real vacation.

The Houseboat

You can think of a houseboat as a floating mobile home, one that is not tied down to roads and crowded campgrounds. Some of the earlier models were exactly that: they built a mobile home on a platform instead of wheels and stuck pontoons and an engine on it. Today's modern houseboat is a far cry from those early models. Designed from the start as complete floating homes, they are marvels of simplicity and convenience.

Virtually all houseboats are planned with the same general concepts in mind: maximize the main living area (both inside and outside) and still provide sleeping accommodations for as many people as possible. The main living area usually takes up half, or more, of the interior of the boat. The rest of the boat consists of a sleeping area and several outside deck areas. The arrangement and use of space can vary greatly, but the basic idea of living, sleeping, and outside areas is common to all. (Chapter 3 covers specific sizes and designs and features to consider in making your choice.)

Most people are surprised to discover they can rent a houseboat and take it out for a week's vacation by themselves—even if they have never driven a boat before. The simple truth is that houseboating is easy. No operator's license is required, the boats are, in many ways, easier to drive than a car, and the waters where houseboats are available for rent are calm and protected. Slow and stately (10 mph is fast for a houseboat), they are the essence of peace and tranquillity.

The steering wheel on a houseboat works just like the one in your car. Engine controls are usually a simple three-position gearshift (forward, neutral, and reverse) and a throttle. In effect, it is the same as driving a car with an automatic transmission. Sometimes the gearshift and throttle are combined. You push it forward to go forward and pull it backward to go backward. There is more involved in the operation of a houseboat than just turning a wheel and moving a couple of levers, but that's all there is to the mechanical part.

Driving a "house" around on the water is a strange experience, particularly the first time you do it. There is something unreal about standing in a living room, watching the scenery go by. If it is your first time on a houseboat, you probably will not feel quite in control of the situation. Don't worry, you will probably be more in control than I was the first time.

The first houseboat I ever drove wasn't a rental. I did not have the advantages you'll have of a well-tested boat and a thorough checkout. It was a

The helm station on a houseboat is simple. In many ways, driving a houseboat is easier than driving a car. (Photo by Michael White)

brand-new 42-footer I had bought to live aboard on the Sacramento River. It had never even been in the water before the day the company brought it up by truck from Stockton, launched it, and turned it over to me. Over the next several years I would explore, with my floating home, most of the 1,000 miles of waterways that make up the California Delta. But the biggest vessel I had driven before that fine summer morning many years ago had been a 16-foot ski boat.

My friend Jerry, who lived on his own houseboat, had offered to help me get from the launching ramp to the marina a couple of miles upstream from my rental slip. "Remember," he said as I settled in behind the wheel, "the first rule of driving a houseboat is to take it slow and easy."

I nodded my understanding, put the shift in forward, added some power, and turned the wheel a little to the left to ease out into the river. The boat started going toward the bank on the right. "Isn't it supposed to go left when I turn the wheel left?" I asked, as I turned the wheel more to the left. The boat veered to the right.

Fortunately, I was following Jerry's advice to "take it slow and easy" and after several circles and some graceful "S" turns, we managed to get back to

The houseboat I owned and lived aboard for three years in Sacramento, shown here during a cruise of the California Delta in 1976. (Photo by Michael White)

the ramp, where the launching crew was packing up their gear. After a little poking around, a red-faced mechanic told us that the steering cables had been hooked up backwards on my new boat. In a few minutes he had them switched, and we set off again. Amazing—with the steering cables hooked up properly, driving a houseboat really was simple.

Your first experience will be a lot easier than mine. The houseboat you rent will have been thoroughly tested on the water before you arrive at the marina, and the rental company will have an instructor there to give you a complete checkout, which will cover all the basic information you need to know to run the boat. (Chapter 5 explains houseboat operation in detail.)

Houseboating Areas

Houseboats, because of their nature and design, are intended for use on calm water, which is where houseboat rental companies always have their operations. Occasionally, you will see a privately owned houseboat on an intercoastal canal or even a relatively calm ocean bay, but the ones available for vacation rental are always on well-protected inland waters.

Lakes are by far the most popular sites for houseboat vacations, but there are also companies based on rivers, canals, and even water systems that include all three. Although each location is unique, all provide near-perfect conditions for houseboating: calm, protected waters, short traveling distances, lots of places to tie up or anchor, and little in the way of current or navigational hazards.

Although there can be places on even the safest and most protected body of water where you can get into trouble if you really tried, the only thing you need to do to avoid them is follow the instructions of the rental company. You can be sure the people who rent you the houseboat are very familiar with their operating area and fully aware of any places that can present a problem either because of navigational hazards or because they are too open to be safe in a houseboat. Besides their concern for your safety, they have a strong self-interest in protecting their substantial investment in the houseboat. They will warn you emphatically about any potentially dangerous areas that might exist or, more likely, simply prohibit you from going there.

My own first houseboating area, the California Delta, is a good example. The delta is a houseboater's dream. There are hundreds of miles of canals and quiet rivers to explore. But a boat rented in the delta could be taken out into the Sacramento River and then on down to San Francisco Bay. From there, you could just head west under the Golden Gate Bridge and be on your way to Hawaii! (No, they would not let you do that—and you really wouldn't want to do it, even if you could.)

On a houseboat vacation, you set your own pace. You get up when you want, get under way when you want, and go where you want. You will probably spend a lot of time just exploring, seeing what is around the next bend or in the next cove. Between these adventures, you may just relax with a good book or sit down with your friends and solve the world's problems. You'll probably do some "water things": swimming, fishing, maybe some water skiing. And expect to do a lot of plain old loafing. After all, this is a vacation.

You can do these things regardless of where you choose to go. The key ingredients—a houseboat and water—will be there. Looked at from that standpoint, it doesn't matter much where the water is located. Every body of water is different, each has its own special attraction, but they are all good. I have never seen houseboats for rent at a bad place; a company wouldn't last long with an operation on the Los Angeles River.

The easiest answer to the question of where to go, therefore, is a place close to home. Even if you are already familiar with the area, it will still be a

new experience if this is your first time on a houseboat. Things look different from a boat, and there are good reasons for making this choice if you live
within a day's drive of a houseboating area (as the great majority of Ameri-
cans do). A location within driving range will mean less vacation time and
money spent getting there. In addition, there are no worries about packing
light for an airplane—just throw everything in the car and go. You will have
your own car there to use when you are getting provisions and taking side
trips.

There are also good reasons for traveling to a different location. Part of the
fun of a vacation is seeing new areas; variety really is the "spice of life." People
who live on the seashore like to go to the mountains on their vacation. City
folks like to go to the country. Southerners want to go North and Northerners
want to go South. It is the change that's significant: different scenery, cli-
mates, accents, foods, and so on.

Combining a vacation on a houseboat with a trip to another region can
add new dimensions to both experiences. The houseboat adventure is
enhanced because you really are exploring. It does not look like new territory
just because you are seeing it from a boat—it *is* new territory. There is a sense
of adventure that comes from watching animals you cannot identify run up
the bank or waking in the morning to the calls of strange birds.

Seeing a new area from a boat somehow makes you more a part of it. You
are not spending your time, as you probably would if you were land based,
just going to the same old tourist traps and meeting the same people you'd
meet at home. You're more aware of your surroundings, more in tune with
what makes the area special. And when you meet somebody from the local
area out on the water, you won't be just another tourist, you'll be another
boater.

Even if you live near a great houseboating site, consider going someplace
different—perhaps navigate a 150-year-old canal through nineteenth-
century villages set in quiet forests and countryside. Or voyage out onto a lake
so big that if you explored a dozen islands a day, it would take *years* to see
them all. Or cruise through majestic desert canyons three quarters of a mile
above sea level. Perhaps you would prefer to drift a river lined with giant trees
draped with Spanish moss and seek the solitude of a quiet backwater—your
only company the great blue heron stepping carefully through the marsh in
search of its dinner. Or maybe—just once—you'd like to be someplace where
the fishing really is as good as they said it would be.

You can do any of these things. The only problems are the time and cost involved in going beyond a reasonable driving range. You will probably have to fly and then, because most houseboat areas are somewhat remote, rent a car for transportation to the boat, provisioning, and taking side trips by land. Let's look more closely at the places mentioned above, how to find others like them, and the features that might make them worth the additional cost of an airline ticket and a rental car.

GETTING AWAY FROM IT ALL

You can get away from the crowd on even the smallest lake. But, generally speaking, the larger the cruising area, the easier it will be. If you really want to explore secluded areas, then you want a big, remote lake—like Lake of the Woods.

The size of a lake is usually given in surface acres of water. Brochures often will give you two other pieces of information: the number of miles of shoreline and the number of islands. Miles of shoreline is probably most important. It is the creeks and river to explore, the coves and inlets to anchor in, that give a lake character. A perfectly round lake without any islands would be boring even if it was immense.

A lake of 30,000 surface acres is good sized; one over 100,000 acres is big. Two or three hundred miles of shoreline will give you some room to explore; a big lake will have over a *thousand*. Most lakes have at least a few islands.

Now consider Lake of the Woods. This beautiful lake—located mostly in the province of Ontario but spilling over into Manitoba and the state of Minnesota—has 950,400 acres of water. That's a big lake. And it is not round. There are over 65,000 miles of shoreline to explore. Islands? Sure—over 14,000 of them. The best word to describe this lake is "incredible."

There are a couple of towns on the lake. Kenora, on the north end, is the largest and is well set up to handle the needs of boaters. Even the hospital has a dock. There is a free (during the daytime) city dock within easy walking distance of a market, several restaurants, the downtown shopping area, and a museum. But if you want abundant shoreside activities and tourist attractions, this is not the place to find them.

This is a wilderness lake. The plaintive call of the loon replaces the automobile horn. You could easily cruise for a week without having any contact with civilization. This is the kind of place you would go to get away from it all.

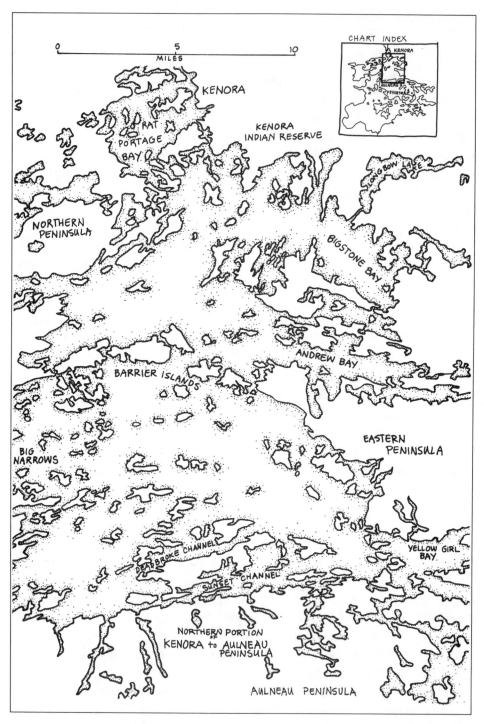

This small portion of the Lake of the Woods chart, showing only about 20% of the total area, gives some idea of the incredible opportunities for exploring which a large lake with lots of islands provides.

WILDLIFE

Remote wilderness lakes such as Lake of the Woods are fantastic places for observing wildlife. Deer and bear are seen along the water's edge, and moose can be spotted shoulder-deep in the water, grazing on the bottom grass. But there are many less remote areas where wildlife abounds.

Although all lakes and rivers have animals and birds living along their shores, the best ones—if wildlife is one of your priorities—will be those bordered by large areas of natural habitat that have remained unchanged for many years. Usually, these will be found where some kind of sanctuary has been created to stop, or at least minimize, the encroachment of civilization.

The St. Johns River is such a place. From its headwaters south of Cape Canaveral, it flows north (one of the few U.S. rivers to do so) about 170 straight-line miles to the city of Jacksonville in northern Florida. But the St. Johns River seldom follows a straight line. Instead, it meanders up the state, creating delightful coves, small islands, backwaters, and lakes.

The best houseboating is on the stretch of river running from Sanford to Palatka, where the river is protected along most of its west bank by the Ocala National Forest. This is an area of primeval beauty. Forests of cypress draped with Spanish moss, stately oak, and lines of palm reach high above the dense undergrowth guarding the riverbanks. Huge springs spout millions of gallons of fresh warm water, creating clear pools in the tea-colored river. Alligators lie drowsing in the sun. Deer and opossums make their way quietly through the trees. Ospreys circle high overhead in their endless hunt, while the stately herons and egrets stand patiently below.

This is not a remote area. It is only about twenty miles from Interstate 95 to this stretch of the St. Johns. And there are docks along the river (docks, not Miami-style marinas) where you can buy basic provisions or go for a night out at places with names like Blair's Jungle Den and the Blackwater Inn. Remember, if you choose a place that's in a park or recreation area for its feeling of remoteness and its wildlife, its accessibility makes it a compromise. On weekends, the river explodes in a frenzy of outboard motors and parties. But by Sunday night, it will be yours again; quiet, peaceful, and timeless.

RIVERS AND CANALS

Cruising on rivers, such as the St. Johns, and canals is different from cruising on a lake. There are some obvious differences—you don't just head out in any direction, you go where the river or canal goes—and some that may not be so obvious.

Most rivers and canals were first used for the transportation of people and goods, not for recreation. They were so used before the majority of our present-day lakes (most of which are man-made) even existed. The first inland settlements on the continent were usually along rivers. Many of these early towns and villages have preserved their heritage of centuries-old buildings and traditions. As a result, you will usually find much more of historical interest on a river trip than on a lake trip.

Cruising some of these areas, such as the Rideau Waterway in eastern Ontario, can be a little like taking a trip back in time. Over 150 years ago, a number of the lakes and rivers of the Rideau region were linked by a system of canals and locks connecting Kingston, on Lake Ontario, with the nation's capital in Ottawa. The architects of these canals did not design them for your cruising pleasure, but they couldn't have done a better job if that had been their intent. Using their system today, you can visit a variety of fascinating places—and go right into downtown Ottawa to see the capitol itself—from the comfort of your cruising home. This is the kind of vacation you would choose if you wanted a leisurely cruise through pastoral countryside with plenty of time set aside to tour historic towns and museums.

On a river, there is also a greater sense of going somewhere. It is difficult while cruising the Upper Mississippi River (the main houseboating area of the Mississippi is the stretch above the confluence of the Ohio River) not to think about what it means to be on the Mighty Mississippi. "Let's see," you say to yourself as La Crosse, Wisconsin, slides past your port beam, "we're making about nine knots and we have a little current going with us. At that speed, traveling fifteen hours a day, we could be in New Orleans in about ten days." Well, OK, maybe you won't do it, but knowing you *could* makes it more exciting.

Finally, you usually see more of what's ashore when you're cruising on a river rather than a lake. You will almost always be close to *two* shorelines— kind of like a "two for the price of one" sale.

Land-based Attractions

Many houseboating areas are also popular for land-based attractions that can be visited for a few days either before, during, or after your houseboat vacation. I do not mean places that have a few things to do ashore; almost all have those. I'm talking about places with major land-based attractions. Table Rock Lake is a good example.

Table Rock Lake, located in southern Missouri and extending into Arkansas, has 52,000 acres of water, 857 miles of scenic shoreline, and some great fishing. It is an excellent houseboating lake. It also has the advantage of being at the center of an extremely popular tourist area in the heart of the Ozark Mountain country. This area of rolling hills and long hollows forested with oak and cedar was the inspiration for Harold Bell Wright's novel, *The Shepherd of the Hills*. Its publication in 1907 started a tourist boom that is continuing; at present, about 2.5 million people visit the area every year. The original appeal was the beauty and quiet of the hill country. This is still there, but the major attractions now are man-made. All are within a short drive of the lake.

Silver Dollar City welcomes you to step back to the 1880s at a theme park devoted to preserving America's crafts heritage. The Shepherd of the Hills Homestead and Outdoor Theater has entertainment ranging from medicine shows to frog jumping contests, culminating at night with a play based on Wright's original novel. White Water invites you to "experience nine of the world's best water adventures," and Wilderness Safari tempts you to drive through its "wild animal kingdom." At night, you have "76 Country Boulevard." This strip of Highway 76 west of Branson boasts foot-stomping live country music shows that rival Nashville's—both in number and quality. Everything from bluegrass to country pop can be found at one of the twenty or so theaters on the strip.

If this sounds too hectic for you, but you still want a place with a lot to do ashore, consider an area where there is extensive public development. The northern end of Kentucky Lake—extending from western Kentucky down into Tennessee—is a good example. Kentucky Lake and its younger and smaller sister, Lake Barkley (they're linked at the north end by a canal), have a total of about 220,000 surface acres of water and a 3,600-mile shoreline. This is a big lake system with plenty of small creeks and wooded inlets to explore. The area between these two lakes, called, appropriately enough, Land Between the Lakes, has been developed by the Tennessee Valley Authority as a showplace of outdoor recreation, resource management, and environmental education.

This is an area of 170,000 heavily forested acres with 200 miles of hiking trails, twenty-three inland ponds stocked with fish, a nature center with a theater and natural history exhibits, a "living history" working re-creation of an 1850 farm, a buffalo herd, and a visitor center that has everything from a planetarium to a moonshine still. There are areas for camping, archery, hunting, horseback riding, and even a 2,350-acre off-road vehicle site. Although there are 300 miles of undeveloped shoreline to explore, you will need a car to visit most of the attractions. You get the best of both worlds—the unique-ness and convenience of a houseboat and all the attractions of a land-based vacation.

If you spend a lot of time visiting shore sights as part of your houseboat vacation (the cost of the boat should be about the same as a motel room in these tourist areas), it is convenient to have unlimited free use of the com-pany's docks during the week. This lets you pull back into your home dock, get into your car parked nearby, and just go. Ask the company ahead of time; some allow this, and some do not.

Even in places without many land-based attractions, you needn't spend all your time on the boat. A significant part of your time will probably be spent sightseeing, hiking, exploring, picnicking, laying about on the beach, and simply enjoying places you can't get to except by boat. It is, once again, a matter of the houseboat providing more options than you would have just on shore.

Frequently, your houseboat will take you right to an area's major attrac-tions. Some places, such as Lake Shasta Caverns on Lake Shasta in northern California, cannot even be reached by car. Landlocked vacationers can take a ferry out to explore these extensive caverns, but it is a lot easier—and a lot more fun—just to pull your houseboat up to the dock and step ashore for the tour. Lanier Islands, on Lake Lanier in Georgia, is another example. Although a causeway connects these resort islands to the mainland, why bother fight-ing traffic when you can just pull your boat up on a beach next to the Wild Waves water park, probably the most popular attraction on the islands? Featuring the South's largest wave pool, Wild Waves has a variety of water rides and a mile-long white sand beach. Being able to spend a day with a place like this for a front yard—particularly if the group includes children—is one of the attractions of a houseboat vacation.

Dining out is something special on a houseboat vacation. What could be more civilized than tying your boat up to a dock for the night and going ashore for dinner and a bit of partying? No problems with getting everybody organized—just decide on a time for dinner and turn the crew loose for shore leave. Everybody can do whatever they want: go shopping, do some sight-seeing, or conduct a comparative study of the local saloons. At the end of the evening, there is no driving to do—it's only a short walk home.

Of course, night spots vary from place to place. If there are towns along

Exploring the local bars and restaurants along rivers and canals adds a new dimension to houseboating. (Photo by Michael White)

the shore, you will be able to tie up and have your pick. If not, there are almost always marinas and resorts catering to boaters; these range from sumptuous to simple. Rivers and canals usually have the most places and the greatest variety. Some of those funky river-rat hangouts are a great experience, both eating and otherwise.

If eating out is high on your list, ask the rental company what is available in their area. Some will even send you restaurant descriptions.

2 Putting It Together

A houseboat vacation is a do-it-yourself adventure. If you were planning a cruise ship vacation (or a week at a resort, or a package tour), you would probably use a travel agency. After discussing several alternatives with the travel agent, you would make a decision and then sit back and write a check while the computer spun out your itinerary.

Not so with a houseboat vacation. You will gather all the information yourself, deal directly with the houseboat rental companies, make your choice of a boat, provision it, and plan your own itinerary. None of these tasks is difficult; they can even be fun. All of them will be easier if you approach them systematically, understand how rental companies operate, and know where potential problems might arise.

First, choose the location for your houseboating vacation. Second, get information on the companies and houseboats available there. If, at this point, you have several areas under consideration—or only a general idea as to the kind of area you want—that's OK; get information on every place that interests you. Obviously, you will still have to decide on a specific body of water before you choose a boat and make your final plans, but the information you gather will help you make that decision. Some of the topics discussed in the previous chapter might be important; other considerations are discussed below.

All houseboat rental companies have brochures describing their area, houseboats, services, and prices. Write, or call, each company at a potential vacation spot and request one (they're free). These brochures will be your primary source of information about individual companies and houseboats. Call them to get answers to any questions not covered in the brochures. Chapter 6 contains a directory with the addresses and telephone numbers of more than 200 houseboat rental companies.

Your Group

It should go without saying, but I will say it anyway: the most important thing about your group is that everyone should be compatible. In most cases, this simply means that they be family or friends who know they will enjoy spending a week aboard a houseboat together. Occasionally, problems arise because there is a certain amount of work to be done during a houseboat vacation. If one or two people get stuck with all of it, there could be some bad feelings—if not outright fights—by the end of the trip.

This doesn't mean you have to establish a formal work schedule. That would detract from the fun of being on vacation. People who know each other well enough to spend a week on a boat together should easily be able to work out (maybe without even talking about it) some kind of informal who-is-supposed-to-do-what arrangement. Above all, do not let one person get stuck with all the work. (It *is* Mom's vacation, too.)

Someone will sign the rental contract and become the captain, making him or her legally responsible for the boat. This doesn't mean he or she has to *really* be the captain. Someone has to be in charge during certain maneuvers, but the rest of the time, you can have co-captains or no captain at all. Just avoid the dreaded "Captain Bligh Syndrome." Signing a rental contract does not give the "captain" the right to declare a mutiny and shoot anyone who disagrees with him.

Should you take children on a houseboat vacation? By all means. Most children love the adventure of being on a houseboat for a week, trying new things and having new experiences. A houseboat vacation is a great learning opportunity for children.

Safety is not a big problem. Of course, very small children and nonswimmers should wear life vests on any outing near water. But houseboats do not tip over, go fast, or do anything else that would make this vacation any more dangerous than staying at a lake resort for a week. The children might even be safer; there is no traffic for them to walk into, it is hard for them to get lost, and they are almost always within shouting distance.

In choosing a boat, give special attention to safety features such as the adequacy of the guardrails, the layout of the top deck, and the ease of using the swim ladder (see chap. 3). If the brochure does not provide enough information, call the company, tell them you are bringing children, and ask them to describe these features to you. Aside from that, safety is a matter of instruction and a few simple rules. See chapter 5 for some specific suggestions.

Call the company and ask about taking pets if they are not covered in the brochure. Some companies do not permit them, and occasionally, an additional fee or special security deposit will be required. You are responsible for any damage or mess they cause.

When to Go

An important consideration in planning your houseboat vacation is what time of year to go. If your schedule is open, pick the best time of year for thth location; if it is not, pick a good location for the time of year you must go.

Weather is a crucial factor. Do not go to the far north in April if you want warm sunny days (most northern operations do not open until May 1), and avoid the desert in August if you dislike the heat. Cost, countryside appearance, crowds, and water level are also subject to seasonal variations.

The "high season" for houseboat rentals is the summer, which varies in length from place to place. At Lake Powell, for example, on the Utah-Arizona border, the peak season for pricing purposes is from May 15 until October. Compare that to Lake of the Woods in Ontario, where the peak season runs from July 1 to August 14.

Each area's dates are based on peak business times—in other words, the dates most vacationers think are best for that area. Although these dates (listed in every company's brochure) are a good guide, remember that they are based on when "most" people want to go. In some areas, early spring can be a delight. In others, a cruise in the fall, with the leaves changing color and the first nip of winter in the air, could be the ideal choice.

These days, you can expect all but the most remote areas to be crowded during the midsummer peak season. Just how crowded depends on the size of the body of water and the number of boats operating there.

There are advantages to areas with lots of boats: more marinas, more and better places to shop, and more to do ashore. If you do not want these advantages—if you seek peace and solitude—plan your trip for the early spring or late fall. At either time, you can expect to find considerably fewer people on the water.

Possibly the most important concern—particularly if you are going to a lake—is the water level. Most lakes are now controlled by dams. The agency in charge of the dam considers many factors in deciding how much water to release during a summer; recreational boating is usually way down the list. On some lakes, especially in dry years, the water will be much lower at the end of the summer than it was in the spring. Whether this is a problem depends on how low "low" is and how important it is to you. You can still pursue most water activities even if the water is very low. The main differences are in the scenery and the ease of getting between the boat and the normal shoreline (both for loading the boat and for exploring). There could also be navigational restrictions at low water, making some areas of the lake impossible to get to.

If you plan to take a lake trip late in the season (after August 1), ask the rental people about the water level. Do not settle for answers like "a little low" or "about normal." Such descriptions mean different things, depending on the lake and what area residents are used to. Late in the drought summer of 1988, I went to a place where, before coming, I was warned that the lake was "way down." I found the level less than ten feet below the tree line and the newly exposed shore mostly covered with grass. At another lake that same

At the lake shown above, the water level was described as ''a little below normal.''
(Photo by Michael White)

year, I was told that the water level was "a little below normal," as I gazed across rock and dirt at a tree line 135 feet above my head.

Ask how many feet below the high-water line the lake is or, if your vacation is still some time off, how many feet below high water they expect it to be when you arrive. "Feet below the high-water line" is a standard way to objectively describe a lake's level.

If you have any doubts, or if the houseboat company is suspiciously vague, call the agency in charge of the lake and ask them. They have the best information and no reason to be anything other than honest with you. Some even maintain special consumer lines to provide such information.

Fishing

Every lake, river, and canal has fish in it, and since all fishermen are liars, each will be touted as having the biggest, the most, and the hungriest fish on the planet. There is no question more difficult to get a straight and honest answer to than, "How's the fishing?"

The best approach is to be more specific. Has the area yielded any record fish? Do they have any fishing tournaments? If they do, request a copy of last year's results. If not, and the fishing is so great, why not? Ask what time of year is best (see below for how to judge the answer to this trick question).

If you are considering a place like Lakes Marion and Moultrie in the Santee Cooper country of South Carolina, it will not take much questioning to find out you have a shot at catching trophy-size fish. These lakes (connected by a canal) were created in 1941 to provide hydroelectric power for the war effort. A huge stand of cypress trees was flooded, and today this excellent natural habitat is a major reason these are among the best bass and catfish lakes in the country, having yielded several world and state records. (The fishermen in the area will be more than happy to give you species, year, and weight for each of them.) Among these records are a 55-pound striped bass (the world record until 1977) and a 58-pound channel catfish (a state record). Now those are fish worth getting excited about!

Tournaments, particularly bass tournaments, have become very popular. Tournament results provide proof of the size and type of fish you can expect to find at the host lake. If there are no tournaments in the area, the fishing probably is not good enough to attract top fishermen.

As any fisherman knows, the time of year you go fishing is important. Generally, it is better in the early spring and late fall. You should automati-

You have to be in the right place at the right time, and know what you are doing, to catch fish like this. (Photo courtesy of Santee Cooper Counties Promotion Commission)

cally distrust anyone who tells you the fishing is *always* great where they are. It may always be good—it may be much better than you have at home—but the only "always" is that certain times of the year are better than others. If fishing is your main reason for choosing a site, be there at its peak fishing season. And remember that "always" may mean "seldom."

If the company cannot answer your fishing questions, ask for the names of some local guides and call them. If they cannot give you the name of a local guide, forget it. Any lake or river with good fishing will have some guides working it.

If you are serious about catching fish, consider hiring a guide, at least for the first day or two. What they can show you, both in terms of areas and techniques, may well make the difference between a week of frustration and a week of fish dinners. I consider myself a fair fisherman, but my first time after walleye on a lake in Minnesota would have been a disaster if I hadn't had a guide. As it was, I spent most of the day—with him picking the spots and showing me how to fish them—trying to figure out why he was catching all the fish. By midafternoon, I was landing fish, but I wouldn't have been without Charley along.

A good fishing lake is not necessarily some bleak place without appeal to the nonfisherman. For example, the southern end of Lake Marion—mentioned above for its trophy fish—is a fascinating place. The flooded cypress forest is alive and flourishing in this part of the lake. You can drive into it with your houseboat, tie up in the shade, and go ashore at one of the many small, uninhabited islands sitting among the trees. Many of these islands' beaches would make excellent campsites for the nonfisherman during the day or places for everyone to sit around a fire at night. You could even sleep ashore if you wanted.

Cost

The cost of a houseboat vacation varies considerably, depending on the area, the season, the number of people in the group, and the size of the boat. Since prices are generally based on the boat's sleeping capacity—not the size of the group—the cost per person will primarily depend on how many are aboard (this is covered in detail in chap. 3). The other major variable is the season; off-season rentals in some areas are as much as 50 percent less than in peak season.

Rental fees do not include food and beverages, which you will generally provide. In a few cases, the company will do it for an additional fee. You should plan on spending about $250 per person per week for the peak-season rental of a houseboat large enough to provide considerable comfort and privacy. An off-season rental of a houseboat just large enough to accommodate your group will cost less than half that much. These prices add up to one of the best vacation bargains you will ever find.

Houseboat Rental Companies

The houseboat rental company provides you with a houseboat equipped as called for in your contract as well as the instruction and help you need to safely operate and enjoy it. There is much more to this job than meets the eye.

Consider what happens in the middle of a busy season between the time that other group pulls the houseboat into the dock in the morning and your group gets on in the afternoon. Company workers clean the boat from top to bottom; check and fill the fuel, water, and propane tanks; change the linen; inventory all removable or disposable items and replace them where necessary; perform routine maintenance (oil changes, engine checks, safety inspections); and fix any mechanical problems that occurred during the last week. A large company could have twenty or thirty boats turning around on one

These early morning fishermen appreciate the versatility of having an auxiliary boat along, and so do those that would rather stay ''home'' and sleep in.
(Photo by Michael White)

On rivers such as the St. Johns, you just pick a place you like and tie your house-boat up to the bank. (Photo by Michael White)
Inset: A modern houseboat can provide all the comfort and convenience of a shoreside apartment, and you can take it with you when you go exploring.
(Photo courtesy of Three Buoys Houseboats)

Shasta Lake is one of the most popular houseboating lakes in North America, but you can still find that ideal private cove. (Photo courtesy of John F. Reginato)

For the sheer thrill of running whitewater, it's hard to beat being part of the team on one of the smaller paddle-driven rafts. (Photo courtesy of Whitewater Voyages)
Inset: The guides on this Green River trip didn't tell us why we were pulling over to the bank, but after the first person stepped into the hot spring, we figured it out in a hurry. (Photo by Michael White)

You don't spend all your time on a river rafting expedition running whitewater; much of it will be spent leisurely drifting along and enjoying the scenery.
(Photo by Michael White)

*There's a distinct sense of adventure and exhilaration that comes with traveling
the North Woods by canoe the way the original explorers did.
(Photo courtesy of North Country Canoe Outfitters)
Inset: Bighorn sheep, cow moose, and wood duck. (Photos courtesy of David Rosen)*

A motor yacht like this 72-footer will usually provide more luxury than a sailing yacht of the same length. You'll also be paying more for the additional comfort of such things as the elegant main salon shown above. (Photos courtesy of Rick Friese)

It's impossible to sail a resort over to the next island to explore a deserted beach, but it's easy with your own yacht. (Photo courtesy of James Ulik)

A group of six can charter a yacht like this 60-footer, complete with crew and all provisions, for about the same amount they would spend on a vacation at a resort. (Photo by Rick Friese)
Inset: Sailing yachts typically have more traditional wood interiors. (Photo by Rick Friese)

day. At the same time, they are meeting new arrivals, helping them get settled, and giving checkouts to groups who are ready to go.

The company's assistance does not stop when you leave the dock. If you have a problem or question during the week, they will be there to take care of it. Usually, you'll have a two-way radio on the boat with which you can call "base." If the problem cannot be solved on the radio, someone will be sent in a chase boat to help you.

It is a big job, and you want a houseboat company that can handle it. Most companies can. They are competing not only with the "usual" vacations (which are much better known and accepted by the public) but with a few hundred other houseboat companies as well. They have to do a good job to survive, let alone show a return on their quite sizable investments. As a result, companies that have made it for a few years should be good at what they do.

Although the major difference between companies will be in the houseboats they offer, there also will be variations in the way the boat is equipped, company procedures, and the terms of their rental agreements. These can be important. Even if you choose a location where only one company operates (this applies to about half the destinations listed in chap. 6) or select a company (as most people do) simply because it has the houseboat that most appeals to you, pay attention to these details; they can greatly affect the planning of your trip.

Booking Procedures and Contracts

The procedures for booking your houseboat will be spelled out in the company's brochure. These can range from simple statements of how much the deposit is and when the balance is due to full-fledged contracts that would make a lawyer cringe. The following terms, conditions, and procedures are— with the variations noted—fairly standard. Again, there will be differences from company to company, sometimes significant ones, so read the brochure carefully. Avoid surprises at the dock, such as not having a boat waiting for you.

Captain's requirements. No license is required for the operation of a houseboat. The only requirement is that the person who signs the contract, thereby taking responsibility for the boat, be a responsible adult.

Reservations and deposits. Your reservation for a houseboat is not confirmed until a deposit is received by the company. The amount of the deposit is usually $200 to $300. Some companies let you confirm by telephone as long as your deposit is received within a reasonable period of time, usually seven days. Others will confirm by telephone and put the deposit on your credit card. Most simply require you to include the deposit with your written request for a reservation. Remember: you *do not* have a houseboat reserved until you have made a deposit. This can be critical if you want to go during a popular vacation time such as the 4th of July. Reservations for these weeks should be made—and confirmed with a deposit—several months ahead.

Deposits do not usually apply toward the rental fee. They are kept as a security deposit and will be refunded in full if the boat is returned on time, undamaged, and reasonably clean. I have seen contracts that call for a *second* deposit to be made at the time of boarding (without saying what happened to the first one). Always know what you are paying for.

Rental fees. You are usually required to pay the full rental fee 30 days prior to your boarding date (a few companies say 45 days). Some companies allow payment to be made at time of boarding; cash or traveler's checks, please.

Miscellaneous charges. Any extra charges for things such as insurance, pets, early boarding, or the rental of extra equipment will normally be paid at the same time as the houseboat rental payment.

Insurance coverage is usually included in the rental cost. Ask about insurance if it is not mentioned in the brochure. Some companies do have extra insurance charges, usually to reduce the amount of the deductible. Most companies do not, however, so consider these charges part of your rental fee when comparing prices.

The cost of fuel is extra. You will receive the boat with full tanks and be charged for the amount you have actually used when you return it.

Cancellations. If you cancel after making your deposit but before making the final payment, there is usually no problem. A service fee will be deducted (20 to 50 percent), and the balance of your deposit will be refunded.

If you cancel after you make the final payment, you could have problems. Most companies will return the rental fee and keep the deposit (or a portion of it) even if you cancel after the date the full rental payment is due. Some only return the rental fee "if your boat is rebooked." Since you usually do not have a specific boat booked—just a general reservation—this means they will have to book *all* their boats for your time period before you get your money back. If you were booked for a busy time, the chances of getting a refund are good; they are not so good if you were booked for off-season. A few companies keep the deposit and the full rental fee regardless of the reason for cancellation or whether they rebook the boat.

Nobody books a boat expecting to cancel. But unexpected things do happen. If possible, choose a company with a reasonable cancellation policy.

Condition of the boat. The boat will be turned over to you clean and in good condition; you are expected to return it the same way. You are not responsible for any mechanical problem or damage unless you cause it. If there is a problem with the boat which could affect your safety or comfort, get it fixed before you leave the dock. Make sure even minor damage or problems are noted by the staff so you are not blamed—and charged—for them when you return the boat.

The company is responsible for fixing any mechanical breakdowns that occur while you have the boat. Problems are unlikely, but they occur; the company should make every effort to get you going again as soon as possible. Usually, they will send a mechanic in a chase boat to fix the problem; occasionally, you will have to bring the boat back to the dock for repair. If there is a major problem, they will give you another boat if one is available.

If a delay becomes substantial, you should be entitled to a partial refund of your rental fee for the lost time. A problem fixed within an hour or two (as most of them are) is usually no more than a minor inconvenience. You can usually do the same things while the mechanic works that you would have been doing anyway. If you do need a minor repair, do not get upset with the company or bother making a claim for what would be a small refund.

Occasionally, you will see a contract clause that says the company is not responsible for loss of use due to mechanical breakdowns. That is, if you got on board and the engine wouldn't start, you could technically spend the entire week waiting for them to fix it and they would not be required to give you a refund. Although that would never happen, you should be reluctant to sign a contract with this clause in it, both because it is unfair—they should be responsible for any mechanical problems—and because it may say something about their faith in their boats. After all, who knows their equipment better than they do? Ask them to strike the clause. If they won't, consider using another company.

Boarding and return times. The boarding time is when you can first go on board; return time is when you must have the boat back at the dock. Boarding time is usually stated as a time period (for example, 2:00 p.m. to 5:00 p.m.) as opposed to "any time after" a certain hour. This is because they need to have someone there to show you around the boat and give you your checkout. If you plan to arrive late, or if you are delayed, talk to the company and see if they can make special arrangements for you. If you arrive late without doing this, you may not be able to get checked out in time to get under way that day; in fact, you may not even be able to board the boat.

Some companies offer an "early boarding" option. If available, this can be a real convenience and a money saver. Early boarding allows you to sleep aboard the boat at a reduced rate (at the dock) the night before your scheduled departure. The charge for this is usually less than half the normal daily rate; sometimes it is even free. If this option appeals to you, ask about the possibility even if it's not mentioned in the company's brochure. If the boat is available, they might agree to it.

Return time will be a definite hour. Returning your boat late subjects you to an hourly penalty stiff enough to get your attention (properly so; your late return could delay someone else's vacation).

Some companies board in the afternoon, some in the morning; some have their return time in the afternoon, some in the morning. Any combination is possible. You will have to plan your trip around these times. Also, pay attention to boarding times when comparing prices. A "week" that starts at 5:00 p.m. and ends at 9:00 a.m. is not really a week.

Sources for Further Information

The brochures provided by houseboat rental companies primarily tell you about their boats and services and usually provide only general information about their area. For more complete information, write or call the tourism departments, chambers of commerce, and national forests, parks, or recreation areas near your destination for their information packages. These are almost always free and usually contain all the information you need.

Start with the tourism department for the state or province. Most have elaborate magazine-style booklets, often 100 pages or more, containing detailed, up-to-date information. Then contact the local towns, regional associations, and other sources listed for your specific area of interest. Local organizations frequently have the best and most complete information; often they will send you individual brochures for the area's tourist attractions. Don't forget to use directory assistance for toll-free numbers (1-800-555-1212) when trying to reach these offices.

Once you have received all the information, picked a location, and familiarized yourself with the booking procedures and contracts, you are ready for the fun part—choosing a houseboat.

3 Your Floating Home

Condominiums do not float. Neither do mountain cabins, resorts, or motel rooms. Every time you want to go someplace, you have to pack everything in the car and drive there. If you want to go fishing or swimming, you have to walk or drive to the water. Every morning when you get up and look out the window, you have the same view. The room you rent is a place to sleep; it does not go with you and become a central part of your vacation. A houseboat does.

This is one of the great things about a houseboat vacation—the freedom to be able to move your entire house somewhere else whenever the mood strikes you. Because you can do this, and because the houseboat is very much a self-contained unit, you will probably spend a lot more of your vacation time on the boat than you would in that motel room. You will sleep, eat, play, and travel on your houseboat. Choosing the right one is, therefore, considerably more important than picking a motel. Let's take a quick "walk-through" to get oriented and then examine, in detail, some of the features to consider in making your choice.

Houseboats today are built both in the conventional way—on pontoons —and on regular boat hulls. Rental houseboats range from about 36 feet to over 60 feet in length. Most are still simple boxlike designs, but some of the newer models have quite graceful lines. In some cases, the distinction between houseboats and power cruisers is starting to blur.

The main living area is almost always located "forward" (toward the front

Houseboats built on hulls instead of pontoons have many of the characteristics of a power cruiser. (Photo by Michael White)

of the boat) in a houseboat. Most of the main living area will be furnished for eating and lounging. The furniture will usually include one or two couches that convert to beds (called "gaucho beds" on the West Coast) and a dining area. The dining area will be either a dinette or a regular table and chairs. A dinette usually converts to a bed. The "helm" (the place where you drive the boat) will be located all the way forward on the right side. The final, and some would say most important, thing found in this area is the "galley" (kitchen).

Every houseboat is equipped with a galley sufficient to store and prepare all the food needed for a week on the water. Some are fairly basic, but most larger houseboats have galleys that rival the kitchens found in modern apartments. These will have spacious open areas with lots of counter and sink space and plenty of cupboards and drawers (already stocked with a full table service and a complete selection of cooking utensils). There will be a built-in stove with oven, a refrigerator/freezer, and, on some boats, even a microwave. Most will also have basic small appliances such as toasters, coffee makers, and blenders. In short, virtually everything you need will be provided.

Located "aft" (toward the back of the boat) of the main living area are the sleeping quarters. These will consist of one or more "cabins" (the bedrooms, although the word can be used to refer to any compartment) and "heads" (bathrooms). Sleeping arrangements differ significantly from boat to boat. Some have large private cabins with just one "berth" (bed), and others use almost a dormitory approach. Bunk beds, pullouts, and fold-downs are common. In addition, almost all boats have convertible sleeping arrangements (as described above) in the main living area. The head will be equipped with a toilet, a shower, and a sink with a mirror and vanity. Some boats even have a tub.

The outside decks consist of the "foredeck" (on the front of the boat), the "aft deck" (on the back of the boat), "side decks" (along the sides of the boat), and the "top deck" (right, the one on the roof). The foredeck will be one of the most popular places on your boat. Large, open, and equipped with a permanent awning, it is the perfect place to lounge about "under way" (when the boat is moving), enjoying the cool breeze and the perfect view ahead. This deck also becomes a natural extension of the main living area—sort of like your backyard or patio at home—when the boat is "anchored" (stopped with its anchor down; on a houseboat, you will probably beach the boat or tie it up a lot more than anchor it, but more of that later). The foredeck on many boats is equipped with extra chairs and tables for outside lounging and dining. The barbecue, if provided, is also there.

If the foredeck is the backyard, then the aft deck is the garage. It is smaller than the foredeck and is usually unshaded and functional. This is where the engine access and fuel tanks will be and where any other large items will be stored. The ladder to the top deck is generally on the aft deck.

The top deck is for sun lovers: it has a 360-degree view from a large open area ten feet above the water. On some boats, this deck is completely bare—just a ladder to get up on top. On others, it will be elaborately equipped with tables, chairs, carpeting, and complete safety rails. Some even have a "flying bridge" (a separate control station located on the top deck) and a penthouse sleeping area.

The side decks are primarily for moving fore and aft on the outside of the boat, which is helpful when docking or otherwise maneuvering in close quarters or when a cabin is occupied (on most boats, you must walk through the cabins to get from one end to the other).

In all probability, you will select your houseboat without ever actually seeing it. Each company's brochure describes their company, their area, and their houseboats, along with pictures and floor plans. Most of the information you need to make a decision will be there; the rest you can get from calling the company. As with all brochures, however, it is designed to sell a product. It will praise the boats' virtues (some of which may be of no importance to you) and fail to mention their shortcomings (some of which might be). At some point, you and your group will probably end up sitting around a kitchen table covered with these brochures, each one describing a number of different boats. Although there are similarities, every boat is different. The variety of features and floor plans is bewildering. How do you choose the right one?

The key is knowing what to look for. This, in turn, means realistically looking at the requirements of your particular group and matching them to the boats available. You might not find a boat that is perfect for you in every way. It comes down to deciding what is important and what is not; what are you willing to give up to get something else? A good way to start is by making two lists: one for those features you regard as "essential" and another for those that are "desirable." Here are some guidelines to consider.

What Size?

The question of size seems simple. The brochure tells you how many the boat "sleeps." If you have eight people, you get an "eight sleeper," right? Not necessarily.

The first question most people ask when looking at a new boat is, "How many does she sleep?" They apparently believe that the more beds a boat has, the bigger (therefore better) it is. Those familiar with boats know this frequently is not true.

The people who build and market houseboats, and the companies that rent them, know that bed space usually is the first criterion, valid or not, by which their product is judged, so houseboats are built to sleep as many people as the designer can find space for. They have beds everywhere. It sometimes seems that the only things designers have not made convertible to a bed are the helm and the galley sink (and they are no doubt working on that).

Of course, bed space is not all a marketing gimmick. Many people do want a boat capable of sleeping the largest number of people possible. Houseboat rental prices, as previously mentioned, almost always are established as a price for the boat (the same as for a rental car). The more berths filled, therefore, the cheaper it will be for each person. A few companies will even allow you, for a slight additional charge, to take *more* people than there are berths for. If economy is your prime concern, the question really is, "How many will she sleep?"

Before deciding to fill every berth, however, seriously consider what this savings in money is going to cost you in privacy. Some boat designs do allow for a reasonable amount of privacy—providing curtains, folding partitions, and doors to separate the sleeping areas. But many have two double beds (either double bunk beds or side by side) in the same cabin, and a few even add a third convertible—making one cabin the sleeping quarters for six people! This may be fine for a group of kids, but many adult couples would find sharing a cabin for a week with two other couples—and sleeping within 18 inches of them—unacceptable even if they were best friends. If you were traveling with another couple on a land-based vacation, would you plan on saving money by sharing a single room with double beds? If the answer is no, then you probably do not want to do it on your boating vacation.

Look closely at what the real savings are. Planning to fill every berth on a boat might well be a false economy. The question of size is not just one of sleeping accommodations. Larger boats also mean more room generally—more living space, more storage space, larger (and usually better-equipped) galleys, and more outside deck area. Examine the floor plans carefully and work out the actual additional cost of choosing one that allows for a little more room and privacy—not necessarily a private cabin for everybody, just a little more room. Often, the cost increase per person is considerably less than you would have expected and probably worth the extra comfort.

Most companies do not even recommend taking the maximum number of people they allow on the boat, primarily because their experience has shown that any negative comments about a trip usually come from someone who was on a boat filled to capacity. When you get 14 people on a 56-foot boat, some friction is not surprising.

If yours is a family group that is used to living together or a young (in fact or at heart), gregarious gang in search of a week-long party, then, by all means, pack them in, save some money, and have a great time. If not, you should plan on a larger boat than is absolutely necessary.

The Multiple-Boat Option

If your group is large, you may not find a boat at your chosen location which is big enough to take all of you in comfort. The answer is simple: take two boats. Or three. Or six. No rule says you all have to be on the same boat.

The multiple-boat option has some definite advantages, the most important of which is greater flexibility. Say you have fourteen people on one boat; half want to go explore the town, and half want to go fishing. Problem. If you have the same group on two boats—no problem. Simply pick a cove that looks good and set a time to meet there. Then the town people take one boat and the fishermen the other. Simple.

There are other advantages in being able to better satisfy individual preferences. Some might want to party all night, while others would rather go to bed early. Some might want to pay the additional money to get a boat that allows them a private cabin, while for others it is not worth it. Adults might want to get away from the kids for a while (and vice versa). Taking more boats is the solution to many of these problems.

If you do plan a multiple-boat trip, try to get boats equipped with two-way radios (or take along CBs). They are a big help in organizing and keeping track of your fleet.

Design Features

The Galley

Houseboat galleys range from adequate to elegant. All will meet the fundamental requirements of providing some means of cold storage, a stove, and basic cooking, serving, and eating utensils. Many will furnish virtually everything you would have in your kitchen at home, including standard electric appliances. Microwaves are becoming common, and some boats even have trash compactors and dishwashers.

There is one item you should pay particular attention to—the refrigerator. Although very few modern boats are without any refrigerator (supplying ice boxes only), there are big differences in the size. A large refrigerator with a freezer is an advantage on a houseboat.

The question of how important a large well-equipped galley is depends on the size of your group and how elaborate your meals will be. The answer should probably be left to those who are going to do the cooking. There is nothing worse than a grouchy cook.

The Top Deck

There is probably more diversity in top decks than in any other component of a houseboat. At one end of the scale are those with a ladder to the top of

The galleys on many houseboats rival the kitchen in a modern apartment.
(Photo by Michael White)

the boat and nothing more. Not even guardrails. At the other end are models
that effectively double your living space by turning the top deck into a true
second story. This is a feature that deserves your special attention. An enjoyable top deck area will add significantly to the pleasure of your houseboat
vacation and often will become the most popular spot on the boat. Consider
putting a superior top deck on the "essential" list, particularly if your group
likes to spend a lot of time outside.

What makes a "superior" top deck? The first thing to look for is substantial guardrails (some have low walls) all the way around the outside of the
deck. Not only are these an important safety consideration but they make the
area more comfortable by providing a sense of security. It is difficult to relax
if you feel like you're hanging on for dear life.

Guardrails should be high enough and strong enough to keep an adult
from falling over the side. It is common to see boats with a single rail about
six inches high running along each side of the deck. These are sufficient to
keep someone lying down from rolling over the side, but that's about all. Substantial guardrails are, by themselves, enough to transform the top deck into
a true living area instead of just a place to sit or lie in the sun.

A flying bridge adds a lot of room and versatility to a houseboat. (Photo by Michael White)

A "superior" top deck should also have some kind of seating—chairs, lounges, benches, cushions; something to sit or lie on besides the deck. These may either be built-in or movable (see Extra Equipment, below).

Having a flying bridge allows you to operate the boat from the top deck. There are three advantages in being able to do so: first, it allows the person at the helm to join in with the rest of the group when everybody is on top; second, the 360-degree view from the flying bridge can be a real help in navigating and maneuvering; and, third, it is fun. Unfortunately, very few houseboats have flying bridges.

Other desirable top deck features include outdoor carpeting or astro turf, folding canvas awnings, a table, and convenient access by way of a stairway with rails instead of a ladder. I have never seen a top deck that had all these features; but a few come close.

EXTRA EQUIPMENT

The brochure should tell you what is furnished with the boat. If not, call the company and ask. Look carefully at what is provided, particularly if you are comparing prices. Some things that cannot be considered "extras" (such as linens) may be supplied for an additional charge or not supplied at all.

Although you could rent some of these items separately or bring them from home, having them included as part of the rental cost—and already aboard when you get there—is a plus. Following are the major extras you will want to consider.

Generator. The standard electrical supply on a houseboat is 12-volt direct current—the kind you have in your car. A generator provides 110-volt alternating current—the kind you have in your house. Without a generator, you will not have air-conditioning, a microwave, or the ability to run most small appliances such as blenders, toasters, coffee makers, and hair dryers. You will also not have a television unless you bring, or are supplied with, one that runs on 12 volts. If these things are important to you, put a generator on your "essential" list.

Barbecue. A gas or charcoal barbecue is almost always provided. If not, it may be because the company has a rule against using them on the boat (very uncommon). Check with them first if you plan to bring your own.

Ice chest. Even if you have a large refrigerator, you will still probably want an ice chest for beer and/or soft drinks. It is handy to have out on the deck, particularly the top deck, and when you go ashore. Most companies provide one.

Appliances. Toasters, blenders, and coffee makers are often supplied on boats with generators. You will usually have to bring anything else (electric beaters, food processors, hair dryers, etc.). Remember: you cannot use these appliances if the boat does not have a generator.

Lounge chairs. All boats will have some kind of outside seating. Some will just have a few plain folding chairs or built-in benches, while others provide complete patio sets with side tables, a dining table, and cushioned seats. You will spend a lot of time outside; plan to be comfortable, even if that means bringing your own lawn furniture.

Cassette tape players. These are fairly common; bring your own cassettes.

Fishing boats. A few companies supply a small fishing boat as part of the houseboat rental. This is an expensive "extra" if you want to rent it separately. Be sure to consider it when comparing prices.

UPGRADES

You will occasionally see two boats in the same brochure which look the same, are the same length, and have the same number of berths but have different prices. Look closely at these situations. The more expensive one is probably a newer boat and may well be worth the extra dollars.

For example, Holiday Harbor on Shasta Lake in northern California had two versions of a 47-foot houseboat in their 1988 brochure. The newer, more expensive one had two refrigerators (each with a freezer) instead of one, a second head with shower, and a swim platform added to the stern which was wide enough to use as a sun deck. Are these improvements worth the additional cost of $225 a week? To a lot of people they would be.

Or consider the Skipperliner 50' at Rainey Lake Houseboats on Rainey Lake in Minnesota. These are steel boats built on a regular hull instead of pontoons and operating on a lake with 1,500 miles of shoreline. The newer version has twin engines. Serious powerboaters would not be able to get the extra $150 out of their pockets fast enough.

CONSTRUCTION

You will seldom see anything about the construction of a houseboat mentioned in a rental brochure. And for good reason: you don't care. The only important thing is that, for all practical purposes, it is *impossible* to sink one. If a houseboat is of particularly sturdy construction, that is for the benefit of the owners, not you. They want to cut down the repair bill following that unintentional game of bumper-boat in the middle of the lake or the hard grounding that comes right after somebody says "slow" and the driver hears "go."

By the way, do not expect the construction and finish to be "yacht" quality. You will not find solid teak cabinets and brass fixtures on houseboats. Although most are very nicely appointed, they are essentially simple, comfortable, and unpretentious.

Some Examples

The perfect houseboat would have private cabins for twenty and a main living area large enough to hold a party for twice that many. A separate dining area would seat them all for dinner. The galley would be a Cordon Bleu chef's delight, complete with everything from a food processor to a pizza oven. Each of the cabins would have its own head equipped with a sauna, a Jacuzzi, and a marble Roman bathtub. A circular staircase in the main living area would lead to a top deck that would rival a Park Avenue apartment's patio (it would have a flying bridge and a complete wet bar, of course). The boat would be elegantly decorated yet maintenance-free and indestructible. It would be about 35 feet long, making it easy to maneuver and fit into crowded marinas, would sell for about $2,000, and would rent (including a ski boat and two windsurfers) for $100 a week. If you find it, let me know.

In the meantime, accept the fact that every boat is a compromise. Each is the result of many design decisions, most of which center on how to build a boat within a certain size and cost range that will appeal to the maximum number of people. Keep in mind that you are renting it for a week—not buying it—so there is no need to find the "perfect" boat.

The best way to understand the differences between the hundreds of boats available—short of going out and looking at all of them—is to compare the features of several distinct designs that contain most of the variations you are likely to encounter. These can then serve as a framework for analyzing other models.

The following pages contain pictures, floor plans, and descriptions of five houseboats. I selected these particular boats as examples because they represent a good cross section of the sizes and designs you will see in rental fleets and because, within this group, there are illustrations of most of the better features found on houseboats. None of these boats is "perfect"; all are very good.

BOATEL 36'

The Boatel company, founded in Mora, Minnesota, in 1954 to build houseboats for rental operations in that area, is one of the pioneers in houseboat construction. The company now manufactures a full range of boats (a second plant was opened in Page, Arizona, in 1981), including open sport and fishing boats, coastal cruisers, and houseboats up to 65 feet long. Boatel's extensive design experience is well demonstrated in the Boatel 36' Hercules, the smallest in their line of houseboats.

The biggest problem in designing a houseboat of this size is getting all the amenities into the plan and still having adequate lounging areas. This is particularly important, because many of the groups choosing it will be single families, and, all too often, the layout is such that there is no way for the adults to get any privacy, short of sending the kids to bed. Boatel has solved this problem by moving the galley and dining area aft (a very unusual arrangement) and using gauchos for all the sleeping areas. The result is two distinct lounging areas for day use and no space used just for bedrooms. The trade-off (and there are always trade-offs) is that those wanting an afternoon nap will have to do it in an area of heavy traffic.

Note that the boat is equipped with sizable, well-guarded decks on the sides as well as fore and aft. This is an important safety consideration if chil-

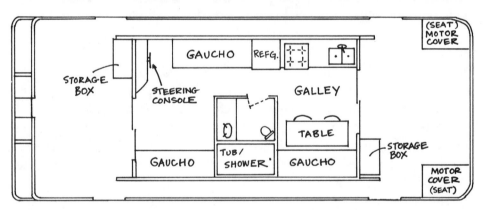

(Photo and floor plan courtesy of Boatel)

dren are aboard. Also note the substantial rails on the top deck, a feature frequently omitted on boats this size (apparently because the manufacturer believes, correctly, that they will make the boat look clunky). Rails are, if anything, more important on smaller boats where space is limited than on larger boats with lots of deck area.

Large opening windows throughout, an entirely adequate galley, and the biggest head I have ever seen on a boat this size complete the picture of a very good boat for two people and an economical alternative for a family of up to six or two adult couples.

PLAYCRAFT 41'

Playcraft's facility in Richland, Missouri, builds houseboats from 36 to 58 feet long, a line of pontoon day-use boats to 28 feet, and (under the name of "Charger") runabouts, fishing boats, and ski boats. They do a fair amount of custom houseboat work and are continually changing their models and floor plans. The model shown here is "typical" of a Playcraft in the 40- to 43-foot range, but there are many variations.

The floor plan of this houseboat, although fairly conventional, incorporates a couple of unusual features, the most important of which is an aft cabin that is as big as you will find on any size houseboat. A full bed, vanity, nightstands, and ample storage make it a good example of what can be done to provide a very nice bedroom in a relatively limited amount of space. This type of boat is an excellent choice for groups who have no problem with unequal sleeping accommodations (such as a family where Mom and Dad want to have a comfortable private area of their own). Two or more adult couples should have some sort of understanding about the sleeping arrangements before choosing a boat like this. Otherwise, the fight over that beautiful, spacious bedroom could take up most of the week.

(Photo courtesy of Playcraft)

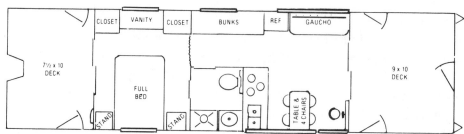

(Floor plan courtesy of Playcraft)

Another notable feature is the furnishing of a proper table and chairs instead of a dinette. The dining set will probably be a minor consideration to most, but for sticklers who find serving a pleasant dinner in a dinette akin to drinking coffee from a Styrofoam cup, it is a nice touch.

The walls around the top deck are both functional (they keep small objects from blowing or falling over the side) and attractive. The railings are rather low, and without the walls to increase security, they would be barely adequate. If you expect to spend a lot of time on the top deck, you should consider this example the minimum acceptable. This would be an excellent boat for an average-size family or a couple who wants to travel in luxury.

THREE BUOYS 46'

Three Buoys Houseboat Vacations was established in Canada in 1982 and, through innovative design and equally innovative marketing, quickly became the biggest houseboat company in North America. Three Buoys was unique in both building houseboats and operating their own rental fleets. In March 1989, most of the operational side of Three Buoys was taken over by Go Vacations. At that time, the company had over 700 houseboats on the water and rental operations at nine different locations.

The Three Buoys Sunseeker 46' is one of their most popular boats and a departure from traditional houseboat design. As is evident from its rakish styling, this is a thoroughly modern houseboat. Its most impressive feature (styling aside) is the top deck. A combination of high (and attractive) railings and walls, latching gates, a good helm station, and ample permanent seating make this one of the best top decks I have seen. The top deck is a true second living area; you will want to spend a lot of time there.

Other notable features include the addition of the "penthouse" (the small sleeping area on the top deck), which gives you one more private cabin than is normally found on a boat this size (there are also convertible beds for six in the main living area). Also, the galley is large, and since a generator is standard, the boat will be equipped with modern conveniences, including a microwave oven and *two* central air-conditioning units. One unusual feature is that although the fore and aft decks are sizable and comfortable, the side decks are virtually nonexistent; a narrow ledge-and-handrail arrangement allows a reasonably agile person to move fore and aft.

The combination of the superb top deck and the penthouse cabin adds a lot of room to this boat. You still may not want to fill all ten berths, but if you do, you will be more comfortable on the Sunseeker than on most 46-footers.

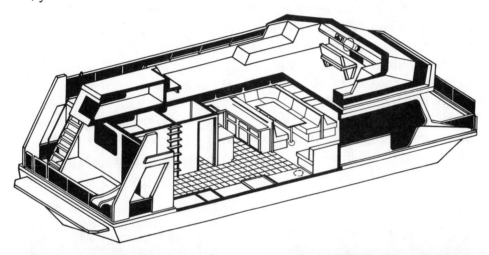

(Photo and floor plan courtesy of Three Buoys Houseboat Vacations)

LEISURECRAFT 56'

R & R Leisurecraft in Redding, California, is a custom houseboat manufacturer. The company is located right next door to Shasta Lake, which is
home to probably the largest fleet of rental houseboats on any single body of
water in the world—about 450 boats. Many of those houseboats were built
to the different operators' specifications by Leisurecraft.

The Leisurecraft 56' is intended to be functional, and it is. It incorporates
most of the features you would expect to find as well as several you would
not. This boat is both an excellent example of a traditional rental houseboat
design and a demonstration of what can be done with that design by a company that understands the needs of houseboaters.

The Leisurecraft is very well equipped, with a spacious main salon with
two large gauchos and a folding table that can be moved out of the way or
taken out on the foredeck when not in use. The huge galley has plenty of
counter space, two refrigerator/freezers, a large stove with oven, a microwave,
a trash compactor, and even a dishwasher. Two heads (one with a bathtub)
and an aft cabin with three double beds (upper, lower, and gaucho) complete
the basic layout. There is also a large penthouse cabin; the entire floor is one
big bed.

(Photo courtesy of R & R Leisurecraft)

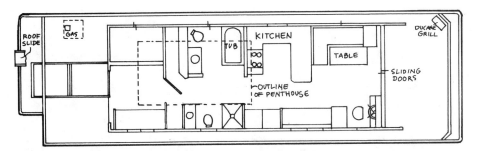

(Floor plan courtesy of R & R Leisurecraft)

All the decks are good sized and equipped with exceptionally strong protective rails. The aft deck has a large swim platform attached to it, and convenient boarding steps are built into the starboard pontoon. The top deck has a flying bridge with built-in 7-foot settees on either side of it (space on the top deck is somewhat limited because of the size of the penthouse cabin—again, a matter of trade-offs).

The Leisurecraft 56' would be a bit crowded if you filled all the available beds, but it still would be a good boat for a large, gregarious group, particularly one that could put that outstanding galley to proper use.

Stardust 64'

Stardust Cruisers of Monticello, Kentucky, specializes in building large, aluminum-hull houseboats that range from 54 to 72 feet in length. Stardust is very active in building custom-designed houseboats for some of the bigger rental fleets.

Your first impression when boarding a Stardust 64' is that this is a *big* boat—partly because a 64-foot boat *is* big, partly because the design optimizes what can be done with this length. The Stardust is 16 feet wide (a couple of feet wider than most boats this length) and has a relatively small aft deck. As a result, there is a tremendous amount of space for interior accommodations, and the top deck, which is well railed and has a flying bridge, is huge. The interior is very open; over half is devoted to daytime living area, and there are numerous windows. There are two heads, and sleeping arrangements are reasonable and equal enough that there should be no "who gets what bed" problem. Each of the aft cabins has two large beds (upper and lower), and there are two more beds in the main living area. As would be expected on a boat of this size, a generator and all modern conveniences are provided.

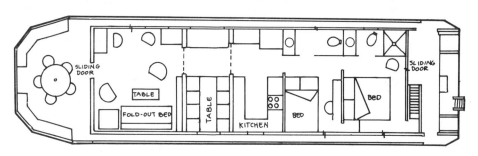

(Photo and floor plan courtesy of Stardust Cruisers)

One of the outstanding features of the Stardust 64' is the ease and convenience of moving about the boat. There are sliding glass doors located forward, aft, starboard of the helm, in each of the aft cabins, and even in the forward head. The top deck can be reached either by a conventional aft ladder or a stairway behind the helm in the main salon (with, by the way, a wet bar under it). Being able to go in or out of the boat virtually anywhere significantly increases the feeling of openness.

This is the kind of boat to look for if you are going with a large group. Even if you have on board all 12 people this boat can accommodate, you should still have plenty of room. For three couples, it would be palatial.

4 Ready to Go?

A houseboat vacation requires more planning and preparation than most vacations ashore. It is, after all, a bit of an adventure. The better prepared you are, the more likely the trip will go smoothly.

Many things can go wrong if you do not think of them until after leaving the dock. Mostly they are small annoyances, such as getting ready to open that special bottle of wine and not being able to find a corkscrew. Or learning for the first time—just as you are putting the water on for the lobster—that somebody has an allergy to shellfish. Or getting into an argument over who was supposed to have packed the deck of cards.

The goal of your planning is to have everything you need or want on board when you leave the dock. Very few groups, however, are so well organized that nothing is forgotten. If you make it through the week without a single "I wish we would have remembered to bring the. . . ," you should award a medal to the person in charge of planning.

In most areas, you will be able to buy forgotten items before leaving the dock (if you remember you forgot them), and sometimes you can pick them up along the way. I once met a group that had forgotten to bring a blender (an essential piece of equipment for them). They lived on the waterway they were cruising, so they just pulled up to their backyard, and somebody ran in and got it.

Most of us will not be so lucky if we forget something. Plan on having everything you need aboard before you leave the dock.

Planning Checklists

Planning is really two jobs: first, deciding what you want to have on board; second, making sure it is on board. Consider everything you *might* want and then decide which of these you *do* want. The checklists below will help you do both jobs.

These lists were developed from studying the advice in many different companies' brochures and from my own extensive experience forgetting things (I was actually out the door one time before I remembered I had forgotten my fishing tackle).

The first list is for preplanning. It consists of items that companies frequently supply as part of the basic rental fee or have available at an extra charge. Go through the list the first time, checking off all those items you want. Then check those that are supplied as part of the rental (these should be listed in the brochure) as being "Provided" and "Aboard." If it is an additional-charge item, do not check it off as "Aboard" until *after* you have made arrangements with the company for furnishing it. Any desired item that is not provided by the company should be listed under "Miscellaneous" on the main planning list, below.

An extra boat does not have to be a big ski boat. Any small auxiliary (a dinghy) will be fun to have along for fishing, getting back and forth to the beach, and exploring. How important the boat is depends on the area. If a boat is not provided, and you do not want to rent one (or even if you would like a second small boat), you might consider buying an inexpensive, two- or three-person inflatable boat. You can get one for about $50. Fishing boats provided with the houseboat rental usually do not come with outboard motors; either rent one or take your own.

Remember: you cannot use electrical appliances unless the boat has a generator.

The second list is the main planning list. Start by checking off the items you want to take. Although the company should supply some of the smaller kitchen utensils listed, consider bringing your own anyway. Utensils do not take up much space, and if they are already on board, you can keep yours for spares. A few other items on here might be supplied by them; check them off as packed. Check the items you want and need to buy. Do not check items off as packed until they are bought and packed.

Try to sucker one person into taking responsibility for making sure the main planning list items are all checked off. There is a lot less chance for confusion if you do.

Preplanning Checklist

WANT	PROVIDED	ABOARD	ITEM
☐	☐	☐	Barbecue
☐	☐	☐	Bedding (or sleeping bags)
☐	☐	☐	Blender
☐	☐	☐	Boat (fishing or ski)
☐	☐	☐	Cassette player
☐	☐	☐	Chairs (for deck and/or beach)
☐	☐	☐	Coffee maker
☐	☐	☐	Engine for auxiliary boat
☐	☐	☐	Ice chest
☐	☐	☐	Pillows
☐	☐	☐	Radio (AM/FM)
☐	☐	☐	Radio (marine VHF or CB)
☐	☐	☐	Ski belt or jacket (besides life vests)
☐	☐	☐	Television
☐	☐	☐	Toaster
☐	☐	☐	Towels (bath)
☐	☐	☐	Towels (kitchen)
☐	☐	☐	VCR
☐	☐	☐	Water skis

Main Planning Checklist

Want	Buy	Packed	Item
☐	☐	☐	Air mattresses or sun pads
☐	☐	☐	Bags (zip-lock)
☐	☐	☐	Barbecue utensils
☐	☐	☐	Batteries (flashlight, etc.)
☐	☐	☐	Binoculars
☐	☐	☐	Boat (inflatable)
☐	☐	☐	Book (this one)
☐	☐	☐	Books (general reading)
☐	☐	☐	Bottle opener
☐	☐	☐	Calculator
☐	☐	☐	Camera
☐	☐	☐	Camping equipment (for ashore)
☐	☐	☐	Can opener
☐	☐	☐	Carry bag (for shore trips)
☐	☐	☐	Cassette tapes
☐	☐	☐	Charcoal
☐	☐	☐	Clothes hangers
☐	☐	☐	Clothespins
☐	☐	☐	Compass
☐	☐	☐	Cookbook/recipes
☐	☐	☐	Cooking utensils (your list)
☐	☐	☐	_____
☐	☐	☐	_____

☐ ☐ ☐ Corkscrew

☐ ☐ ☐ Cutting board

☐ ☐ ☐ Eating utensils (plastic)

☐ ☐ ☐ Film

☐ ☐ ☐ First-aid kit

☐ ☐ ☐ Fishing bait

☐ ☐ ☐ Fishing license(s)

☐ ☐ ☐ Fishing tackle

☐ ☐ ☐ Flashlight

☐ ☐ ☐ Flotation vest(s) (child's)

☐ ☐ ☐ Flotation vest (for everyday use)

☐ ☐ ☐ Games (your list)

☐ ☐ ☐ _____

☐ ☐ ☐ _____

☐ ☐ ☐ _____

☐ ☐ ☐ Garbage bags

☐ ☐ ☐ Hair dryer

☐ ☐ ☐ Ice

☐ ☐ ☐ Ice chest (a second one)

☐ ☐ ☐ Ice pick

☐ ☐ ☐ Inner tubes

☐ ☐ ☐ Insect repellent

☐ ☐ ☐ Lantern (gas or battery)

☐ ☐ ☐ Lighter fluid (for charcoal)

☐ ☐ ☐ Lip protection

☐ ☐ ☐ Matches

☐	☐	☐	Medications
☐	☐	☐	Napkins
☐	☐	☐	Plates (paper)
☐	☐	☐	Playing cards
☐	☐	☐	Sleeping bag (for deck/beach)
☐	☐	☐	Soap (dish)
☐	☐	☐	Soap (bath)
☐	☐	☐	Spices
☐	☐	☐	Storage containers (for food)
☐	☐	☐	Suntan lotion
☐	☐	☐	Swimming toys
☐	☐	☐	Towels (beach)
☐	☐	☐	Towels (paper)
☐	☐	☐	Writing materials
☐	☐	☐	Miscellaneous (your list)
☐	☐	☐	_____
☐	☐	☐	_____
☐	☐	☐	_____
☐	☐	☐	_____

The final list is for personal belongings. Each person should be given a copy of this one. Some items are duplicated from the main list, because some people might want to take their own.

You do not need much in the way of clothes; this is a casual vacation. A swimming suit or two, a couple pairs of shorts, a pair of long pants, a few lightweight shirts, and a sweatshirt or sweater should do it for general wear on a normal summer cruise. Only easily forgotten items of clothing have been included on the list.

Personal Belongings Checklist

WANT	BUY	PACKED	ITEM
☐	☐	☐	Books (general reading)
☐	☐	☐	Camera
☐	☐	☐	Carry bag (for shore trips)
☐	☐	☐	Cassette tapes
☐	☐	☐	Coat (windbreaker type)
☐	☐	☐	Eyeglasses
☐	☐	☐	Eyeglasses (extra pair)
☐	☐	☐	Eyeglasses strap (or string)
☐	☐	☐	Film
☐	☐	☐	Fishing tackle
☐	☐	☐	Flashlight
☐	☐	☐	Hat or visor
☐	☐	☐	Lip protection
☐	☐	☐	Medications
☐	☐	☐	Pocket knife
☐	☐	☐	Razor (optional)
☐	☐	☐	Shoes (rubber soled)
☐	☐	☐	Sunglasses
☐	☐	☐	Suntan lotion
☐	☐	☐	Sweater or sweatshirt
☐	☐	☐	Swimsuit
☐	☐	☐	Toiletries
☐	☐	☐	Towel (beach)

If it sounds too much like work to use the lists in the systematic way outlined here, at least look them over before you leave. Chances are good you will have forgotten something.

Meal Planning

Provisions (food and beverages) may either be purchased before you leave home or at the destination. Buying at home gives you the advantage of shopping in a familiar place, where you know what is available. Shopping ahead also means less vacation time spent doing it. Even if you are not driving, consider doing at least some of your provisioning before you leave. I have seen many well-taped ice chests with airline tags on them sitting on docks, ready to go on board.

Most houseboating areas have a large market within easy driving distance. Ask the company ahead of time; sometimes you might not even need a car. If you are flying, it is usually easier to do most of your provisioning at the destination.

There are a few places—usually remote areas—where the company will provision the boat for you. Some will do it from your shopping list; others have a standard menu from which you choose a selection of meals and snacks. The brochure will tell you if this service is available.

The group cooks usually get together and plan the meals and shopping. When the group is made up of two or more families or couples traveling from different areas, it is better to wait until everybody gets together before doing the shopping. It is also more fun. The cooks head for the market, and the captains do whatever it is captains do.

Meals are usually fixed and the cleanup done by volunteers. Generally, this works out fine. But occasionally, it results in one or two people doing most of the work. Over the course of a week, this can start annoying even the best-hearted souls. Try not to let it happen. One of the surest ways to create problems within the group and ruin a vacation is to burden one person with all the work.

Another meal-planning system is to have each couple responsible for all the meals and cleanup for a particular day (or days, depending on the size of the group). If, for example, there were three couples going for a week— and you planned on eating out one night—each couple would have two days of "galley duty" and be free the other five. A variation is to do this for dinners only and have breakfast and lunch done by everybody.

Meals can be as simple or as elaborate as you want. If you do plan a meal that requires some special cooking or serving equipment (such as an extra-large pot), write it in on one of the blank lines under "Cooking utensils (your list)" so you do not forget it.

Avoid planning an elaborate meal for the first night, particularly if you are arriving late in the afternoon. Most people will not feel like cooking after a day of traveling, loading the boat, getting checked out and used to the new environment, and cruising to the first overnight stop. Everybody will want to relax and enjoy the new experience. Make up something simple ahead of time for that night or pick up a take-out dinner. A big bucket of chicken and a bowl of potato salad make a great first-night dinner.

Itinerary

Very little needs to be said about planning an itinerary. Who needs one? One of the real joys of houseboating is the freedom to go where you want, when you want. The best plan is frequently no plan at all.

If there is a place or attraction you especially want to visit, pick a day to go there and let the rest of the cruise plan itself. This would also apply to plans for having dinner out. And you should have some idea where you want to go the first night in case you get a late start.

5 On the Water

If you owned a boat worth close to $100,000, would you let somebody who had never been on a vessel bigger than an air mattress take it out for a week? Neither would I. Yet houseboat rental companies do exactly that every day. You have to admire their courage.

Each year, thousands of people who have never run a boat before show up on the docks of these companies ready to become instant captains. And they do, thanks to the checkout, which gives you the basic information needed to handle your houseboat for the week.

Checkouts

A houseboat checkout typically takes an hour or more. Your instructor will usually start with a basic walk-through of the boat, explaining where things are and how they work. The controls and instruments will then be explained and demonstrated for you. Finally, you will be briefed on the operating area and any special rules or procedures. If this is your first time on a houseboat, the instructor may go out on the boat with you for a little "hands-on" practice.

Use the checkout to ask any questions you have about the boat or its operation. Do not be afraid to ask a "dumb" question; it is easier to answer dumb questions than to correct stupid mistakes. Most houseboats have manuals on board which will answer the majority of questions that come up after leaving the dock.

A big pain for rental companies is the occasional know-it-all who will not listen to the instructor during checkout. Usually, this is someone who knows a little about boats (or has told his friends he knows a lot about them) and feels compelled to act like it is all beneath him (sorry, guys, the masculine pronouns are intentional—this is usually a macho problem). It is a mistake to feel or act this way. The instructors give you a lot of valuable information in a short time. Pay attention, even if you do not think you need to. Houseboats are simple to run; anyone with a good general knowledge of boats could probably take one out without any checkout and have no problems. But someone who knows boats will not settle for "probably" just to save a few minutes. Checking out a professional captain would likely take *longer* than checking out a boating novice. The professional would want to know everything about the boat.

The following general information about boats and their operation goes beyond the normal checkout. Many excellent books are available on boating skills; this is not intended to be one of them. The information here is very basic. If you have substantial boating experience and you have driven houseboats, you probably will not learn anything new. Skip it (except for the sections on safety, which we should all review periodically). If you know nothing about boats and would like to know at least a little before walking out on the dock for the first time, read on.

Boating Basics

Houseboats are big and unwieldy. They have small engines for their size, so they are slow to accelerate and—once they get going—slow to stop. Because they are big boats, they have a big turning radius. They turn by swinging the stern (not the front, like a car), so a beginner's wake usually looks like that of an inebriated snake. Their high sides are the equivalent of about 400 square feet of permanently raised sail, making them vulnerable to the slightest crosswind. And they have no brakes; the only way to slow or stop the boat is to reverse the engine. Houseboats are not designed to run slalom courses.

Now the good news. None of these characteristics are a problem as long as you remember the basic rule: Take it slow and easy!

When maneuvering in close quarters, go no faster than is necessary to accomplish the job. This does not mean you have to drive like the proverbial

little old lady; it means avoid *unnecessary* speed. Leave the hot-rodding to
people who do not care if their vacation is cut short and they never see their
damage deposit again. More on maneuvering the boat after we look at what
you will be maneuvering it with.

Your houseboat will probably be powered either by an outboard motor
or an "I/O" (an inboard engine with an outboard drive). An outboard motor
has the engine and drive (propeller assembly and propeller) contained in the
same unit. This is the type commonly seen on the back of small, open boats.
An I/O has a fixed engine, internally mounted, with a linkage to a separate
propeller assembly. In both cases, turning the wheel turns the propeller to
steer the boat. The arrangement, common on larger boats, where both the
engine and the propeller are fixed and a rudder is used to steer the boat is
very seldom found on houseboats in North America.

On a boat equipped with a rudder, boat speed through the water deter-
mines the degree of turn for a given turn of the wheel. With either an outboard or I/O, the thrust of the propeller turns the boat, which will not turn
effectively unless power is being applied (although if the boat is moving, you
will get some turning action even without power, because the out-drive will
act like a rudder). The important thing to remember about all this (assuming
from here on that your houseboat will have an outboard or an I/O) is that the
boat will not turn properly unless you give it some power.

After leaving the dock and getting out into a clear area, you should try
a few practice maneuvers. Bring the boat to a complete stop, and start with
a slow (quarter-throttle) forward turn in either direction. Note how fast it
turns for different amounts of wheel control. Repeat this several times in each
direction, coming to a complete stop between each maneuver. If there is any
wind, try it with the wind hitting the boat from different directions. Now do
the same thing in reverse. Notice that you get less power for a given throttle
setting when going in reverse (because of the propeller design) and that the
swing of the boat is different (because the steering action is now on the
"front," like a car). After completing these slow turns, try them with a little
more throttle. Note each time how much turn you get for different amounts
of wheel and throttle, which will teach you what combinations are most effective for different circumstances.

Once you feel comfortable with the boat, you are ready to try a minimum-
radius turn, a maneuver used to turn the boat in the least possible space. It
is a little tricky and not really essential to know, but it's good practice and
sort of fun.

From a complete stop, start a forward turn in either direction; have the wheel all the way over and use about one-third throttle. As soon as the boat gets some speed up (about 2 mph), pull the throttle back to idle and quickly turn the wheel completely over in the opposite direction. As you turn the wheel, shift into reverse. Add power (about half throttle) when the wheel is all the way over. As soon as the boat starts to back up, repeat the steps: throttle back to idle; turn the wheel in the opposite direction; shift while turning the wheel (this time into forward); and add power. When you have forward speed, start over. It may take two or three times through this sequence of maneuvers to complete a full 180-degree turn. What you are doing is using the engine to alternately pull and push the stern in the direction you want it to go. If this seems unclear to you now, it should make more sense when you do it on a boat.

Finally, take the boat up to cruising speed, throttle back to idle, put it in reverse, and add full reverse power (following the instructions you were given in your checkout; you do not want to damage anything). Note how long it takes to come to a complete stop. This is an emergency stop. Do it one time for practice, so you will know how far the boat will travel in the event of a real emergency—a good distance. This will help you avoid an emergency in the first place by realizing how much room you do need and slowing down early.

When you stop for the night, you will either anchor, beach the boat, or tie it up. Anchoring for a day stop—as long as someone is on board and awake to watch the boat—is no problem. Anchoring overnight is a different thing. It is much more difficult than most people think to anchor properly. Some houseboats do not even carry anchors; others have them for emergency use only. Beaching a houseboat and tying it up are comparatively simple. Know a few basic knots before you start out—at least the bow line, the square knot (sailors call it a reef knot), and the cleat hitch.

Proper anchoring depends on water conditions (primarily bottom type and depth), the equipment used, and technique. At areas where company houseboats usually anchor, the conditions there have been judged to be satisfactory. Anchor where and how they tell you to, and you should have no problem.

Beaching the boat is accomplished by driving the bow onto the beach and then running stern lines to the shore. Be careful to select a beach where the water is deep enough offshore so the propeller does not touch bottom. The stern lines can be tied to trees or other solid objects or to spikes driven into the beach. The helmsman should hold the boat against the beach with a little

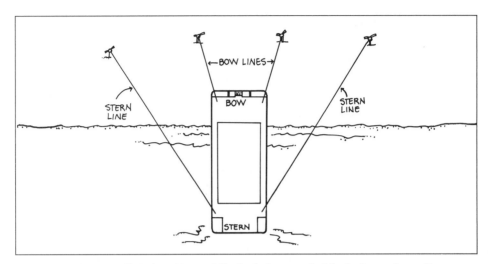

A crew member ties off the bow lines while the helmsman holds the bow ashore. Stern lines are then secured to keep the houseboat from swinging.

forward power while the lines are being tied off. Be sure nobody is in the water near the stern of the boat while this is being done. Propellers are dangerous, and the person at the helm will be watching forward, not aft.

Make sure the boat is pointing directly into the beach. You could cause damage if you let it get sideways. The person at the helm can use the wheel to keep the boat straight until it is tied off. Once the boat is secured, use the forward boarding gate to get back and forth. This is a very easy and convenient way to spend the night.

If you have trouble getting the boat off the beach in the morning, try putting the wheel hard over and applying power for a few seconds, then idling back and turning it the other way and adding power again. Do this several times. Usually this will work the boat loose.

You can tie the boat up to trees or to a dock. When tying up to live trees along the shore of a river or lake, pick a spot where wayward branches will not become part of the interior decor if the boat swings. Tie up to the trunk or a solid branch of a tree, and always run at least one more line ashore and tie it off. This line should come from the opposite end (or at least the opposite side) of the boat. The second line is for safety and to keep the boat from swinging with the wind or current.

When tying up to dead trees (common on many man-made lakes) away from shore, try to use two of them. This will keep the boat from swinging with the wind and bumping other trees or the one it is tied to. Pick two trees

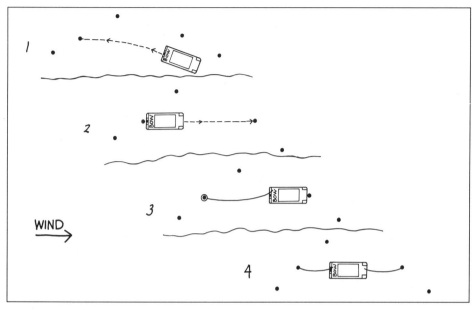

1) Select two trees at least fifty feet farther apart than the length of your houseboat. Approach the windward one on a course into the wind. 2) Tie off to the first tree and pay out line as you back down wind to the second one. 3) Tie off to the second tree. 4) Adjust both lines so the houseboat sits between the trees.

at least fifty feet farther apart than the length of your houseboat. Usually, you will want them oriented with the wind. Have two long lines ready—one on the bow and the other on the stern. Drive upwind to the first tree; this will put the second tree behind you. Have someone check the first tree to see if it is solid and, if so, tie off the bow line. Now back slowly, with the wind, to the second tree while letting out the forward line, and if the tree is solid, tie off the stern line. Take up the forward line while slacking the aft one until the boat is about halfway between the trees. Tie both lines off on the boat and have a nice night.

Tying up to a dock is the easiest of all. Getting close enough to the dock to tie off is the main problem. If there is very little wind, or if there is a breeze parallel to the dock, docking is fairly simple.

The secret to successful docking is planning. Have your lines and "fenders" (the rubber bumpers supplied with the boat) ready before you head for the dock. You should have one line forward and another aft (assuming you are tying the side of the boat to the dock) on the side that will be next to the dock. Have a crew member standing by with each line.

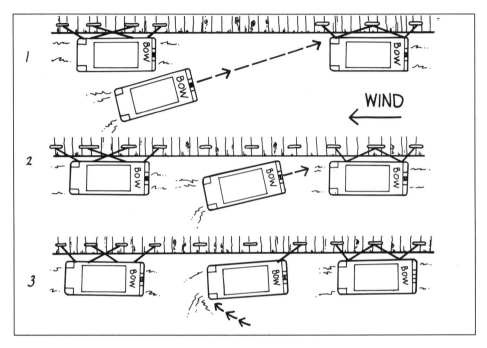

1) Approach the dock into the wind and at about a 20 degree angle. 2) When you get close, turn the helm hard toward the dock and add power in reverse to slow the houseboat and move the stern toward the dock. 3) Tie off the bow line first.

Approach the spot on the dock where you want to tie up, going *upwind* and at a slight angle—about 20 degrees. Remember the basic rule: **Take it slow and easy**. Gradually reduce speed as you get closer to the dock. Throttle back to idle, shift into reverse, and turn the wheel toward the dock as soon as you know your boat's momentum will take you the rest of the way in. Just before the boat touches the dock, add enough reverse power to bring it to a stop. Since you have the wheel turned toward the dock, this will also swing the stern in. The crew then steps ashore or hands the lines to a helpful person on the dock, and you tie up. The crew should not make long leaps to the dock or long, desperate throws of the lines. Simply pull out and try again if the approach is so bad that it requires these daring feats to salvage it.

If the wind is pushing the boat toward the dock, approach at a greater angle—up to 40 degrees. This makes it easier to back out if necessary and gives you more ability to slow the boat's speed as you approach the dock. No problem getting the stern in—the wind will do that for you. The one exception to the "greater angle" approach is in parallel parking. Just pull up parallel with the dock and stop the boat. If the wind is directly into the dock, it will push you right to your spot.

If the wind is pushing the boat away from the dock, decrease your angle to the dock. In this case, it's easy to get back out if you have difficulty: just sit there and let the wind blow you out of trouble. You decrease the angle to make it easier to get the stern in. With an offshore wind, you can easily find yourself in the embarrassing position of having the stern drift away from the dock, leaving the boat hanging in the wind by its bow line.

Current should be handled the same as wind. The good things about current are that it is consistent (you never get a gust of current) and almost always parallel to the dock. If there is both wind and current, take both into consideration, but plan your approach based on which one will have the most effect on your boat—usually, the stronger one.

It is best to back a houseboat away from a bank or out of an area with restricted maneuvering room. Backing is difficult, but it does have two advantages. The swing of the stern acts with instead of against you, and the boat drives more like a car (the steering action is now on the "front"). Have someone stationed on the stern as a lookout and sound three short blasts on your horn (the signal that you are maneuvering astern) before backing up.

Always think ahead. What could go wrong, and what are you going to do when it does? Always take current or wind into account when planning any maneuver. It is the captain's responsibility to have crew members in the right places to handle lines and otherwise assist. They should be properly briefed on what is happening and what they are supposed to do. When all is ready, proceed. If you foul up, no big deal. Pull out and start over again. If you follow these simple guidelines, you will have no problems; if you ignore them, you may be the cocktail-hour entertainment.

Navigation

"Navigation" is a word that unnecessarily scares people. Basic navigation is easy, and a little knowledge of it can add a lot to the fun—and your peace of mind. You will be able to go safely to places avoided by less intrepid explorers, identify those sights on the shore because you know where you are, and make better plans because you will know your ETA (navigator talk for estimated time of arrival). There is no need to master celestial navigation, just a few basic skills.

Most houseboat navigation is done by eye. The distances involved are short, and you often have intermediate reference points all along your route.

Just look out over the water, identify the next place you want to go, and drive to it (I told you this would be easy). This reference could be a point of land, an island, or a marker or the next bend in the river. When you reach it, pick the next one and proceed to it. Few houseboating areas require compass skills. Most houseboats do not even have a compass.

You will use a "chart" (map to landlubbers) to find your destination and the route for getting there. A chart of the operating area will be provided by the company. If possible, get it before the trip, both to familiarize yourself with it and to formulate any questions you may have about it for the checkout.

You can actually plot a course on the chart or (like most people) use the "go-out-to-the-island-over-there-and-turn-right" method. The chart includes all the information found on a normal map (highways, towns, prominent land-marks, etc.) as well as information about water depth and navigation aids.

Water depth normally is shown in feet (the chart will indicate whether it uses meters or fathoms; one fathom = six feet) and also is depicted by different colors for different depths. Shallow water and underwater hazards will be marked. Most houseboats go aground or strike bottom with the pro-peller in about 18 inches of water; note the way in which shallow or hazard-ous areas are marked on your chart; slow down and keep a close watch when near one. Do not assume that because the chart shows five feet of water you can go blasting through at full speed. You might get surprised by a snag, a rock, or an uncharted shallow spot.

The navigation aids of primary importance to houseboaters are channel markers—buoys or posted signs placed to help navigate shallow or hazard-ous areas. They have distinctive shapes, colors, and patterns, depending on their purpose. Markers on the sides of the channel will be consecutively numbered. Under the International System, a red buoy marks the right side of the channel when you are returning from sea (going upstream). Just remember Red-Right-Returning. Red buoys have even numbers that get larger as you proceed upstream. The other side of the channel will be marked by green or black odd-numbered buoys. The International System is widely used, but there are local variations, so ask about this during checkout.

It is sometimes unclear—particularly in lake navigation—which direc-tion "returning from sea" is. If you see two different-colored numbered mark-ers, there is no problem; just go between them (unless you're at a fork in the channel, in which case, stop and take a close look at the chart). The sure way to know which markers should be on which side is to look at the chart ahead of time.

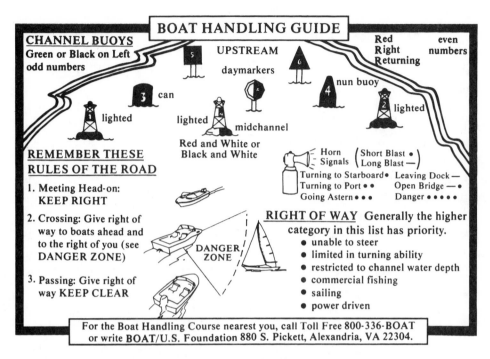

The stick-on guide pictured above shows most of the basic rules. It is available free from the BOAT/U.S. Foundation.

Channel markers are also useful if you are temporarily disoriented (navigators never get lost, only "temporarily disoriented"). Drive up to one, look at the number, find it on the chart, and you know where you are.

There are a variety of other warning and restriction signs. Any important markers that are not easily understood should be explained during your checkout.

It is easy to figure out how long it will take to get from where you are to where you want to go, how far you have traveled (or will go in a given time), or even boat speed. One simple formula does it all. The speed-time-distance formula is Speed times Time equals Distance. Any one of these variables can be found if you know the other two (the same formula lets you figure out that at 55 mph, you will make that city 110 miles away in two hours.) If your high school algebra is rusty, here are the three variations:

Time equals Distance divided by Speed $T = D/S$
Distance equals Speed times Time $D = S \times T$
Speed equals Distance divided by Time $S = D/T$

If your houseboat is going 8 mph, how long will it take to make it to a cove 20 miles away? Divide 20 by 8 (T = 20/8), and you find it will be 2.5 hours (time is always in hours; convert to hours and minutes by multiplying the fraction by 60).

If sunset is 5 hours away, how far can you go and still have at least an hour and a half to get properly relaxed for watching it? Figure 3.5 hours traveling time times the boat's 8 miles per hour (D = 8 x 3.5). You can go anywhere within 28 miles of where you are now.

The last formula gives you the actual speed of your boat. Measure the distance between two points on your chart—two channel markers work well—and then time how long it takes to go from one to the other. The speed of your boat is the measured distance divided by the time it took to travel it. For best results, use two points at least a mile apart. (Note that the speed you get will be the speed over the bottom—not the same as the speed over water if there is a current.)

For a simple way to estimate traveling time, try this: using the mileage scale on your chart, cut something to the distance your boat would travel in one hour. If, for example, your boat goes 8 mph, lay a matchstick on the scale and cut it off so it is 8 miles long on the scale. You now have in your hand one hour of boat traveling time. With this, you can measure time—for your boat at that speed—directly from the chart. One matchstick equals one hour of traveling time.

Safety

Your houseboat will be equipped with all Coast Guard-required safety equipment, including life jackets (commonly called a "PFD" because of its technical name, "Personal Flotation Device") and fire extinguishers. Know where these are and how to use them. You should try on a life jacket and know how to adjust it for a snug fit before you leave the dock. Some companies keep the life jackets in sealed lockers or packages to prevent people from playing with them. If your company does this, ask to borrow a spare life jacket so each person on board can become familiarized with it before you leave. If children will be on board, make sure the company provides child-size life jackets. Some companies only supply adult sizes.

Ninety percent of all boating accident fatalities are caused by drowning. Falling overboard accounts for a substantial number of these. Be careful when moving around the boat. Keep the gates in the safety rails fastened when not in use and closed when under way. Never climb over the safety rails or sit on them when the boat is moving.

If someone in your group would feel more comfortable wearing a flotation device when swimming or under way, you may have to bring one for them. Life jackets provided with the boat are exactly that—life jackets. Like all safety equipment, they should be kept in top condition so they will be ready in an emergency. Do not use them for water toys and boat bumpers.

Let someone responsible know your travel plans—at least your general direction and tentative stops—in case of an emergency. One way to do this is to use your radio to periodically check in with the company.

Many safe houseboating practices are matters of common sense that would apply equally at home. A vinyl floor is slippery when wet, regardless of where it is located. There are, however, several features of houseboats which create potential safety problems.

- First of all, it is a boat. Drive safely.
- Gasoline and propane tanks will normally be on the aft deck. Both are highly flammable. If one of the tanks develops a leak, and there is a cigarette or other open flame nearby, a fire or explosion could occur. Check the tanks occasionally for leaks—your nose is the best leak detector—and never smoke or allow open flames near them.
- Never start the boat engine when swimmers are in the water. The propeller could seriously injure someone. Remember that the swim ladder is usually right next to the propeller.
- Diving off the top deck can be dangerous. Check the water first to make sure it is deep enough and contains no hidden hazards.
- Go up and down the top-deck ladder facing it. Be aware that suntan lotion or even water can make the ladder slippery.
- Be careful around the front of the boat when it is under way. A person falling over the front of a moving pontoon boat would be swept underneath the boat, between the pontoons, and into the propeller. The first thing you do in any overboard situation is put the boat in neutral.
- Now, the real killer. Over 70 percent of all boating accidents—and half of all boating deaths—are alcohol related. A substantial number of deaths occur simply because a drunk falls overboard and drowns. Use some sense. Above all, do not drive while intoxicated or let an intoxicated person take the helm. Operating a boat while intoxicated is a federal offense in the United States.

CHILDREN'S SAFETY

Whether to take extra precautions for children depends on their age, physical ability, swimming ability, and experience. I have watched an eight-year-old do a fine job of running a second anchor out with an outboard-powered dinghy (a fairly tricky maneuver that many adults foul up) while carrying on a discussion with his dad, who was back on the boat, as to its proper placement. I have also seen a kid twice that age completely destroy a dinghy through carelessness. The amount of supervision required is a decision only you can make.

Children tend to follow the example set by adults, particularly when a new experience such as houseboating is involved. Show proper respect for safe boating practices and chances are your children will, too.

It is a good idea to "explore" the boat with children when they first get on board. They will want to do this anyway, and it gives you the chance to discuss safe boating with them and point out anything that might be dangerous.

Nobody likes a lot of rules—especially on vacation—but some rules are a good idea. Following are guidelines to consider in deciding what rules, if any, your children need.

- Children should wear life vests anytime the boat is under way and anytime they are on the top deck (unless it is equipped with child-proof guardrails).
- No swimming unless someone is there to watch. Use a flotation device if not a good swimmer. Do not swim in marinas or other areas with heavy boat traffic.
- No jumping or diving off the boat until someone has checked the depth and made sure there are no underwater hazards. Adults should also follow this rule.
- No touching the engine controls except under adult supervision.
- No running while the boat is under way; no running on the top deck.
- No playing with the lines used to tie off the boat. (Parents like to wake up with the boat where it was when they went to sleep.)

You can give your children some advance instruction in the basic concepts of water safety with the "Water 'n Kids Coloring Book." This is a free U.S. Coast Guard publication. Call 800-368-5647 or write:

Commandant (G-BC)
U.S. Coast Guard Headquarters
Washington, D.C. 20593-0001

Weather

Weather is seldom a problem on the protected waters where houseboats operate. If you do get caught in a sudden storm, just head for the nearest cove and
tie up until it blows over. If there are several coves or banks to choose from,
pick the one on the side the wind is coming from. Your boat will then be protected from the wind by the shore.

If you are caught out in the open with the wind coming up and waves
building, head toward the nearest shelter that is on a course *into* the wind.
The boat can handle the weather more comfortably on the bow, and this
course will take you to the best place to wait it out. Do not try to make it into
a marina if the wind is howling. Wait until the storm is over.

You should be prepared to change your plans if the weather is unsettled.
To keep from getting caught out in the open in bad weather, plan shorter
cruises that avoid open water or just relax and enjoy where you are until conditions improve. If your boat is equipped with a marine radio, you will be able
to get weather information from the company base. If not, you can get it by
listening to the regular commercial radio, from marinas along the way, or
from other boaters. In many areas, weather information is broadcast continuously on special marine radio channels.

Learning More about Boating

As I have said, houseboating is easy and requires no prior boating experience.
Boating is, however, a complex subject. Every topic I have touched on
above—even knot tying and anchoring—has had entire books devoted to it.
This is one of the attractions of the sport: no matter how much you know,
there is always more to learn.

For more boating information, either read up on the subject on your
own or take a boating course. Courses for novices are offered by the U.S.
Power Squadron (you want the Public Boating Course) and the U.S. Coast
Guard Auxiliary (Boating Skills and Seamanship). Both of these courses
cover all the basics: equipment, boat handling, safety, seamanship, weather,
rules of the road, and elementary navigation. Courses are given in the evenings and are free.

Boat/U.S. Foundation is a nonprofit boating safety organization that has
information on free boating courses offered by nonprofit organizations
throughout the United States. Call them at 800-336-BOAT (in Virginia,

800-245-BOAT) for a free brochure describing courses and class schedules in your area. Their "Boater's Source Directory" pamphlet has a lot of good information for recreational boaters, and they will send you a decal of the *Boat Handling Guide* (pictured on p. 67) to place near your helm. These are also free.

For information on boating courses in Canada, call the Canadian Coast Guard at 613-990-3116.

6 Directory of Houseboat Rental Companies

The following directory of houseboat rental companies in the United States and Canada will help you locate and contact companies in areas that interest you. The companies are listed by geographic area and then alphabetically by location and company name. The Mississippi River has been placed, somewhat arbitrarily, in the north central area.

Sometimes the address given is not the actual physical location of the company; some companies' offices are not at their operating locations, and others have several operations and use a central information and reservations office. The address given is the one to use for general information and to request a brochure.

Toll-free telephone numbers (800 numbers) have been listed where available. If a company has more than one 800 number, the one for out-of-state callers has been given. If the 800 number for a company in your own state does not work, try directory assistance (1-800-555-1212) for an in-state number. The 800 numbers are for general information and for requesting brochures.

Regular (you pay) numbers listed are generally for the local office or operating area. Try the 800 number first if there is one; if it is not at the marina where the boats are kept, the local number can be useful for more specific information.

When available, the size of the body of water has been provided (in parentheses). Remember that the length of a river or waterway is not really as good for comparison purposes (see the section on rivers and canals) as shoreline miles are for lakes. Bigger is not necessarily better in any case, but size *is* a consideration.

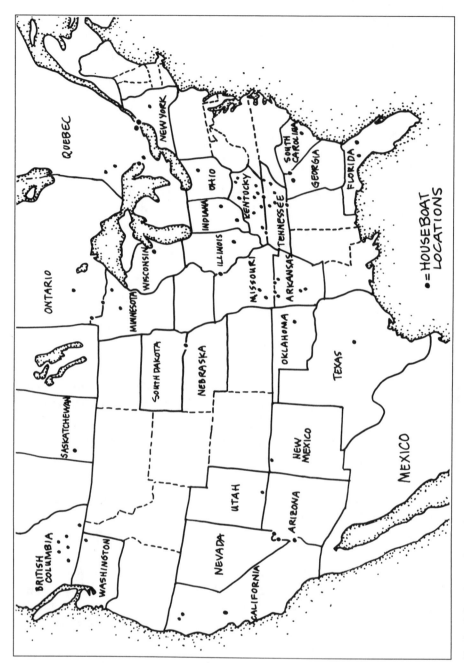

Each of the places shown above has commercial houseboat rental operations.

Northwest

ARROW LAKE, BRITISH COLUMBIA
(105,500 acres)

Scotties Marina Ltd.
R.R. #1, Site 33, C-7
Castlegar, British Columbia V1N 3H7
Canada
604-365-3267

ATLIN LAKE, BRITISH COLUMBIA
(138,800 acres)

Norseman Adventures
P.O. Box 184
Atlin, British Columbia V0W 1A0
Canada
604-651-7535

FRASER RIVER, BRITISH COLUMBIA

Condo Marina Ltd.
4178 Winnifred Street
Burnaby, British Columbia V5J 2S4
Canada
604-430-4247

Condo Yacht Charters
#202 1676 Duranleau St.
Granville Island
Vancouver, British Columbia V6H 3S4
Canada
604-682-0275

KOOTENAY LAKE, BRITISH COLUMBIA
(105,500 acres)

Kaslo Shipyard Corp.
Box 449
Kaslo, British Columbia V0G 1M0
Canada
604-353-2686

OKANAGAN LAKE, BRITISH COLUMBIA
(87,000 acres)

The Marina-Okanagan Lake
293 Front St., Box 460
Penticton, British Columbia V2A 6K6
Canada
604-492-2628

LAKE ROOSEVELT, WASHINGTON
(82,000 acres, 630 miles of shoreline)

Lake Roosevelt Resort & Marina
P.O. Box 340
Kettle Falls, WA 99141
509-738-6121
800-635-7585

Roosevelt Recreational Enterprises
P.O. Box 587
Grand Coulee, WA 99133
509-633-0201

SHUSWAP LAKE, BRITISH COLUMBIA
(78,000 acres, 640 miles of shoreline)

Anglemont Marina
Box 128
Anglemont, British Columbia V0E 1A0
Canada
604-955-2277

C.M.W.B. Enterprises
Box 1042
Salmon Arm, British Columbia V0E 2T0
Canada
604-832-8544

Channel Cat Houseboat Rentals
R.R. #1, Kappel Street
Sicamous, British Columbia V0E 2V0
Canada
604-836-2658

Cruise Along Houseboat Charters
Box 459, 718 Riverside Road
Sicamous, British Columbia V0E 2V0
Canada
604-836-2969

Go Vacations Ltd.
129 Carlingview Drive
Rexdale, Ontario M9W 5E7
Canada
604-836-2202
800-387-3998

International Houseboat Holidays
P.O. Box 542
Sicamous, British Columbia V0E 2V0
Canada
604-836-2202

Portside Houseboat Charters
Box 167
Sicamous, British Columbia V0E 2V0
Canada
604-836-3339

Salmon Arm Marina
Box 2064
Salmon Arm, British Columbia V0E 2T0
Canada
604-832-4144

Twin Anchors Houseboat Rentals
Box 318
Sicamous, British Columbia V0E 2V0
Canada
604-836-2450

Waterway Houseboat Limited
Box 69
Sicamous, British Columbia V0E 2V0
Canada
604-836-2505

THOMPSON RIVER, BRITISH COLUMBIA

Sun Chariot Houseboats
R.R. #2, Site 10, Comp 9
Kamloops, British Columbia V2C 2J3
Canada
604-573-4551

North Central

ASH RIVER TRAIL, MINNESOTA

Minnesota Voyageur Houseboats
Ash River Trail
Orr, MN 55771
218-374-3571

BIRCH LAKE, MINNESOTA
(7,628 acres)

Timber Bay Houseboats
Box 248
Babbitt, MN 55706
218-827-3682

CRANE LAKE, MINNESOTA
(3,396 acres)

Voyagaire Houseboats
Crane Lake, MN 55725
218-993-2333

LAKE DIEFENBAKER, SASKATCHEWAN

Houseboat Holidays
Box 189
Elbow, Saskatchewan S0H 1J0
Canada
306-854-2211

LAKE OF THE WOODS, ONTARIO/ MANITOBA/MINNESOTA
(950,400 acres, 65,000 miles of shoreline)

Canadian American Houseboats
Route 2, Box 44
Litchfield, MN 55355
612-693-6641

Floating Lodges
Box 188
Sioux Narrows, Ontario P0X 1N0
Canada
807-226-5476

Go Vacations
129 Carlingview Drive
Rexdale, Ontario M9W 5E7
Canada
800-387-3998

Houseboat Adventures
Box 1030 L
Kenora, Ontario P9N 3X7
Canada
807-543-2911

Lake of the Woods Houseboats
Box 179
Sioux Narrows, Ontario P0X 1N0
Canada
807-226-5462

Lake Pine Houseboat Adventures
100 Colonization Road
Kenora, Ontario P9N 4C5
Canada
807-468-5823

Nestor Falls Houseboat Rental
Box 55
Nestor Falls, Ontario P0X 1K0
Canada
807-484-2448

Ontario Wilderness Houseboat
General Delivery
Morson, Ontario P0W 1J0
Canada
807-488-5594

Peterson's Island Houseboat
R.R. #1
Sleeman, Ontario P0W 1M0
Canada
807-488-5605

Sherman Houseboats
P.O. Box 490
Keewatin, Ontario P0X 1C0
Canada
807-547-2117

Sunwest Houseboats Ltd.
115 Barker Blvd.
Winnipeg, Manitoba R3R 2C9
Canada
204-895-3190

Tomahawk Resort
P.O. Box 27
Sioux Narrows, Ontario P0X 1N0
Canada
807-226-5622
800-465-1091

LEECH LAKE, MINNESOTA
(640 miles of shoreline)

Fisher's Houseboats
Box 488
Walker, MN 56484
218-547-1162

LEWIS & CLARK LAKE, SOUTH DAKOTA/ NEBRASKA
(29,000 acres, 90 miles of shoreline)

Lewis & Clark Marina
P.O. Box Drawer 19
Yankton, SD 57078
605-665-4186

MISSISSIPPI RIVER, IOWA—WISCONSIN

Boatels
McGregor, IA 52157
319-873-3718

Captain's Cruises
710 Division St.
La Crosse, WI 54601
608-784-3088

Cruising Houseboats
Alma Marina
Alma, WI 54610
608-685-3333

Great River Cruises
400 Winona St.
La Crosse, WI 54601
608-783-3879

Houseboating Adventures
Box 2094
La Crosse, WI 54602
608-788-4420

S & S Houseboats
990 S. Front St.
Lansing, IA 52151
319-538-4454

Lake Pepin, Minnesota

Great River Houseboats
P.O. Box 106, 1009 E. Main St.
Wabasha, MN 55981
612-565-3376

Rainy Lake, Minnesota/Ontario
(220,800 acres, 4,000 miles of shoreline)

Canadian Wilderness Floating Lodges
Box 487
Fort Frances, Ontario P9A 3M8
Canada
807-274-6523

Northernaire Floating Lodges
510 Island View Route
International Falls, MN 56649
218-286-5221

Rainy Lake Houseboats
Route 8, Box 408
International Falls, MN 56649
218-286-5391

Lac La Ronge, Saskatchewan

La Ronge Houseboat Charters
Box 505
La Ronge, Saskatchewan S0J 1L0
Canada
306-425-2292

Lac Seul, Ontario
(410,000 acres)

Lac Seul Floating Lodges
Box 107
Hudson, Ontario P0V 2T0
Canada
807-582-3284

Sioux Lookout Floating Lodges
P.O. Box 137
Sioux Lookout, Ontario P0V 2T0
Canada
807-737-2902

Lake Vermilion, Minnesota
(49,110 acres, 1,200 miles of shoreline)

Vermilion Houseboats
Star Route, Box 1632A
Tower, MN 55790
218-753-3548

Whitefish Chain of Lakes, Minnesota

Chain O'Lakes Houseboats
Box 154
Crosslake, MN 56442
218-692-4677

Northeast

ATWOOD LAKE, OHIO
(1,540 acres, 28 miles of shoreline)

Atwood Lake Boats
P.O. Box 57
Dellroy, OH 44620
216-364-4703

BROOKVILLE RESERVOIR, INDIANA
(8,000 acres)

Horns Houseboats
P.O. Box 188
Liberty, IN 47353
317-458-5155

GEORGIAN BAY, ONTARIO

Go Vacations Canada
129 Carlingview Dr.
Rexdale, Ontario M9W 5E7
Canada
416-674-1880
800-387-3998

GREAT SACANDAGA LAKE, NEW YORK
(150 miles of shoreline)

Holiday Houseboats
47 Algonquin Drive
Queensbury, NY 12801
518-793-4469

LAKE NIPISSING, ONTARIO
(205,700 acres)

Sea Turtle Houseboats
P.O. Box 953
Lively, Ontario P0M 2E0
Canada
705-692-5600

Valhalla Houseboat Holidays
R.R. #1
Monetville, Ontario P0M 2K0
Canada
705-898-2683

PATOKA LAKE, INDIANA

Lick Fork Marina
R.R. #1, Box 45-D
Celestine, IN 47521
812-678-4991

RIDEAU WATERWAY, ONTARIO
(about 123 miles of waterways)

Big Rideau Boats
5 Ancona Court
Nepean, Ontario K2G 0N4
Canada
613-825-3317

Garmmac Houseboat Rentals
670 Third Avenue
Pembroke, Ontario K8A 5H3
Canada
613-735-3720

Hurst Marina
P.O. Box 1028
Manotick, Ontario K0A 2N0
Canada
613-692-3627

Long Island Marine
Box 579
Manotick, Ontario K0A 2N0
Canada
613-692-2316

Rideau Waterway Houseboats
P.O. Box 49
Odessa, Ontario K0H 2H0
Canada
613-386-7321

Summer Magic Houseboat Rentals
P.O. Box 358
Port Hope, Ontario L1A 3W4
Canada
416-885-9503

Lake Shelbyville, Illinois
(12,000 acres, 250 miles of shoreline)

Lithia Springs Marina
R.R. #4, Box 103A
Shelbyville, IL 62565
217-774-4121

Lake Temagami, Ontario
(50,136 acres)

Leisure Island Houseboat Rentals
P.O. Box 356
Temagami, Ontario P0H 2H0
Canada
705-569-3261

Three Buoys—Temagami
Box 249
Temagami, Ontario P0H 2H0
Canada
705-569-3455

Thousand Islands, New York/ Ontario
(large cruising area)

Houseboat Holidays Ltd.
R.R. #3
Gananoque, Ontario K7G 2V5
Canada
613-382-2842

1000 Islands Rent-A-Cruise
R.R. #1
Lansdowne, Ontario K0E 1L0
Canada
613-659-3163

Rebob Houseboat Rentals
Rockport, Ontario K0E lV0
Canada
613-659-3410

Remar Houseboat Rental
510 Theresa St., P.O. Box 159
Clayton, NY 13624
315-686-3579

Trent-Severn Waterway, Ontario
(about 240 miles of waterways)

Charlore Park Marina
R.R. #4
Omemee, Ontario K0L 2W0
Canada
705-799-5052

Go Vacations
129 Carlingview Drive
Rexdale, Ontario M9W 5E7
Canada
705-657-8027
800-387-3998

Hammock Harbour Resort
P.O. Box 921
Orillia, Ontario L3V 6K8
Canada
705-325-6051

Happy Days Houseboats
R.R. #2
Bobcaygeon, Ontario K0M 1A0
Canada
705-738-2201

Maranatha Marina Houseboat Rentals
R.R. #1
Lakefield, Ontario K0L 2H0
Canada
705-657-8747

Muskoka Houseboat Rentals
P.O. Box 1309
Oshawa, Ontario L1J 6P8
Canada
416-723-6874

Princess Houseboat Rentals
362 Martindale Rd., R.R. #3
St. Catharines, Ontario L2R 6P9
Canada
416-934-5447

R & R Houseboat Rentals
P.O. Box 129
Ajax, Ontario L1S 3C2
Canada
416-839-2469

Sunburst Houseboat Rentals
Omemee, Ontario K0L 2W0
Canada
705-799-5745

Trent Line Houseboat Rentals
Box 72, R.R. #1
Lakefield, Ontario K0L 2H0
Canada
705-657-1590

Turtle Bay Vacations
R.R. #5
Peterborough, Ontario K9J 6Y3
Canada
705-748-2290

Water Way Houseboat Rentals
143 Sentinel Rd.
Downsview, Ontario M3J 1T3
Canada
416-636-8700

WOLF/FOX RIVERS, WISCONSIN

Party Doll Fleet
9082 Marion Lane
Fremont, WI 54940
414-446-2224

Southwest

BULLARDS BAR RESERVOIR,
CALIFORNIA
(4,816 acres, 656 miles of shoreline)

Emerald Cove Marina
P.O. Box 1954
Nevada City, CA 95959
916-692-2166

CALIFORNIA DELTA, CALIFORNIA
(about 1,000 miles of waterways)

Delta Country Houseboats
P.O. Box 246
Walnut Grove, CA 95690
916-776-1741

Herman & Helen's Marina
Venice Island Ferry
Stockton, CA 95209
209-951-4634

New Hope Landing
Box 417
Thornton, CA 95686
209-794-2627

Paradise Point Marina
8095 N. Rio Blanco Rd.
Stockton, CA 95209
209-952-1000
800-752-9669

Rainbow Resort
1100 W. Brannan Island Rd.
Isleton, CA 95641
916-777-6172

S & H Boat Yard
Route 1, Box 514
Antioch, CA 94509
415-757-3621
800-257-3626

Take Five Charters
P.O. Box 6339
Stockton, CA 95206
209-948-1712

LAKE HAVASU, CALIFORNIA/ARIZONA
(20,400 acres)

Go Vacations
129 Carlingview Drive
Rexdale, Ontario M9W 5E7
Canada
619-858-4571
800-387-3998

Sandpoint Marina
P.O. Box 1469
Lake Havasu City, AZ 86403
602-855-0540

LAKE MEAD, NEVADA
(157,900 acres, 822 miles of shoreline)

Callville Bay Resort & Marina
Box 100S, Star Route 10
Las Vegas, NV 89124
702-565-7340
800-255-5561

Echo Bay Resort
Overton, NV 89040
702-297-1005
800-752-9669

LAKE MOHAVE, NEVADA
(28,200 acres, 254 miles of shoreline)

Cottonwood Cove Resort & Marina
Box 1000S
Cottonwood Cove, NV 89046
702-297-1005

Lake Mohave Marina
Katherine's Landing
Bullhead City, AZ 86430
602-754-3245
800-752-9669

NAVAJO LAKE, NEW MEXICO
(15,000 acres, 150 miles of shoreline)

Navajo Dam Enterprises
Star Route 1, NBU #6
Navajo Dam, NM 87419
505-632-3245

LAKE POWELL, ARIZONA/UTAH
(1,960 acres)

Bullfrog Resort & Marina
Bullfrog, UT 84734
801-684-2233
800-528-6154

Hall's Crossing Resort & Marina
Blanding, UT 84511
801-684-2261
800-528-6154

Hite Resort & Marina
Hanksville, UT 84734
801-684-2278
800-528-6154

San Juan Marina
356 S. Main St.
Blanding, UT 84511
801-678-2217

Wahweap Lodge & Marina
2916 N. 35th Ave.
Phoenix, AZ 85017
602-645-2433
800-528-6154

SHASTA LAKE, CALIFORNIA
(29,500 acres, 365 miles of shoreline)

Antlers Resort
P.O. Box 140
Lakehead, CA 96051
916-238-2553

Bridge Bay Resort
10300 Bridge Bay Road
Redding, CA 96003
916-275-3021
800-752-9669

Digger Bay Marina
P.O. Box 1516
Redding, CA 96003
916-275-3072
800-752-9669

Holiday Flotels
P.O. Box 336-B
Redding, CA 96099
916-221-5666

Holiday Harbor
P.O. Box 112
O'Brien, CA 96070
916-238-2383
800-251-BOAT

Jones Valley Resort
Box 739
Project City, CA 96079
916-275-1204

Lakeshore Resort Marina
Star Route Box 760
Lakehead, CA 96051
916-238-2301

Lakeview Marina Resort
P.O. Box 2272
Redding, CA 96099
916-223-3003

Shasta Marina Resort
P.O. Box E
O'Brien, CA 96070
916-238-2284

Silverthorne Resort, Inc.
P.O. Box 4205
Redding, CA 96099
916-275-1571
800-332-3044

Sugarloaf Marina Resort
P.O. Box 599
Redding, CA 96099
916-243-4353

TRINITY LAKE, CALIFORNIA
(17,000 acres, 145 miles of shoreline)

Cedar Stock Marina
Star Route Box 510
Lewiston, CA 96052
916-286-2225

Estrellita Resort
Star Route Box 542
Lewiston, CA 96052
916-286-2215

Recreation Plus
P.O. Box 156
Trinity Center, CA 96051
916-266-3432

Trinity Alps Marina
P.O. Box 670
Lewiston, CA 96052
916-286-2282

South Central

BEAVER LAKE, ARKANSAS
(28,000 acres, 480 miles of shoreline)

Rocky Branch Marina
P.O. Box 1459
Rogers, AR 72757
501-925-1300

BULL SHOALS LAKE,
ARKANSAS/MISSOURI
(45,500 acres, 1,050 miles of shoreline)

Bull Shoals Lake Dock
Box 748
Bull Shoals, AR 72619
501-445-4424

DeGray Lake, Arkansas
(13,800 acres, 240 miles of shoreline)

DeGray State Park
Route 3, Box 490
Bismarck, AR 71929
501-865-3700

Lake Eufaula, Oklahoma
(102,000 acres, 600 miles of shoreline)

Go Vacations
129 Carlingview Drive
Rexdale, Ontario M9W 5E7
Canada
918-689-9152
800-387-3998

Lake Norfork, Arkansas
(30,700 acres, 550 miles of shoreline)

101 Boat Dock
Route B, Box 164
Gamaliel, AR 72537
501-467-5252

Lake of the Ozarks, Missouri
(60,000 acres, 1,375 miles of shoreline)

Bridgeport Boat Rentals
P.O. Box 186
Osage Beach, MO 65065
314-348-2280
800-346-3365

Fantasy Cruz
P.O. Box 1043
Camdenton, MO 65065
314-365-2955

Go Vacations
129 Carlingview Drive
Rexdale, Ontario M9W 5E7
Canada
314-873-5202
800-387-3998

Link's Landing
U.S. 54
Osage Beach, MO 65065
314-348-2741

Lake Ouachita, Arkansas
(48,000 acres, 975 miles of shoreline)

Spillway Resort & Marina
P.O. Box 321
Mountain Pine, AR 71956
501-767-2997

Table Rock Lake, Missouri/ Arkansas
(52,000 acres, 857 miles of shoreline)

Indian Point Boat Dock
HCR-1, Box 1137
Branson, MO 65616
417-338-2891

Tri-Lakes Houseboat Rentals
49 Lake Road
Kimberling City, MO 65686
417-739-2370
800-992-BOAT

Stockton Lake, Missouri
(24,900 acres, 296 miles of shoreline)

Stockton Lake Houseboats
Route 4, Box 213-B
Stockton, MO 65785
417-276-4825

Lake Travis, Texas
(270 miles of shoreline)

Hurst Harbor
16405 Marina Point
Austin, TX 78734
512-266-1069
800-342-3242

Southeast

LAKE BARKLEY, KENTUCKY
(57,920 acres, 1,004 miles of shoreline)

Eddy Creek Resort & Marina
Route 1, Box 327
Eddyville, KY 42038
502-388-2271
800-626-2300

Green Turtle Bay
Box 102
Grand Rivers, KY 42045
502-362-8364

Leisure Cruise Marina
Box 266
Kuttawa, KY 42055
502-388-7925

Prizer Point Marina
1777 Prizer Point Road
Cadiz, KY 42211
502-522-3762

BARREN RIVER LAKE, KENTUCKY
(10,000 acres, 140 miles of shoreline)

Barren River State Dock
P.O. Box 30
Glasglow, KY 42141
502-646-2357

Peninsula Marina
Route 2, Box 252
Glasgow, KY 42141
502-646-2223

CAVE RUN LAKE, KENTUCKY
(8,270 acres, 166 miles of shoreline)

Cave Run Marinas
P.O. Box 174
Morehead, KY 40351
606-784-9666

CENTER HILL LAKE, TENNESSEE
(18,220 acres, 370 miles of shoreline)

Center Hill Marina
Route 1, Box 200
Lancaster, TN 38569
615-548-4315

Cookeville Dock & Resort
Route 2
Baxter, TN 38544
615-858-4008

Cove Hollow Marina
Route 1
Lancaster, TN 38569
615-548-4315

Hurricane Dock Resort
Route 1
Silver Point, TN 38582
615-858-2221

CORDELL HULL LAKE, TENNESSEE
(11,960 acres, 381 miles of shoreline)

Granville Marina Resort
P.O. 71
Granville, TN 38564
615-653-4360

LAKE CUMBERLAND, KENTUCKY
(50,250 acres, 1,085 miles of shoreline)

Beaver Creek Resort
P.O. Box 377
Monticello, KY 42633
606-348-7280

Buck Creek Dock
Route 7, Hwy. 769
Somerset, KY 42501
606-382-5542

Burnside Marina
P.O. Box 577
Burnside, KY 42519
606-561-4223

Conley Bottom Resort
Route 5, Box 205
Monticello, KY 42633
606-348-6351

Grider Hill Dock
Route 4, Box 682
Albany, KY 42602
606-387-5501

Indian Hills Alligator Dock #2
Route 5, Box 495
Russell Springs, KY 42642
502-866-6616

Jamestown Resort Marina
Highway 92 East
Jamestown, KY 42629
502-343-LAKE
800-922-7008

Lake Cumberland State Dock
P.O. Box 21, Hwy. 127
Jamestown, KY 42629
502-343-2525

Lee's Ford Dock Resort
Box 753
Somerset, KY 42501
606-636-6426

Popplewells Alligator Dock #1
Route 5, Box 606
Russell Springs, KY 42642
502-866-3634

DALE HOLLOW LAKE, KENTUCKY/ TENNESSEE
(27,700 acres, 620 miles of shoreline)

Cedar Hill Resort
Route 1
Celina, TN 38551
615-243-3201

Dale Hollow Dock
Route 1, Box 94
Celina, TN 38551
615-243-2211

Eagles Cove Marina
Route 1, Box 291
Byrdstown, TN 38549
615-864-3456

East Port Dock
Star Route
Alpine, TN 38543
615-879-7511

Hendricks Creek Resort
945 Hendricks Creek Road
Burkesville, KY 42717
502-433-7172
800-321-4000

Holly Creek Resort
Route 1
Celina, TN 38551
615-243-2116

Horse Creek Dock and Resort
Route 3, Box 290
Celina, TN 38551
615-243-2125

Livingston Dock
Route 1
Allons, TN 38541
615-823-6666

Star Point Resort
Route 1, Box 278
Byrdstown, TN 38549
615-864-3115

Sulpher Creek Resort
3498 Sulpher Creek Road
Kettle, KY 42752
502-433-7272

Willow Grove Resort
Route 1arBox 156
Allons, TN 38541
615-823-6616

Wisdom Dock
Route 2, Box 125
Albany, KY 42602
606-387-5821

Wolf River Dock
Route 2, Box 317
Albany, KY 42602
606-387-5841

FORT LOUDON LAKE, TENNESSEE
(14,600 acres, 360 miles of shoreline)

Concord Marina
Concord Park, Northshore Drive
Knoxville, TN 37922
615-966-5830

GREEN RIVER LAKE, KENTUCKY
(8,210 acres, 147 miles of shoreline)

Green River Marina
Route 5, Box 362K
Campbellsville, KY 42718
502-465-2512

Holmes Bend Boat Dock
P.O. Box 353
Columbia, KY 42728
502-384-4425

Taylor County Boat Dock
P.O. Box 282
Campbellsville, KY 42718
502-465-3412

LAKE HARTWELL, GEORGIA
(56,000 acres, 962 miles of shoreline)

Harbor Light Marina
Box 80, Route 3
Lavonia, GA 30553
404-356-4119

KENTUCKY LAKE, KENTUCKY/ TENNESSEE
(160,300 acres, 2,380 miles of shoreline)

Kenlake Marina
Route 1, Box 522
Hardin, KY 42048
502-474-2245
800-325-0143

Kentucky Dam Marina
P.O. Box 9
Gilbertsville, KY 42044
502-362-8386
800-648-2628

Southern Komfort Resort & Marina
Route 4, Box 228
Benton, KY 42025
502-354-6422

Sportsman's Marina
Route 5, Box 402
Benton, KY 42025
502-354-6568
800-331-4553

The Moors
Route 2
Gilbertsville, KY 42044
502-362-8889
800-626-5472

Town & Country Marina
Route 5, Box 391
Benton, KY 42025
502-354-8828
800-331-4553

LAKE LANIER, GEORGIA
(38,000 acres, 600 miles of shoreline)

Go Vacations
129 Carlingview Drive
Rexdale, Ontario M9W 5E7
Canada
404-531-0223
800-387-3998

Lake Lanier Islands Authority
P.O. Box 605
Buford, GA 30518
404-945-6701

LAUREL RIVER LAKE, KENTUCKY
(6,060 acres, 163 miles of shoreline)

Grove Marina
P.O. Box 1483
Corbin, KY 40701
606-523-2323

Holly Bay Marina
P.O. Box 674
London, KY 40741
606-864-6542

LAKES MARION AND MOULTRIE, SOUTH CAROLINA
(171,000 acres, 450 miles of shoreline)

Bell's Marina
Route 1, Box 332
Eutaw Springs, SC 29048
803-492-7924
800-845-7026

Lake Marion Resort & Marina
Box 408
Santee, SC 29142
803-854-3083

NICKAJACK LAKE, TENNESSEE
(10,370 acres, 192 miles of shoreline)

Hale's Bar Resort and Marina
P.O. Box 247
Guild, TN 37340
615-266-0771

NOLIN RIVER LAKE, KENTUCKY
(5,795 acres, 172 miles of shoreline)

Moutardier Resort & Marina
Route 6, Box 221
Leitchfield, KY 42754
502-286-4069

NORRIS LAKE, TENNESSEE
(34,200 acres, 800 miles of shoreline)

Powell Valley Marina & Resort
Route 1, Box 287
LaFollette, TN 37766
615-562-5975

Sequoyah Lodge & Marina
Route 1, Box 194 A
Andersonville, TN 37705
615-494-9920

Shanghai Resort
Route 2, Box 337
LaFollette, TN 37766
615-562-7651

Springs Boat Dock
Route 4
LaFollette, TN 37766
615-562-2405

PAINTSVILLE LAKE, KENTUCKY
(1,139 acres, 52 miles of shoreline)

Paintsville Lake Marina
Box 726
Paintsville, KY 41240
606-297-1521

Paintsville Lake Marina
P.O. Box 150
Staffordsville, KY 41256
606-297-1521

St. Johns River, Florida
(cruise about a 160-mile stretch of river)

Go Vacations
129 Carlingview Drive
Rexdale, Ontario M9W 5E7
Canada
904-736-9422
800-387-3998

Hontoon Landing Marina
2317 River Ridge Road
Deland, FL 32720
904-734-2007
800-458-2474

Sanford Boat Rentals
4370 Carraway Place
Sanford, FL 32771
407-321-5906
800-237-5105

Suwannee River, Florida
(cruise about a 70-mile stretch of river)

Millers Suwannee Houseboats
P.O. Box 280
Suwannee, FL 32692
904-542-7349

Taylorsville Lake, Kentucky
(3,050 acres, 75 miles of shoreline)

Taylorsville Lake Dock
P.O. Box 336
Taylorsville, KY 40071
502-477-8766

Watts Bar Lake, Tennessee
(39,000 acres, 771 miles of shoreline)

Blue Springs Marina
Route 2, Box 324
Ten Mile, TN 37880
615-376-7298

Fisher's Bayside Marina
Route 2, Box 404
Ten Mile, TN 37880
615-376-7031

Harbour Point Marina
Route 4, Box 267
Rockwood, TN 37854
615-354-2974

Rhea Harbor
Route 4, Box 951
Spring City, TN 37381
615-365-6851

II
River Rafts and Canoes

7 Choosing a Wilderness Trip

There are important differences among the many wilderness boating trips offered in North America. Trips can be as short as a few hours or as long as a few weeks; they can have different physical requirements that affect both choice and planning; they can be taken in relatively "civilized" areas or in the most remote places on the continent; they can be do-it-yourself trips or be led by a professional guide. There are also differences in cost and convenience.

In choosing your trip, first, decide what kind of trip you want and, second, what specific trip of that kind looks best. Virtually every company offering wilderness boating trips has brochures describing its trips, equipment, cost, and procedures. Next, write or call the companies to get these brochures, which will be your primary sources of information. The directory in chapter 10 lists companies providing rafting and canoeing trips.

For many people, wilderness is the primary attraction of a river trip. In fact, a wide variety of wilderness boating trips involve little—if any—whitewater. Instead, the emphasis is on escaping modern society, getting closer to nature, and enjoying a simpler way of doing things. Frequently, these trips are on rivers, creeks, and lakes that have no rapids at all.

On land, most true wilderness in America can be reached only on foot or horseback—modes of travel that are not for everyone. The alternative—going by boat—has been used since the first explorers ventured into the wilderness. A boat can get you into wilderness inaccessible to even horses and hikers. The boating alternative is available to anyone with a sense of adventure—even those who have never been on a boat or spent a night in a sleeping bag. If your idea of a serious packing expedition is bringing the groceries in from the car, a professionally run boat trip is the way to go.

The Boats

Several kinds of boats are used on wilderness trips. Having a basic understanding of the differences among them is essential to evaluating the different trips and deciding which is best for you. Your choice of trip may ultimately be based more on what kind of boat appeals to you than any other factor. We will examine the two most popular wilderness boats—the inflatable raft and the canoe—in detail later on, after surveying all the choices.

Do not worry about whether you can handle these boats. On all the trips, you will either have a "guide" or be working with an "outfitter." A guide (or "boatman," even though many of them are women) is a professional who leads your trip; an outfitter provides all the necessary equipment, expertise, and instruction for you to do the trip yourself. Most people can do any of these trips with the help of these experts.

The inflatable raft is the workhorse of most professional river-running companies. These are extremely durable boats made of fabric that is coated to provide airtightness and resistance to abrasion. The development of these boats and exotic fabrics is primarily responsible for the boom in commercial whitewater river running in the last fifteen or twenty years. Smaller rafts will either be powered by oars (the boatman does the rowing) or paddles (you paddle); larger ones usually have an outboard motor. The different types of inflatable rafts and the features affecting your choice of one are covered in more detail in chapter 8.

The canoe is easily the most popular choice for wilderness exploration on relatively calm water. Modern canoes are sturdy, lightweight, and easy to paddle. (A paddle, by the way, is what you hold in your hand to *paddle* a boat. An oar is attached to the boat by an "oar lock" and used in pairs to *row* a boat. Calling an oar a paddle, or vice versa, is like calling a fork a spoon and is sure to earn you one of those looks.) A beginner can learn enough basics in one instructional session to safely and effectively handle a canoe in flat water. We will look at canoes in detail in chapter 9.

For backpackers who would prefer a little more comfort and a little less

There are few experiences that can compare to the thrill of running a chute like this one on the middle fork of the American River. (Photo courtesy of Whitewater Voyages)

effort, canoe tripping can be the perfect answer. An average backpacker carrying a fifty-pound pack has quite a load. Walking ten miles with that pack is a good day's work. A canoe can carry two people and 500 pounds of gear (although you would never want to load it that heavy). Ten miles is considered a modest day's travel in a canoe.

Kayaks are the small, covered boats (usually holding one person) originally developed by the Eskimos. These boats are highly maneuverable and highly unstable. It requires considerable skill to handle a kayak in rough water. My first time in one, I managed to turn it over in a "rapid" that had waves nearly six inches high. Few professional companies take novices on whitewater kayak expeditions unless doing so as part of an instructional program.

Sea kayaking is growing in popularity. As the name implies, these trips involve kayaking in saltwater areas, including marshes, bays, and the open ocean. Trips are available for those without prior kayaking experience, but some paddling experience and swimming ability are helpful.

Inflatable kayaks (usually called "duckies") are quite maneuverable but considerably more stable than the true kayak. A novice can successfully run moderate whitewater in one the first time out. Many river-running companies carry a ducky along for people who want to get a little closer to the water. Some day trips are run using duckies.

Sportyaks are another fun alternative to the true kayak. These boats are a bit more serious than the ducky; the Grand Canyon has been run in one of them.

The dory is the choice of the purist. Dories are the traditional sharp-prowed wooden boats (also made today from aluminum and fiberglass) that have been used by fishermen and ocean sailors for centuries. Their design makes them not only sturdy but quick to turn—excellent rough-water boats. A typical dory is about 17 feet long, oar powered, and carries four passengers plus the boatman. Although dories are not a common sight on rivers today, they are still available for commercial trips.

CANOES VERSUS RAFTS

The great majority of wilderness first-timers choose either a whitewater raft trip or a flat-water canoe trip. Both require going into the wilderness on a small boat, camping out, a certain amount of self-sufficiency, and (at least for the novice) learning new skills. But there are also some big differences between them.

A group of first-timers in an inflatable raft led by an experienced guide can successfully paddle rapids that even an expert would be reluctant to try in an open canoe unless it were specially designed and outfitted for white-water. A team of nine athletes could vigorously paddle that inflatable raft in flat water, and two people in a canoe could easily, and quietly, pass them. The rugged, inflatable raft, so at home on whitewater rivers, would be out of its element on the remote systems of wilderness lakes and rivers that are the canoe's natural habitat. The differences in these boats—and the waters where they are used—make these different types of vacations.

The usual canoe trip requires a good deal more self-sufficiency than the rafting expedition. Controlling a raft in big rapids takes considerable skill, and a beginner must rely on having an experienced guide aboard. But it is easy to learn to paddle a canoe well enough to handle it comfortably on a flat-water trip. Consequently, most people taking a wilderness vacation by canoe—even novices—do it on their own.

The Requirements to Go

Remember, you do not need boating experience to go on any of these trips. On some trips, the guide handles the boat; your only job is to stay in it. On the rest, professionals will teach you everything you need to know before the trip starts. All the whitewater rafting trips are guided (at least one guide is on every boat when floating anything but the easiest water).

Some of these trips are physically demanding, but most are not. If you have any special health problems, check with your doctor before going. Age should not keep a person from going on a river trip if he or she is in reason-ably good physical condition. Steve, a boatman in the Grand Canyon, told me of taking a man of 92 down the Colorado whose only concession to his age was that he "paced himself on the hikes" up the side canyons. On the other end of the scale, our group on a recent four-day whitewater rafting trip included a six-year-old girl. She had a great time. Tara was a cheerful, bright, and helpful addition to the group (one of her "jobs" was passing out the cookies after lunch).

It is not necessary to know how to swim to go on these trips. One of the primary safety rules on river rafts is that everyone wear a life vest when going through even the smallest rapids (on some trips, "whenever you're aboard the boat"). This rule is scrupulously observed on all professionally run trips.

Tara enjoys a little exploring on her own during a lunch stop. (Photo by Michael White)

Some outdoors experience is helpful on camping trips, but even those without any experience usually find the rewards well worth the slight inconvenience involved. Attitude is more important than experience. The key word is enthusiasm. If this is something you want to do, you can.

Safety

Wilderness boating trips are remarkably safe. There are several reasons for this, the most important being the competence and professionalism of the guides and outfitters and their use of first-class, modern equipment.

The most important thing is to know what to expect in the wilderness. Some trips can be demanding. Think about the following passage from a U.S. Forest Service information pamphlet for prospective wilderness canoeists:

> Before you plan a trip to any wilderness, ask yourself if you actually want a wilderness experience. You will not find piped water, prepared shelters, or easy travel. Few trail signs will guide you, so you must know how to use a compass and

read a map. You will be on your own in an (sometimes) alien and unfamiliar environment. You must
be prepared to meet the unexpected, such as accidents and illness, rainy weather, and high winds on
the larger lakes.

Neither the Forest Service nor I intend to be discouraging, only realistic.
Do not back off just because it sounds challenging; the challenge is part of the
fun of a wilderness trip. But be aware of safety all the time; use common
sense and take no chances.

Camping

Campsites vary from place to place. They can be as simple as a sandy beach
or as "elaborate" as a park service campground. Many spots will have the
basics: cleared places for sleeping and a fire pit.

Your group should have a private camp each night. In most wilderness
areas, the unwritten rule prohibits pulling into a site occupied by another
party, even if it is large enough for both. In some areas, it is even against the
written law for more than one group to share a site.

Each night you will set up your own private camp near the group's main site.
(Photo by Michael White)

Each person, couple, or family will set up a private camp near the main camp. This will be where you pitch your tent (if you are using one), lay out your sleeping bag, and keep your personal gear. Your personal camp and gear are your responsibility—not the guides'.

You can either supply your own tent, sleeping bag, and pad or get them through the company. You need a tent since rain is always possible. Sleeping in a tent when it is raining is a pleasant experience; the alternative is not. Often these items are part of the package on river-rafting trips or are provided for an extra charge. On a canoe trip run by a "complete" outfitter, everything will be supplied.

Company tents are generally lightweight, two-person models. Sometimes, four-person tents are available. Tents come in several types and shapes, but the basic components are the same: an external frame of aluminum tubing that supports a nylon tent, a "rain fly" (an external, waterproof cover over the tent), and zippered nylon flap or mosquito netting doors and windows.

In some areas, camping is restricted to certain "designated" sites; camping anywhere else usually is forbidden, although some places permit it under carefully regulated conditions. Designated sites will almost always be "improved" sites, furnished and maintained by the park or forest service. They will have a fire pit (sometimes with grate), a toilet facility (basic chemical toilets or outhouses), and, possibly, a picnic table. The locations often are superb: nice beaches, trees, and lots of agreeable places for pitching your tent.

If this sounds a bit primitive for you, there are good alternatives. It is possible, for example, to take several day trips, with nights (and maybe some days) spent off the river.

The choice of trip to take is primarily one of personal preference. Is it to be the wet-and-wild action of a rafting expedition on serious whitewater, the peace and serenity of a flat-water canoe trip, or something in between? The following chapters should help you make your decision.

8 River Rafting

"Left side, forward!" shouts the guide. Left side—that's you. Your paddle digs in as if it had a life of its own. Working with the other three people on your side, you quickly turn the inflatable raft. "Left side, rest. Right side, back." You stop paddling and look up. There is no river, just a solid wall of whitewater. "All, forward!" The bow of the boat comes up and you crash into the wall. Water roars over your head and in a second you are through. The river is back, calm and placid—for at least the next 200 yards.

Somebody starts a chant, "More whitewater! More whitewater!" Soon everyone joins in. Yours is the loudest voice.

Running a whitewater river is like nothing on earth. It has to be experienced to be understood. In that last second before entering your first big rapids, you may wish you were someplace else—anyplace else. It seems impossible that your little boat could survive a head-on meeting with the roaring maelstrom in front of you. When you come out the other side, though, it will be with a new respect for the river—and your boat. You also will be looking forward to the next set of rapids. Whitewater is addictive.

But river running is much more than rapids. The river is your pathway to the wilderness, taking you places and showing you sights most people only dream about, putting you in touch with a world that existed long before we created the "reality" of modern life. A whitewater river-rafting expedition is one of the last great adventures. A set of rapids in an amusement park

On a paddle boat you are a part of the team. (Photo by Michael White)

could be the wildest ride in the world and still not create the feeling of awe you get when you drift quietly around a bend and hear the roar of that next rapid echoing up the river.

Every river-rafting expedition is different, depending on the type of boat you are on, the amount and intensity of the whitewater, and the length of the trip. Unlike most boating vacations, the amount of time you spend on the water and where you go is dictated by the river, not you. And once you start the trip, you are committed to finishing it. On a river-rafting vacation, as the rafters say, you "go with the flow." Because you are planning a great deal of the trip ahead of time, the choices of area, boat, and expedition type are crucial.

Whitewater Rafting Areas

River-rafting trips can be found throughout North America. Most are relatively short trips of two or three days which provide all the excitement and adventure of a true wilderness experience. Most of the *major* whitewater expeditions in America are run on the great Western rivers of the high desert. This area—most of Idaho, Wyoming, Utah, and Colorado and portions of neighboring states—is renowned both for excellent whitewater and fantastic scenery. Rivers such as the Snake, Yampa, Dolores, San Juan, Green, and Colorado are the first choice of many people seeking longer and more remote whitewater wilderness trips—places where bighorn sheep are more common than people and solitude seems almost tangible.

These big rivers offer some of the most incredible whitewater in the world. But they are also long and varied, and location on the river is as important as the choice of river itself. For example, a stretch of the Green River in Utah—through Labyrinth Canyon and into Stillwater Canyon in Canyonlands National Park—is 120 miles long and has no rapids at all. Yet just above the town of Green River, where this stretch starts, excellent whitewater runs are found in Desolation and Gray canyons, and just below, the Green flows into the Colorado and enters formidable Cataract Canyon.

A few hundred miles farther north, that same Green River provides one of the best trips available for spectacular scenery, lots of wildlife, some moderate whitewater, and a trip of modest length. Starting at the Gates of Lodore, the river narrows and begins a winding journey through a canyon that sometimes seems composed entirely of vertical rock walls. Sheer stone faces loom 1,000 feet overhead; at some places, the cliffs stand apart, their dramatically different rock strata forming a collagelike backdrop to the low wooded hills along the river. Sometimes, the cliffs will be close enough to touch as your raft floats by. At night, you will camp on sand beaches carved out of the cliff bases by the river.

This is not the trip to take, however, if you want lots of big whitewater. There are some fairly large rapids—and smaller ones that are great for running in a ducky—but you will spend more time admiring the scenery and watching bighorn sheep than running whitewater. A trip like this is best taken in an oar-powered, inflatable raft. There is enough calm water to make paddling seem too much like work. It is better to relax and leave the rowing to the boatman. On a leisurely trip through the Lodore, you will spend three nights on the river at some of the best riverside campsites I have seen. Overall, this is an easy, comfortable trip.

The Snake is another good example of the varied nature of rivers in this area. Excellent scenic trips with some whitewater are available near its headwaters in Grand Teton National Park in Wyoming. The river then heads into Idaho and wanders north, then south, then north again on its way westward along the old Oregon Trail. By the time it reaches Hell's Canyon on the Idaho-

The Gates of Lodore await us as we ready the rafts for a run down the Green River.
(Photo by Michael White)

Oregon border, the Snake is a big, fast-moving river with lots of whitewater action.

The trip through Hell's Canyon is different from Lodore. Here you will find much bigger (but still not monstrous) whitewater on a river that sometimes flows through wide open, rolling hills and at other times plunges into canyons of sheer rock walls. This is wild, frequently desolate country. The ruggedness of the area, its history, and the more primitive campsites all enhance the feeling of true adventure. You feel a kinship to the hardy pioneers who settled here, as you explore their abandoned ranches and listen to the guide's stories of great Indian battles.

The Snake also has excellent fishing. One of my best days in years was on a recent trip through Hell's Canyon with Holiday River Expeditions. Shawn (the only other serious fisherman on the trip) and I managed to get a boat to ourselves with a boatman who also liked to fish. We spent the time between rapids moving back and forth across this beautiful river, casting light spinners into the holes behind rocks and crevices in the cliffs. The river was swift, and we usually had only one cast before passing the hole. One was enough; between the three of us (Shawn took pity on the poor, frustrated boatman and rowed for a while so he could fish), we caught and released dozens of trout and bass.

The Green, the Snake, and other rivers of this area are among the great expedition rivers. But the greatest of them all—the preeminent river-running expedition in North America—is found a little farther south, in Arizona. Its name has become synonymous with whitewater adventure: the Grand Canyon of the Colorado River.

The Grand Canyon is 217 miles long and 18 miles across at its widest point. The Colorado River, as it flows through the canyon on its 1,450-mile trip from northern Colorado to the Sea of Cortez, carries water drained from a land area of nearly 250,000 square miles. It took this powerful river an estimated 6 million years to dig to its present depth (more than a mile in the inner gorge of the canyon). At that depth, you can see (and touch) rock from the early Precambrian era—formed 2 billion years ago. But such numbers are just too big to comprehend. So just say the name out loud: the Grand Canyon. Now picture yourself at the bottom of it. In a boat.

The first boat trip through the Grand Canyon was made in 1869 by a group headed by Major John Wesley Powell. Until then, the canyon had been a great unknown. Many people believed the Colorado River was impossible to run, and some even thought it flowed underground through parts of the

The Grand Canyon is even more majestic when seen from a boat. (Photo by Michael White)

canyon. The few existing maps of the area were sketchy and frequently inaccurate; the canyon itself was usually depicted as a huge blank area.

Powell's party survived incredible hardship and danger during their 24-day pioneering passage. Boat problems, loss of equipment, and the dwindling supply of rations intensified their constant fear that the next unknown rapid might be the end of them. The difficulties were so great that at one point (now known as Separation Canyon), three members of the group refused to go on and attempted to walk out. They were never heard from again and were presumed to have been killed by Indians. Ironically, the rest of the party emerged safely from the canyon at Grand Wash the next day. Powell's daring feat earned him a permanent place both in the history of the exploration of the West and the lore of river running.

Few were willing to challenge the formidable obstacles of running the canyon during the following decades. Not until the middle of this century did new developments in equipment, increased knowledge of the canyon, and improvements in river-running techniques begin changing things drastically (in fact, in 1955, two men floated down *without* a boat, and in 1960, a team using three jet boats ran *up* the river through the canyon).

The canyon has not been tamed—it probably never will be—but today virtually anyone can experience its majesty. Each year, dozens of professional companies safely and regularly run the canyon, providing trips for thousands of people. On a single afternoon during the peak summer season, more boaters run the river than during the entire three-quarters of a century between Powell's original exploration and the end of World War II.

A trip through the entire Grand Canyon starts just below Glen Canyon Dam (Lake Powell) at Lee's Ferry. This is Mile "0"; all points downriver are measured from here. The inner gorge of the Grand Canyon stretches from Mile 70 to Mile 116. Grand Wash, where Powell breathed his big sigh of relief, is just past Mile 284. After that is Lake Mead.

A trip through the Grand Canyon will remain in your memory forever—places like Elves Chasm or Havasu Creek, where streams entering the canyon create clear pools under gentle waterfalls. Other falls are breathtakingly powerful. You will stop to replenish your water supply, as Powell did, at beautiful Vasey's Paradise and then, a mile downriver, stand in the huge expanse of Red Wall Cavern and decide for yourself if it really would seat 50,000 people as Powell thought. You will take short hikes up side canyons between vertical rock walls so close together and so high that the sky is a narrow strip above your head and, if you want, longer hikes to explore ancient Indian ruins or stand on the edge of the inner gorge, far above the river. These places are even more awe-inspiring when you consider that few people besides you will ever see them.

Rating the Waters

Riding the monstrous whitewater of the Colorado River is the experience of a lifetime. But many other rivers throughout North America offer great whitewater wilderness experiences. Many stretches of these wilderness rivers are protected by the Wild and Scenic Rivers Act of 1968, which ensures that certain "outstandingly remarkable" rivers are protected from development. There are three classifications in the system: "wild," "scenic," and "recreational." Rivers designated "wild" have been found to "represent vestiges of primitive America." They are completely undammed and can only be reached by foot, horseback, or boat. The requirements for a "scenic" river are slightly less demanding; some accessibility by road and more development are allowed. If the river you are considering has either of these designations (the company's brochure often will tell you), rest assured that it will be a true wilderness river.

Moving water is usually rated according to the International Scale of River Difficulty, from Class I (the easiest) to Class VI (the most difficult). The system provides a good way to make general comparisons between rivers.

International Scale of River Difficulty

CLASS I Moving water with a few riffles and small waves. Few or no obstructions.

CLASS II Easy rapids with waves up to 3 feet high and wide, clear channels that are obvious without scouting. Some maneuvering is required.

CLASS III Rapids with high, irregular waves. Narrow passages that often require complex maneuvering. May require scouting from shore.

CLASS IV Long, difficult rapids with constricted passages that often require precise maneuvering in very turbulent waters. Scouting from shore is often necessary and conditions make rescue difficult. Boaters in covered canoes and kayaks should have the ability to Eskimo roll.

CLASS V Extremely difficult, long, very violent rapids with highly congested routes, which nearly always must be scouted from shore. Rescue conditions are difficult, and there is a significant hazard to life in the event of a mishap. Ability to Eskimo roll is essential for boaters in kayaks and canoes.

CLASS VI Difficulties of Class V carried to the extreme of navigability. For teams of experts only, after close study has been made and all precautions have been taken.

The classification of the river is based on the most difficult rapids you will encounter. The scale is also used to describe individual rapids. When your guide says that the rapids coming up is a Class IV, you know it will get your attention. The ratings are useful when comparing rivers, but they are not as simple or as precise as they may seem. Two or three Class IV rapids on a stretch of river would justify it having a Class IV rating, but there could be a lot of calm water between them.

Although the International Scale is used almost exclusively throughout the world, rivers of the western United States are occasionally described using a system designed specifically for use on extremely high-volume rivers. Here the rating will be on a basis of 1 to 10, with 10 being the most difficult.

A particular area may have several rivers, or stretches of river, to choose from. Here is where the flow (volume of water past a given point) and gradient (average drop of the riverbed) become important considerations. The water in many rivers is very low late in the summer (some cannot even be run), so if you want the wildest ride, go early or choose rivers controlled by dams, which have fairly constant flows. Because gradient is the *average* drop of the river, it is a better indicator of the amount of whitewater you will have on shorter trips than on longer ones. But do not try to judge a river sight unseen based on these factors alone. Talk to the people running the rivers, tell them what you want, and take their advice.

Many wilderness rivers offer excellent fishing. Let the company know if you are interested. They will know about river conditions (whether a particular river is too muddy to fish at the moment) and advise you as to the best choices. Also, some companies do not allow fishing while the boat is under way; most will restrict it if it might interfere with the other guests. You will always be able to fish when the boat is stopped.

The river-running season is roughly from midspring to late fall. Higher water in the spring usually means bigger, more powerful rapids, and fishing is generally better in the spring and fall. The weather should be warmer and more predictable in midsummer, but this is also when you will find the most people on the rivers.

Which Raft?

The increased popularity of whitewater river running during the last twenty years is primarily a result of the development of the inflatable raft. Nearly all river expeditions now use these incredibly rugged boats.

The forerunner of these boats was the inflatable assault raft developed by the U.S. Navy during World War II. These seven-man and ten-man rafts were made of canvas with a black neoprene coating; thousands were sold after the war as surplus, and their low price, excellent flotation, and durability soon made them the choice of most river runners.

Since then, the inflatable has evolved into a highly sophisticated piece of equipment. Nylon, polyester, and Kevlar fibers now provide considerably more strength than the original cotton canvas. Coatings such as Hypalon, polyvinyl chloride (PVC), and polyurethane have replaced neoprene, providing increased durability. Modern inflatable rafts range in size from the original ten-man navy version (15 feet long by 7 feet wide) to monsters that could have escaped from a science fiction movie. These boats have changed whitewater river running from an exploit for the rugged adventurer into a vacation opportunity for all of us.

The smallest inflatable rafts are paddle boats. The best way to truly experience the river is with a paddle in your hand. Paddling through rapids is completely different from just riding through them on one of the bigger boats. You are no longer simply a hanger-on but a vital member of the team, helping to maneuver the boat. The thrill and exhilaration of whitewater river running is even greater when you become involved in the action.

On an oar-powered boat the boatman handles the boat; your only job is to hang on.
(Photo by Michael White)

On paddling trips, you get a lot wetter. Instead of ducking when the water gets rough, you have to dig in with your paddle and go. You also stand a good chance of taking an unintentional swim (why you should not worry about falling off the boat is discussed below).

A paddle-boat trip is not all that physically demanding, especially a shorter trip. If you can walk two blocks at a reasonable pace without getting winded and have enough coordination to rake leaves, you can handle a day trip on a paddle boat. Longer paddle trips are more demanding, particularly if there are long stretches of calm water to paddle; on these, some paddling experience can be helpful.

Oar-powered rafts are usually bigger than paddle boats and are equipped with a set of sweep oars mounted on a frame in the middle of the boat. They are rowed by the guide, who sits in the center of the boat and, when going through rapids, faces downstream and rows against the current, a technique perfected in the 1890s on cataract boats. Next to the dory, the oar-powered raft provides the most traditional way to run a river.

If you want to try your hand at the oars, your guide probably will let you handle the boat on calm water and maybe through some of the milder rapids. My first time at the oars of a whitewater rowboat was quite an experience. It only took me a few minutes (and a few blisters) to gain a new appreciation for the skill it takes.

The biggest inflatable rafts are motorized. The ones used by Western River Expeditions (one of the largest whitewater rafting companies) on some of their longer big-water trips are a good example of the state-of-the-art in giant raft construction. It is hard to think of this boat, called a "J-rig," as a raft. Five separate pontoons are lashed to a steel frame to create a boat 37 feet long and over 15 feet wide. Power is supplied by a 30-horsepower outboard motor. It can carry 18 passengers, a crew of two, and all the equipment and provisions needed for a week-long expedition. Fully loaded, the J-rig weighs more than 8,000 pounds.

The J-rig and other large motorized boats offer a different kind of experience. Their size provides more stability and room, but you will have less intimate contact with the water (literally and figuratively). You have a choice of several different places to sit on these boats, from the "chicken nest" in the center to the very front, where you can actually ride the pontoons like a rodeo cowboy. The closer to the water, the wilder the ride. Besides comfort, the main advantage of the motorized boat is its ability to cover the distance between rapids in less time than other boats. This lets you take long trips in

I try the oars in a little whitewater. Notice how calm and relaxed I appear.

about half the time it would take on an oar or paddle boat. The trade-off is that you have to listen to the motor all the time.

This brief survey of inflatables would not be complete without another mention of the ducky. The only way to get closer to the water than on a ducky is to go swimming. You sit at water level, with your legs out in front of you, and use a paddle with a blade on either end (a kayak paddle). Even a small rapid looks big from a ducky. Ask whether a ducky will be provided on the trip you are considering; they can add a lot of fun to the river experience.

If time is not a consideration, choose whatever type of boat you prefer. If you want to take a long trip, such as the entire Grand Canyon, and have limited time, take a motorized boat. Generally speaking, the smaller the boat, the bigger the rapids look and the wilder the ride. An oar-powered boat is the most popular choice for a medium-length trip (three to five days). It is small enough to be great fun in rapids yet large enough to be stable and comfortable. And you can leave the driving to them. If you want to get in on the action, take a paddle boat.

Which Trip?

An important consideration in choosing a river rafting trip is how long you want to be on the water. How much "roughing it" will be fun for you? For camping novices, a shorter trip (three or four days) is probably better. Even

Large motorized rafts, such as the J-rig shown here, have the advantages of speed and comfort but still provide a wild ride in big whitewater.
(Photo courtesy of Western River Expeditions)

hard-core campers start looking forward to a hot shower by the end of a long trip. Day trips offer some exciting alternatives.

Next, consider how much whitewater you want. Do you want to spend a lot of time on the river and run some big rapids, or would you prefer a more leisurely trip on a quieter river with lots of time ashore?

For a rough idea of the nature of the trip, look at the miles traveled per day (total miles divided by number of days). This is particularly useful for comparing different companies' trips on the same river. It is less useful for comparing different rivers, because the speed of the current (and, therefore, travel time) will be different. In general, 15 miles or less per day is fairly leisurely, and 20 or more is pushing it. Motorized trips easily do 30 or more miles per day because of their higher speeds.

DAY TRIPS

Hundreds of day trips are offered in North America. Because you normally would not plan an entire vacation around one of these, the trick is to be in an area that offers a number of different day trips.

There are good reasons for planning vacations around several day trips instead of a single, multiday trip. An important one (if camping out does not appeal to you) is that camping is not necessarily involved. Day trips can be as short as a couple of hours or as long as the full day. Regardless, you will be back at the company's headquarters each afternoon. You can sleep at a motel instead of in a sleeping bag.

Another advantage of day trips is versatility. Day trips are booked on an individual "per trip" basis; you pick the excursions that look good and fit your schedule and choose the days, locations, and class of water that suit you. This gives you the flexibility to design a vacation of any length with as much or as little whitewater as you want. In some areas, you can even combine whitewater rafting and canoeing. Since you will be on the water only during the day—or a portion of it—you will also have time to go sightseeing by land.

Some of the best day-tripping vacations are planned around areas that offer a variety of short whitewater rafting trips. Some tremendous whitewater rivers are not in remote areas and are easily run in a day. Many of these runs are not true wilderness trips (although you will see some beautiful country); what counts on these is the excitement of the whitewater. Areas such as the Appalachian Mountains (from Tennessee to the Virginias), the Sierra Nevadas (California), and the Cascade Range (northern California to Washington) regularly attract thousands of vacationers who come to experience the thrill of running great whitewater rivers in the best possible way—with a paddle in their hands.

Most day trips are run on boats that you help steer and paddle. There may be six or eight paddlers and a guide on each boat (most paddle trips include several boats traveling together). The paddlers sit on either side of the boat (actually up on the tubes) and are directed by the guide, who sits on the stern.

Your guide will demonstrate how to paddle and take you through the basic commands while the boat is in calm water. The boat is turned by having the paddlers on one side stop (or back-paddle) while the other side paddles forward, the guide using his or her paddle like a rudder. For example, if everyone were paddling forward in calm water and the guide gave the command "left side rest," paddlers on the left would stop while those on the right continued, and the boat would turn to the left. Paddling is simple. The physical part is easy to learn, then all you have to do on the river is follow the guide's directions.

There are good whitewater rivers available for day trips in many areas of North America. The choice of where to go, therefore, is frequently based

Companies running large whitewater day trips will provide everything you need, including transportation from a central meeting place to the put-in. (Photo by Michael White)

on geographic convenience. For most people, the choice is simply a matter of filling the available time with the maximum amount of whitewater action.

In most cases, the company provides (for a single fee) the trip, transportation from a central meeting place to the put-in, and, on a full-day trip, lunch. The cost of a day trip ranges from about $35 to $95, depending on the length, location, number of people going, and the season. Some of the larger multiriver operations also provide (at an extra cost) lodging or camping facilities and meals when you are off the river. A few offer all-inclusive packages. If you plan to be on several rivers, choose one of these companies instead of contacting a different outfit for each river. It is usually more convenient. The directory of rafting companies in chapter 10 includes those that do day trips.

EXPEDITIONS
Expeditions are multiday trips scheduled ahead of time and booked on an individual basis. In fact, a majority of people on expeditions are singles and couples. These guided trips, which include overnight camping, can be as short as two days and one night or as long as two weeks. Most, if not all, of your boating and camping equipment will be supplied by the company, which also supplies all the food; cooking and clean-up are done by the guides. Although the great majority of expeditions use inflatable rafts, some companies offer canoe expeditions (usually not on whitewater).

You will find large price differences among companies offering similar trips. Expeditions start at about $100 per person per day and can be more than twice that. Often, the higher price means you get more services for the base price. When comparing the costs of different trips, look at what is provided for the listed price. This is true both in comparing trips on different rivers and different companies on the same river. The most important "extras" to pay attention to are camping gear (sleeping bag, sleeping pad, tent, and, occasionally, river bag), transportation to and from the river, accommodations before and after the trip, and beverages (some companies supply beer and soft drinks). If something you want is supplied on one trip, add its cost to the price of the trip that does not supply it. This will give you an accurate total cost to use for comparing trips of the same length.

For trips of different lengths, divide the cost of the trip by the number of *nights* on the river. Most companies start trips in the morning and end in the afternoon; a "five-day" trip means four nights on the river. You will lose a lot of river time on the first and last days due to traveling, loading, and unloading, so dividing by the number of nights gives you a better figure for comparison than dividing by days.

If you have a large group, you can usually get a better price by arranging a charter (see below). There are also some seasonal price variations worth looking at.

Booking the Trip

Companies establish their schedules for the next season well ahead of time and then book on a first-come, first-served basis. The schedule in their brochure includes the dates planned for each river they run (many companies run several different rivers) and the length and price of each trip. Schedules are always subject to change; do not make any definite plans until you have confirmed the trip and its availability.

Singles and couples should find an opening on fairly short notice if they are reasonably flexible about dates, rivers, or both. If your choice of river and dates is firm, or if you have a large group, book well ahead of time. This is particularly true if your destination is the Grand Canyon, where high demand and restrictions imposed on the companies by their use permits usually mean that trips will be filled early. But go ahead and check with the company even if you want to book a large group for the day after tomorrow. The number of boats used for a given trip is based on the number of people going. Most companies have a maximum number they can handle, but if they are still under that number, another boat could be added to accommodate your group. Last-minute cancellations also occur.

Large groups should consider a charter. Most rafting companies will arrange exclusive trips for your group; these have the advantages of greater flexibility in selecting start and finish times and in limiting the trip participants to members of your group. There is also usually a "group rate" discount when you do this. The number of people it takes to have your own trip varies, depending on the company and the river. Contact the company well ahead of time to make charter arrangements.

Planning a Grand Canyon expedition is a little different, both because the trip takes longer and because there is only one place to enter or leave the canyon (unless you use a helicopter, which some companies do). There are several ways to take the trip. The first is to get on an oar boat at Lee's Ferry and get off at Lake Mead a couple of weeks later. This is the purest and most complete experience. But for many, a trip this long is impossible because of time limitations, inadvisable because of inexperience, simply undesirable because of its length, or all three. There are alternatives.

The easiest trip and the shortest in time is aboard one of the large boats with a motor. Motorized trips, starting at Lee's Ferry and going through most of the canyon (you are flown out by helicopter at the end of the trip), are available from several companies and run about six days. They provide an excellent alternative for those with limited time, experience, or both. And do not think that being on a big boat diminishes the thrill of the whitewater. The rapids in the Grand Canyon are huge; be prepared for a very exciting ride.

The other major option is to do a shorter trip through a portion of the canyon. Usually, this means going down the river from Lee's Ferry to Phantom Ranch, at Mile 88, and then hiking out on the Bright Angel Trail or hiking in to Phantom Ranch to meet the boat for the trip through the rest of the canyon. If you choose this option, you should be in pretty good physical shape. The Bright Angel Trail is over nine miles long and has a very steep grade. The hike in will take three or four hours; hiking out takes twice that long, and the grade seems straight up. If you can handle the hiking, this option will allow you to take an oar boat, have a more leisurely trip, and spend more time in the canyon.

FINDING A BROKER
There are several central booking agencies for whitewater trips. These agencies (not to be confused with travel agents) work with a number of river-

running companies and sell their trips on a commission basis. Some of them run their own trips as well as book trips with other companies; some, such as High Desert Adventures (Western expedition rivers) and USA Whitewater (the Appalachians), act as a central marketing department for several companies; others book dozens of companies in all areas. It costs no more to book through a central agency than to book directly with the company (the company pays the commission).

The advantages of using these agencies are flexibility and convenience. Because they book trips with many companies on many different rivers (and should be very familiar with all of them), it should be easier for them to find the right trip for you than it would be for you to go through each company's brochures. This is particularly true when arranging a trip on short notice, when calling each company would be necessary to confirm availability. Other advantages include assistance in making travel arrangements and booking accommodations before and after the trip.

The main disadvantage of a broker is in dealing with an intermediary instead of the company. This can lead to communication problems. The most important consideration in selecting brokers is how closely they work with the companies they represent. A broker who works regularly with a few companies may know more about those companies and have a better working relationship with them than a broker who books them all.

After booking the trip, simply pack your personal gear and show up at the appointed time and place. Your hosts will take care of everything else.

Your Personal Gear

As already mentioned, the company will provide (either as part of the trip cost or at an extra charge) tents, sleeping bags, and sleeping pads. Life jackets are always provided. In addition, you will be given a "river bag" and an "ammo can." A river bag is a heavyweight, waterproof bag large enough to hold all the personal gear you need on a trip. The top folds down several times to make a seal and is then buckled to the side of the bag. These bags are tied to the raft or stowed under a tarp and are not usually accessible to you during the day. An ammo can is a small metal box with a hinged lid and a rubber seal to keep water out. Most are actually military surplus ammunition boxes. They are large enough to hold the items you will need during the day (such as your camera) and are stowed where they will be readily accessible.

Keep personal gear to an absolute minimum. Everything must fit into your river bag and ammo can. If your river bag gear will fit in a standard brown-paper grocery bag, you're in good shape.

The following checklist contains everything you *need* for most summer trips. Check the items you want, use it as a shopping list, and then make sure everything is packed.

Personal Gear Checklist

Want	Buy	Packed	Item
☐	☐	☐	Bag (plastic for wet/dirty clothes)
☐	☐	☐	Beverages (see below)
☐	☐	☐	Books (paperback general reading)
☐	☐	☐	Camera and film
☐	☐	☐	Eating utensils (see below)
☐	☐	☐	Eyeglasses and an extra pair
☐	☐	☐	Fishing tackle (see below)
☐	☐	☐	Flashlight (small with extra batteries)
☐	☐	☐	Hat with strap
☐	☐	☐	Insect repellent
☐	☐	☐	Jacket (lightweight windbreaker)
☐	☐	☐	Jacket, a warm one (or sweater)
☐	☐	☐	Knife (small pocket type)
☐	☐	☐	Nylon cord, 10 feet of 1/8″ (misc. uses)
☐	☐	☐	Pants (one quick-drying pair)
☐	☐	☐	Pillow
☐	☐	☐	Rain gear (see below)
☐	☐	☐	Shirts (one long sleeve; two short)

☐	☐	☐	Shoes (two pair; light, quick-drying)
☐	☐	☐	Shorts (two pair)
☐	☐	☐	Soap (biodegradable)
☐	☐	☐	Socks (several pairs)
☐	☐	☐	Suntan lotion/block, also for the lips
☐	☐	☐	Sunglasses with safety strap
☐	☐	☐	Swimsuits (two)
☐	☐	☐	Toilet kit
☐	☐	☐	Towel (small)
☐	☐	☐	Underwear (wear a swimsuit during the day)
☐	☐	☐	Washcloth
☐	☐	☐	Miscellaneous (your list)
☐	☐	☐	_____
☐	☐	☐	_____
☐	☐	☐	_____
☐	☐	☐	_____

All companies have something to drink available during the day, usually water and lemonade. Beer and soft drinks are occasionally furnished by the company; if not, bring your own if you want them. These beverages do not have to go in your river bag (they'll provide a way to keep them cold). Liquor must be in a plastic container. (Wine that comes in a box works well.) Eating utensils are supplied by most companies, although a few require you to bring your own mess kit. If you plan to fish, a break-down backpacker's rod is best. Keep your tackle to a minimum.

The rain gear can be either a two-piece rain suit or a poncho. Pick up one of the inexpensive, lightweight types found in any store that sells camping equipment. They are not just for rain protection. On some rivers where the water is very cold (particularly in the morning), rain gear will help to keep you warm going through the rapids.

Do not bring hard suitcases, radios (or tape decks), firearms, illegal drugs, nonwaterproof watches, or pets.

On most trips, you will unpack your gear into the river bag and ammo can and leave your suitcase behind. On some trips, you will not return to where you spent the night before your departure. This is commonly done on the Grand Canyon, where many trips start in Las Vegas, fly to Page for the night before the trip, and then return directly to Las Vegas after it, which means you must take everything down the river with you. Pack your gear in either a small cloth bag that will fit inside your river bag or a plastic garbage bag. You can check extra luggage at the airport in Las Vegas and pick it up when you return.

The Guides

If your idea of a river guide is a grizzled, weather-beaten man with a barrel chest and a beard down to the second button of his plaid shirt, you have a surprise in store for you. All kinds of people work as river guides. Most are young, gregarious, fun-loving folks who look like they would be just as much at home lounging around a ski lodge as sitting on a whitewater raft. In fact, some of them spend their winters working at ski lodges.

Many of the best boatmen are women. A man with years of guiding experience told me why as we drifted down one of the infrequent quiet stretches on the Lower Gauley.

"It's simple," he said. "A lot of men get out on the river the first time with some sort of macho, man-against-the-elements attitude. They figure they're going to beat the river with those big muscles of theirs. Bull. Nobody can beat the river. You have to learn to work with it; to read the water; to think ahead. There's not one time in a hundred that muscles will get you out of trouble once you get into it. Best to stay out of it in the first place. Women usually make good guides because they learn that little secret of river running the first time out instead of having to have it beat into them. A lot of people say I run the river like a woman," he added, flexing his heavily muscled shoulders in anticipation of the next rapid. "I do. And I'm proud of it."

On most rivers, the guides (and the companies) are required to be licensed. One of the conditions for the guide's license is that the applicant have experience—usually four to six runs—on the river under the supervision of a licensed guide. There will always be one very experienced guide in charge of the trip.

River guides know more than just how to get a raft down a river. Their job is to know the territory ashore as well as on the water (many are accomplished naturalists) and to take care of all the group's needs. They are "people" people who are there to see that you have a good time. The guides will lead hikes to places you would not find on your own, point out things you would have overlooked, and answer *all* your questions. (I always wondered how, until a guide told me that three answers would take care of 90 percent of them: everything is going to happen in "about forty-five minutes"; every destination is "around the next bend"; and "it varies" will take care of most of the rest.)

There is a lot more that the guides do (see The Evening Camp, below). The hours are long, the work is demanding, the responsibility is immense, and the pay is minimal. It is proper, as with any other service people, to express your appreciation for their efforts with a gratuity. It is a nice way to say thank you. You can give it to the head guide for distribution. A tip of 3 to 5 percent of the trip cost is appropriate.

Safety

Safety is the guides' top priority. They will instruct you on safe boating practices before you leave and remind you any time they notice you failing to observe them. Most matters of safety are common sense. If you pay attention to the professional advice of the guides and use your head, you will have a safe and enjoyable trip.

The most frequently expressed concern of first-time river rafters is falling off the boat. This is actually far less dangerous than most imagine (people frequently swim smaller rapids just for fun), but even a good swimmer can get into trouble without a life jacket. With a jacket on, you simply point your legs downstream, keep your feet at the surface to ward off obstructions, and use your hands to paddle. The jacket will keep you on the surface, even if you are injured or unconscious. Without a jacket, it is very difficult to maintain the correct swimming position, and you could be pulled under the water, where an injury could have much more serious consequences. The most important safety rule is to **wear your life jacket.**

The chances of falling off the raft depend largely on the kind of raft you are on. It is very unusual to have anyone go over the side on a rowboat or a motorized boat where, unlike a paddle boat, your only job is to hang on. The sheer size of the large motorized boats slows down their motion and further decreases the likelihood of anyone going over. On a paddle boat in Class III or greater water, you stand a good chance of taking an unintentional swim. This is nothing to worry about. Falling off the boat is fairly common, and the chances of being injured as a result are remote. The guides will teach you how to keep from falling off and what to do if you do. On trips where significant rapids will be run on paddle boats, you will be equipped with a helmet in addition to your life jacket.

Guides always have a "throw bag" ready to go. A throw bag is a rope coiled into a bag so that it will uncoil when thrown to a swimmer. Usually, the guide will simply throw the rope from the boat. In some cases (particularly on paddle boats), the first boat through a major rapid will pull over to the side, and the guide will walk back upstream with a throw bag to assist swimmers from the other boats. Either way, you probably will be back in the boat before having had a real chance to enjoy the swim.

Guides working for any reputable company will be qualified in first aid and will be carrying a proper kit. All companies have some kind of emergency medical evacuation plans (some boats carry two-way radios). If these matters are of particular interest to you, ask the company what their procedures are.

The Evening Camp

As soon as the guides secure the boats at the evening campsite, they will start unloading the gear. Everyone is expected to help by forming a "fire line" from the boat to the camp. The guides then hand everybody's river bags, ammo cans, and the general camp gear up the line, and in a few minutes, the job is finished. The same procedure is used, in reverse, to load the boats in the morning.

After the boats are unloaded, you will select a spot for your personal camp and move your gear to it. Meanwhile, the guides will be doing something very important—taking a break. Try to leave them alone. This is about the only time they get to themselves during the day. Let them enjoy it. By the time your camp is set up, they will have the campfire started (if campfires are permitted), the cocktail ice out, and dinner under way.

It only takes a few minutes with everyone working together to load or unload the boats.
(Photo by Michael White)

The first explorers on the Colorado River survived primarily on flour (usually lumpy from being wet all the time), bacon (usually on the verge of spoiling, same reason), and dried apples (or redried, or re-redried). You will eat better than that.

The quality, quantity, and variety of food served on a river expedition is usually terrific. The boat will be stocked with a large assortment of food, and the guides will know what to do with it. Much of their camp cooking is done from scratch, using fresh ingredients.

There may be Dutch oven treats, such as delicious biscuits and fresh cobblers. Breakfasts are huge by anyone's standards, and coffee (in the traditional metal camp pot) will be there from the time you get up until camp is broken. Lunch is almost always a buffet, with an assortment of meats, cheeses, and breads.

Dinner is where the guides really show off their cooking skills. It could be as simple as a grilled steak, with baked potato and fresh green salad, or as elaborate as a Mexican fiesta, complete with sangria.

The guides clean up everything after meals except for your eating utensils; you are responsible for these on most trips and will be shown the wash routine. You are also responsible for cleaning up your own trash. If you smoke, make sure your cigarette butts are properly disposed of. Carry a plastic bag or use a pocket to keep them in during the day.

The guides have their camp routine well organized. Your offer to help will always be appreciated, but except for those duties already mentioned (unloading, clean-up, and your personal camp), your help is not required. Relax and enjoy your evening camp.

Sources for Further Information

Westwater Books specializes in mail-order books for river runners. Their extensive inventory includes books on the history of the rivers, river-running skills, geology and natural history, and individual guides (many of which they publish themselves) for many of the major Western rivers. Call or write them for a free catalog.

Westwater Books
P.O. Box 365
Boulder City, NV 89005
Telephone: 702-293-1406

River Runner magazine has articles on a wide variety of paddle sports, with a heavy emphasis on whitewater action. The magazine includes information on and advertisements for commercially run rafting trips.

River Runner
P.O. Box 458
Fallbrook, CA 92028
Telephone: 619-723-8155

Eastern Professional River Outfitters (EPRO) and Western River Guides Association (WRGA) are the two main trade associations for whitewater rafting companies and guides. Their primary concerns are the promotion of commercial river rafting, river safety, and environmental conservation. They have lists of current members and other information concerning their respective areas which can be useful in selecting a company. Membership does not necessarily mean that the company is "the best on the river" (these are not regulatory agencies), but it does indicate an interest in preserving and improving the sport of river rafting.

Eastern Professional River Outfitters
530 South Gay Street, Suite 222
Knoxville, TN 37902
Telephone: 615-524-1045

Western River Guides Association
7600 East Arapahoe Road, Suite 114
Englewood, CO 80112
Telephone: 303-771-0389

9 Canoeing

The first explorers in the northern forests of the New World faced a land unlike anything they had seen before. Mile after mile of virgin forest stretched out in front of them. Wild game of every type abounded. The majesty and promise of this vast wilderness beckoned them forward. But there was a problem: thousands of lakes and streams crisscrossed the area, making much of it virtually impassable, even on foot. Fortunately for them, the Indians had not only solved the problem but had turned it into an advantage. The answer was the canoe.

Although "canoe tripping" (wilderness camping trips by canoe) is most popular in the original home of the canoe—the northern forests—great trips are available in Southern swamps, Southwestern deserts, and just about everywhere in between. Canoe outfitters can be found at more than 100 locations in North America; Canada, home of some of the best and most remote wilderness canoe trips, has canoeing areas that can only be reached by float plane.

Canoe tripping offers the purest wilderness experience of any boating vacation, partly because you are doing it yourself. The thrill of this gives you a heightened awareness of your surroundings. A bird you might not have noticed before is now not only noticed but seen in a new light. New sights are somehow more meaningful because you are discovering them yourself.

When this sense of independence and self-sufficiency is coupled with the beauty of the wilderness and the grace of the canoe, a true wilderness experience results. The feeling of satisfaction and fulfillment is matched by few other vacations.

Canoeing Basics

Every boat has its particular strengths and weaknesses that make it suited to certain kinds of water. Wilderness exploration on relatively flat water calls for a lightweight craft that is fast when propelled by one or two people, easily carried between lakes and streams, yet still capable of carrying a large load. To navigate as much of the available water as possible, it must be slender, maneuverable, and able to float in shallow water. The canoe meets these requirements perfectly.

Modern canoes are made from a variety of materials, including wood (the aesthetic choice), aluminum (the leading material 20 years ago and still popular), fiberglass (the most common today), Kevlar (the lightest and most expensive), and Royalex (actually a laminated sandwich construction, not a material).

Once you paddle away on a wilderness canoe trip, you are on your own.
(Photo by Michael White)

Your wilderness canoe will be what is called a "cruising" canoe, which is a compromise model, having the ability to maintain a straight course fairly well yet still being reasonably maneuverable. The cruising canoe also carries more gear than some specialized types. It will be between 16 and 18 feet long and about 3 feet wide. It can weigh anywhere from about 50 pounds to over 80.

Weight is the most important factor to consider. You should get the lightest canoe available (there is no such thing as a cruising canoe that is too light). The lighter the canoe, the easier it is to paddle and, more important, the easier it is to portage. Frequently, an outfitter will have a light or ultralight weight option at a slight additional cost (a few dollars a day more for the Kevlar canoes). Take it if you expect any portaging; you may wish you had while lugging that extra 20 pounds over hilly trails. A canoe under 60 pounds should be fine.

Occasionally, an outfitter (who probably has some overweight old junk for rent) will knock the ultralight canoes for their ability to handle waves or their stability. Pay no attention to this advertising hype. Canoe performance is determined by design; construction material and weight have virtually nothing to do with them.

Paddling

In most cases, there will be two people to a canoe, one in front and one in back. The gear is stowed amidship, where it can act as ballast and help stabilize the boat. Most of your paddling will be done while sitting comfortably on the canoe's seats. The kneeling-on-the-floor position need only be used when going through rapids or unusual conditions of wind or waves. The person in front paddles and sets the tempo. The one in back paddles in unison with the other on the opposite side of the canoe and makes most of the course corrections.

You move the canoe with a "power stroke." This is a straight stroke parallel to the canoe's centerline and close to the side of the boat. A canoe tends to turn away from the side the person in the stern is paddling on. The stern pry stroke is the easiest way to correct this tendency. After completion of a power stroke, brace the lower hand on the side of the canoe and turn the paddle with the upper hand until the blade is parallel with the centerline. Then pull the top of the paddle toward you, using the lower hand as a fulcrum. The stern is pushed away from the paddle, and the boat turns toward the paddling side.

The draw stroke is the opposite of a pry stroke: it pulls your end of the canoe toward the paddle. It is accomplished by reaching out over the water, putting the paddle in the water with the blade parallel to the centerline, and pulling it toward the boat.

The sweep stroke is like the power stroke, except that instead of having the paddle perpendicular to the water, you sweep it through the water a short distance from the boat. This turns the canoe away from the stern paddler's side while still providing power. The slightly trickier "J stroke" accomplishes essentially the same thing in the opposite direction, allowing you to correct the natural turning tendency and supply power with the same stroke.

These paddling techniques are easy to learn; ask your outfitter to demonstrate them for you.

Portaging
The final thing you need to know is how to portage. Portages are places where you will have to carry the canoe; the word is also used for the act of carrying the canoe (you portage a canoe over a portage). Portaging is done either to transfer the canoe from one stream or lake to another or to go around unsafe rapids or obstructions. Although portaging looks like someone is wearing a canoe for a hat, the weight of the canoe actually rests on your shoulders on a "yoke" (a piece running across the canoe and curved to fit your shoulders), not on your head. Gear is taken out of the canoe and carried separately (you may have to make a few trips). The yoke will be placed at the balance point of the canoe, which makes it considerably easier to handle. Do not stuff things into the ends of the canoe to save a trip; you will just throw off its balance and make it more difficult to control.

Your outfitter will show you how to lift the canoe to the portaging position. Usually, the lifting is done with the assistance of a partner, but you can do it by yourself. Practice until you can do it comfortably without straining yourself.

Although complete novices can show up at most outfitter's headquarters and learn what they need to know, getting some experience in a canoe ahead of time is a good idea. Once you see how much fun paddling is—and how easy—you will be looking forward with even greater pleasure to your trip. Hundreds of companies rent canoes by the hour or the day. Many also give instruction. The directory of companies in chapter 10 is a good place to start looking for one; most outfitters also do day rentals. Look around in your local area for canoe rentals or, as suggested at the end of this chapter, get the NACLO membership list.

The outfitter will show you everything you need to know to handle your canoe, including how to lift it for a portage. (Photo by Michael White)

Canoe Tripping Areas

Although wilderness is the primary attraction of canoe trips, many excellent trips let you experience the wilderness without being completely out of touch with the outside world. On some "wilderness trips," you will find restaurants, shopping, and even resorts and country inns along the way.

Following are examples of two different trips: one in a less-remote wilderness area, the other where you will be almost completely on your own once you leave the outfitter's headquarters.

THE ADIRONDACKS

New York is not usually thought of as a wilderness (at least not in the conventional sense), but the lakes region of the Adirondacks is an excellent area for a wilderness canoe trip, particularly for first-timers. This chain of lakes and streams extends nearly 100 miles through the heart of the Adirondack forest, amid the 6-million-acre Adirondack Park. Although this vast area is true wilderness, it is far from remote. Old Forge, the preferred starting point, is only a five- or six-hour drive from New York City.

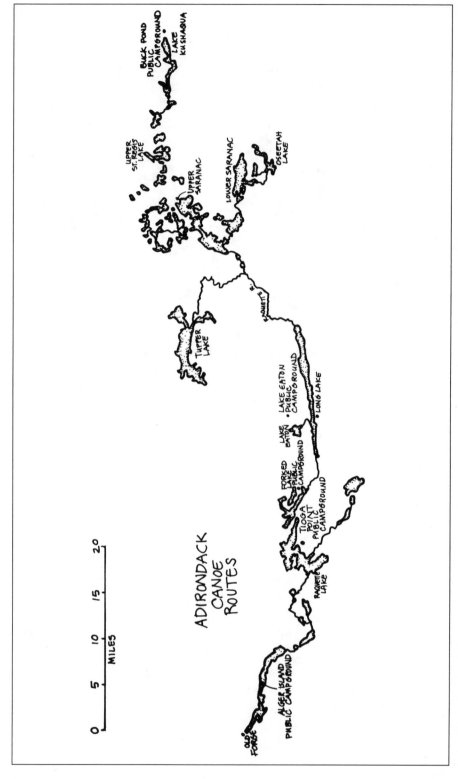

The Adirondacks offer a variety of excellent canoeing. There are several "first trip" possibilities here that don't require leaving civilization totally behind.

There is a lot of "civilization" in this area. Many of the larger lakes are quite developed, with stores along the way to buy forgotten items, occasional restaurants for a dinner ashore, and lodges where one could take a midweek break from camping out. You will be able to call home if you really want to.

This is a big park, however, and the more remote canoe routes get fairly light use and offer true wilderness canoeing. Canoeing here is fairly easy. There are good maps and straightforward routes, and very little, if any, portaging (carrying the canoe) is required. You will stay mostly at designated campsites (some are even equipped with shelters), but you can use "primitive" sites if a designated site is full or unavailable along your route.

A trip in the Adirondacks can be about as easy as you want. For example, if you start from Old Forge at the southwestern end of the lake chain, you can make your first day short by paddling just a few miles and stopping that night at the Alger Island campground. Lean-tos are provided here, a caretaker is in attendance, and a phone is available to call your outfitter next morning if you have any more questions or want to change your plans. Now that's about the easiest way to slip into a wilderness experience that I know of.

From there, you can wander up the chain, with the prevailing wind at your back, for the rest of the trip. If you are out for a week, you will travel about eighty miles. A take-out is then arranged at the end, either on your own if you have two cars with you or by telephoning your outfitter.

The Adirondacks is one of many areas where you can enjoy canoe tripping without leaving civilization completely behind.

The Boundary Waters

Quetico Provincial Park in Ontario and the Boundary Waters Canoe Area (BWCA) wilderness in the Superior National Forest of northern Minnesota constitute one of the most pristine yet easily accessible wilderness canoeing areas in North America. The parks have over 2 million acres (divided about equally between them) of lakes, rivers, and streams that crisscross some of the most beautiful country in the world—most of which can be traveled only by canoe. Each year, thousands of people enjoy this incomparable wilderness canoe-tripping area.

Although Quetico and Superior are separate parks in separate countries, cooperation between the two governments has made them functionally one. The regulations governing the two are not identical, but both are designed to preserve and protect a wilderness that was in serious danger of being destroyed before the parks were created.

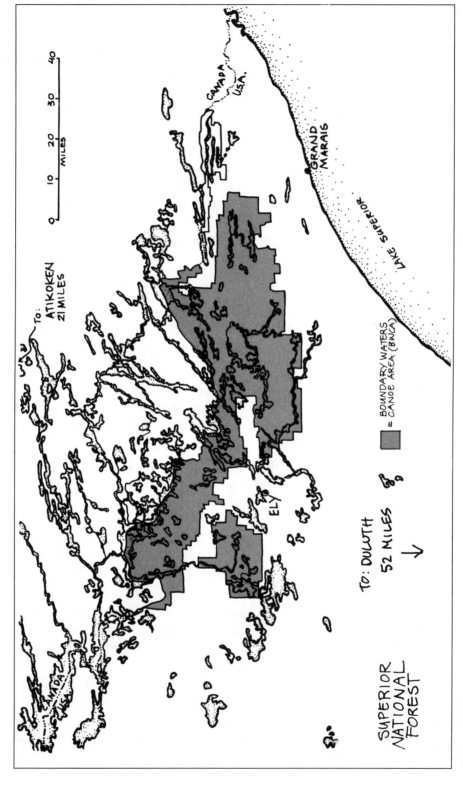

The boundary waters are the most popular destination in North America for those who want a true wilderness canoe tripping experience.

Each group entering one of these areas must have a permit, which controls not only the day of entry but the maximum number of people in a group (ten in the BWCA, nine in Quetico) and the entry point. The number of permits issued each year is strictly limited in the BWCA and *very* strictly limited in Quetico.

Overnight camping in the BWCA is allowed only in designated campsites marked by a red dot on your map (day use is unrestricted). These sites are carefully chosen to be as spread out as possible, and regulations prohibit more than a single group at a site. Camping areas include tent sites, a fire pit equipped with an iron grate, and a latrine.

No food or drink in cans or bottles can be taken in, and all litter that cannot be burned must be carried out. With the exception of a few lakes where outboards are permitted, no motors or "mechanized equipment" of any kind are allowed (minimum altitude for airplanes is even controlled). There is more, but you get the point. This is a beautiful wilderness area, and they intend to keep it that way.

Entering the Quetico/Superior region is a journey back to a time when the waters were clear and ran free, the air was pure, and the land was unspoiled. Wildlife flourishes here, and the fishing is superb. You will meet other people here—this is a popular area—but mostly you will be on your own, just you and your canoe. This is the real thing.

Quetico/Superior outfitters are based primarily in three towns: Atikokan, in Ontario, and Ely and Grand Marais, both in Minnesota. If you want to start from the Canadian side and go directly into northern Quetico, Atikokan is your best choice. But most U.S. outfitters also arrange trips that include southern Quetico (some prefer Quetico because fewer people are allowed there). They will take care of making the reservation for your Canadian permit; all you do is portage across to Prairie Portage Ranger Station, pick up the permit, clear customs (no kidding, there is a customs house for canoeists in the middle of the wilderness), and paddle into Canada.

Grand Marais is near the eastern edge of the BWCA at the head of Gunflint Trail. There are a number of resorts and lodges in this area. If you'd like to ease into your BWCA trip and enjoy civilization for the first day or two, start your trip here. A couple of companies even do inn-to-inn tours (discussed in Canoe Touring, below) in the Gunflint Trail area.

To leave civilization behind with the first stroke of your paddle, start from Ely. A canoeist driving down the main street of Ely gets the same feeling that a gambler would on entering Las Vegas. The town seems to have been created for a single purpose—canoeing. Signs everywhere advertise canoeing products and services. Outdoors stores and outfitters' headquarters abound, full of dazed-looking people searching for that last critical item before escaping into the wilderness.

More outfitters' headquarters are located just outside Ely on the way to the BWCA, some so close that you do not need transport to a put-in; just step off their dock into your canoe and start paddling. Prairie Portage Ranger Station, in the center of the Quetico/Superior region, is just a short distance away. In fact, any outfitter can arrange a "tow" (the canoes are carried on a power boat) right to the international border.

Regardless of where you start your trip, you will have abundant flexibility in choosing your route. This area is so large and has so many navigable streams and lakes that the choices seem unlimited.

OTHER CANOEING AREAS

Although most people think of canoeing as something done on a North Woods stream or a placid lake, many other areas offer canoe trips. The Rio Grande is a long way from the North Woods, but you can arrange canoe trips on it. Or consider the great rivers, marshes, savannahs, and swamps of the Southeast—especially the Okefenokee Swamp in southern Georgia and Everglades National Park in Florida—which offer unique canoeing experiences. Far from being the dark, gloomy habitat of alligators waiting to bite your canoe in half, these delightful canoeing areas—often open, bright, and cheerful—harbor an incredible variety of plant, animal, and bird life.

In the Southeast, you will usually travel on established canoe trails and stay at designated campsites. Even so, you should consider taking one of the guided trips (highly recommended, if not a necessity, for novices going on a serious trip in the Everglades). These trips—expeditions, really—are a good introduction to what is for most people an unknown kind of wilderness. A knowledgeable guide helps you fully appreciate this unique experience.

Another advantage of the Southeast is winter canoeing. The best trip time in the southernmost part of this region is between late fall and early spring; the weather is pleasant, and insects are not a problem. The best time farther north in northern Florida and southern Georgia is fall *or* winter, although midwinter can get quite cold. Avoid the summer rainy season; it is hot and humid, thunderstorms are common, and the mosquitoes will protect their turf to the last drop of your blood.

Which Trip?

One of the most important considerations in choosing a wilderness trip is how remote an area you really want to be in. Remote areas offer a more genuine wilderness experience, but going to them means you must be more self-sufficient. If you have serious doubts as to either your ability or desire, consider going to a less remote area. This kind of trip should not be taken lightly. If you have a healthy respect for the water and wilderness, you are much less likely to have problems.

Will paddling a canoe for a couple of hours wear you out? If you have any doubts, rent a canoe for a few hours and find out. Can you carry 60 pounds on your shoulders for a reasonable distance? Someone in the group has to if you are going to be going over portages. Just about anyone can do a trip without portages by keeping each day's travel down to a prudent distance, setting a leisurely pace, and resting when necessary.

The number and lengths of the portages are important to plan for, even if you are in excellent physical condition. A portage can be as short as a few feet or as long as half a mile. There are numerous trips available where no portaging is necessary (either because of the area or because you can plan the trip that way). But most people do not like portages (too much like work), so doing more of them, and longer ones, will generally get you into the less traveled areas. This is one of the many things you will work out when you and your outfitter start planning the trip.

Day Trips

A variety of wilderness canoe trails can be paddled as day trips and are still within easy range of a campground or motel. The main problem is finding the right location. Although rental canoes are found almost anywhere there is some flat water, few of these places are large enough and diverse enough for vacations built around day trips by canoe. To find a good location, look in the canoe company section of the directory in chapter 10. Companies that only do day trips are not included (both to help narrow the list to true vacation possibilities and because of their numbers), but many of those listed, particularly in less remote areas, also do day rentals. Since all the companies on the list do longer tours, expeditions, or outfitted trips, you can assume their areas also would provide a number of interesting day trips. In addition, recreational areas specifically oriented toward canoes can be found through state and local tourism offices.

CANOE TOURING

"Tours" are multiday trips that do not include camping. These are prearranged packages run according to a schedule established by the tour operator. You do not have to put together your own group to go on a tour. Because reservations are made on an individual basis, any number of people—from one on up—can book a place. You simply sign for the one you want. Most tours are canoe trips, although a few whitewater rafting tours are available.

A tour can let you explore a number of rivers and lakes by canoe during the day and sleep at night in the comfort of a real bed. The tour operator provides all of the equipment, accommodations, and transportation and also serves as your guide. Everything is usually included in the tour price. You just show up and enjoy it.

Canoe tours are run in two basic ways. The first is where you simply paddle from one night's stop to the next. The tour operator plans a schedule around a series of good day trips, each one ending at a different inn or resort. This approach has the advantage of simplicity and convenience, but you will have to hold to a fairly fixed itinerary.

The second approach is to canoe during the day and get transported by vehicle each evening back to the night's stop. This way is less convenient and more time consuming, but it provides for a good deal of flexibility. There will be a rough itinerary (since the tour operator has to make reservations at the inns), usually just day by day. The choice of canoeing waters is open. It is not unusual to have the group sitting around in the evening discussing the next day's possibilities with the guide.

Most tours are from three to six days long, with each day spent on a different stretch of water and each night at a different inn. You will get up in the morning, have a nice breakfast at the inn, load your personal gear for the day's trip, have a great day of canoeing, and then be at that night's lodging in time for a hot shower and a cold drink before dinner. Very civilized.

The accommodations provided with these packages are often selected from the better and more interesting resorts, lodges, and country inns in the area. Many, particularly in the eastern United States, are quaint, elegant older establishments. After a day of canoeing, there is a big difference between spending the evening in one of these charming country inns, with their personal service and excellent food, and grabbing a hamburger before going back to your plastic motel.

Some canoe tours have the added attraction of letting you experience whitewater. Canoes are not for whitewater novices. It takes considerable

On a canoe tour you will frequently be staying at some of the best, and most interesting, country inns in the area. (Photo by Michael White)

experience and special equipment to handle one safely in water much above Class II. But canoes are fun (and safe) in rapids at or below that level, and a canoe tour is one of the best ways for a beginner to get experience. The guides will teach beginners the basic skills for handling whitewater, and then, if the tour offers a choice of rivers, they will tailor the trip to their customers' preferences and abilities.

Some tour operators stress this "custom" aspect of the trip. On a tour in Vermont with Vermont Canoe Trippers, the head guide actually split up the tour for a day (a logistical nightmare) so that those of us who wanted to go on a whitewater river could do so.

If you want to try whitewater on your tour, ask about it ahead of time. Tour companies have different attitudes toward doing whitewater with beginners. If you pick the right company, you will get your shot at it.

Some canoe tours combine touring and camping, and a number of special interest tours are available: photography, women's groups, nature study, and others. Some companies have packages that let you stay in a resort and go canoeing during the day (this option is usually found in tours that offer whitewater rafting packages). There are all kinds of variations and combinations.

Tours are an excellent way to gain canoeing experience, try a variety of waters, see beautiful country, and have a very relaxing vacation. Unfor-

This previously inexperienced couple was enjoying moderate whitewater, and handling it quite well, by the fourth day of their canoe tour. (Photo by Michael White)

tunately, very few companies provide true tours. Those that do are identified in the directory in chapter 10. The cost of a canoe tour will run between $100 and $165 per person per day. Everything is included in that price.

OUTFITTED TRIPS

"Outfitted trips" are those you do on your own. The outfitter will provide everything you need, including instruction in boating and camping skills, and the rest is up to you and your group. On an outfitted trip, you determine the length of the trip, when and where it will start and finish, and do every-thing yourself, including the cooking. An outfitter has the equipment and expertise to take virtually all the work out of the planning and equipping of your trip. You show up at their headquarters with your clothes and personal gear, and everything else you need is waiting for you, packed and ready to go. Of all the vacations discussed in this book, however, canoe tripping offers the greatest challenge to your self-sufficiency. There is no boatman to remind you to put on your life jacket; no "base" you can call on the radio when some-thing goes wrong; no captain to rely on if a problem comes up. Once your outfitter waves good-bye and you paddle away, you are on your own.

Before you paddle off into the wilderness, though, the outfitter will supply you with a canoe, paddles, life jackets, the right camping equipment—from tents and sleeping bags to cooking and eating utensils—and a week's supply of carefully chosen lightweight food. He will also get you maps of the area, any necessary permits, and a strategy for getting to and doing the things you are interested in. Then he will transport you, your canoe, the equipment, and food to the water and make arrangements for picking you up after the trip. If you are new to canoeing, camping, or both, he will teach you the necessary skills.

Outfitters can also arrange for a guide, but most people who can read a map and a compass—or learn to do so before the trip—will not need one. If you are going into an extremely primitive area, however, or are very serious about fishing, a guide is a good idea. You might also want one if your physical condition or other special circumstances require someone's assistance.

When the outfitter supplies everything you need for your trip, including food, it is called "complete" outfitting. You fill out an information sheet, indicating such things as food preferences and equipment options, and the outfitter does the rest. Or you might supply some gear and have the outfitter supply the rest; this is called "partial" outfitting. Complete outfitting is usually done on a price-per-day basis; partial outfitting bills you on a price-per-item basis.

If you are new to canoe tripping, you should opt for complete outfitting. The small amount of money saved by borrowing some of the gear is just not worth the hassle. Even bringing most of the gear yourself probably would not save much; complete outfitters charge more on a per-item basis than they do for the package. It is possible to save some money on the food, but, again, it is hardly worth the trouble. Unless you have substantial experience and equipment, the only time to go with partial outfitting is if complete outfitting is not available.

Most outfitters located in serious wilderness areas provide complete packages. Companies that only do partial outfitting may assist you with what they do not do, usually food provisioning. All complete outfitters also do partial outfitting.

Since you will probably want to stay near the outfitter's headquarters the night before the trip (see below), decide whether to use an outfitter based in town or out on the water. Each has its advantages: the one in town will have convenient access to last-minute shopping and any local tourist attractions; the one on the water will introduce you immediately to the wilderness experience and offer a more leisurely start. In addition, if you are new to canoe-ing, the outfitters on the water will almost always give you canoe instruction the day you arrive (the day before your departure) and allow you to take the canoe out that afternoon for some practice.

Choosing an Outfitter

Canoes are not like houseboats or yachts. There are no big differences between canoes, at least not many that novices will be sensitive to. But there *are* differences, and what kinds of canoes and other equipment a company has can say much about their expertise. Look over the brochures as though you were an expert canoeist who wanted the best possible equipment. You may not actually want to spend the money for this top-of-the-line outfitting, but you can bet that an outfitter that cannot supply it is not doing business with the *real* experts. A good outfitter will have a good selection of modern canoes and equipment.

The services provided by outfitters in a given area are not always the same. Be sure to ask, if the brochure is unclear, exactly what they provide. If this is your first time in a canoe, be aware that a few outfitters will not work with novices. Look at what you need and what you are getting for your money. Pay particular attention to "hidden" costs such as transportation to their headquarters from the airport or extra charges for small items that are included in other packages. These items may not be crucial, but providing them without charge says something about their operation.

Look for a professional attitude. You will be relying on their advice and instruction, which should be competent and tailored to your needs and level of knowledge. Fortunately, that of most outfitters is. If they sound like a tape recorder, do some more shopping. Your questions should be answered com-pletely, giving you confidence in them as well as your own ability to have a safe and enjoyable wilderness vacation.

Some big outfitters do a lot of sports and travel shows. If there is one in your area, stop by and talk to them. Also, if you have a particular outfitter in mind, call them and find out if they are doing any shows near you. Talking to someone face-to-face is the best way to get a feeling for how you will like working with them.

The cost of an outfitter's services depends on how much they provide. For complete outfitting, including food, plan on $40 to $65 a day per person. Prices will generally be lower for larger groups and for off-season trips.

As always, beware of the "real bargain" unless it is backed by good information. You can certainly do some price shopping, but if you select strictly on the basis of the lowest price, you may wind up with a small company with limited services and older equipment.

Booking the Trip

Often, booking the trip is simply a matter of telling the outfitter how many are in your group, when you plan to arrive, how long you plan to be out, and sending in a deposit. Remember: this type of trip has no prearranged schedules or groups you will be joining. But in some extremely popular areas, it is important to make your reservations as early as possible, both because of the limited number of group permits issued each year and because all of the outfitter's equipment may be in use.

The Quetico/Superior area discussed earlier is a good example. Permits for the BWCA and Quetico are issued on a "first-come, first-served" basis starting February 1. By making your trip reservation with your outfitter prior to that date, they should have no problem getting you a permit. If your vacation dates are inflexible, fall in the peak season (July and August), *and* start on a weekend, try to make your reservations a couple of months earlier (outfitters apply for permits in the order in which the reservations are received). Not being in line for a permit on February 1 does not necessarily mean you will not get one, but to know for sure, call an outfitter.

If you do make reservations later in the year, you will have a better chance of getting your first choice of dates if you plan for a midweek (Tuesday through Friday) start. Some outfitters even offer discounts for groups starting on these dates, because it eases their weekend crunch.

It will not help to try another outfitter in the BWCA if one says there are no permits available for your chosen dates. Each permit is issued to a particular permittee and an alternate permittee (two members of your group) and is no good unless one or both of them are with the group. Permits can only be issued, therefore, after a reservation is made; outfitters cannot buy a block of them ahead of time.

Always ask your outfitter if early booking is necessary or recommended for their area at the time you want to go. If it is, book the trip and send in the deposit even if you think your plans might change. The deposit required by outfitters is small (typically, $25 per person); it makes no sense to jeopardize your vacation plans by worrying about losing it.

Either with your original information package or after booking the trip, you will be sent a checklist for selecting your food (assuming complete outfitting) and equipment. As discussed above, the canoe should be a lightweight one, particularly on trips involving portages. The same is true of your other equipment; keep it as light as you can.

Food

Your food should be selected for its light weight and its ability to keep without refrigeration. Many people include some fresh foods for the first day or two, but the bulk of your provisions will either be normal grocery items that do not require refrigeration or special freeze-dried camping food. Canned goods are too heavy.

There is a large variety of freeze-dried food available, everything from fruit cocktails to beef Stroganoff. There are breakfasts, snacks, complete entrées, vegetables, and desserts. You just add water and cook. It is easy to prepare, extremely lightweight, and remarkably good.

Complete outfitters will give you a list of menus to select from ahead of time. As part of your checkout (see below), you will be shown what has been included, how and where it has been packed, and receive an inventory list to use in planning meals (so you don't wind up eating scrambled eggs with chocolate sauce for dinner the last night).

Outfitters who do not provide food provisioning services will often assist you in menu planning. Some have developed very complete systems to allow you to self-provision correctly. Tickner's Moose River Canoe Outfitters (in the Adirondacks), for example, provides a separate brochure on meal planning (complete with suggested menus and a checklist of items available in the local market), order forms for freeze-dried food, and all the personal help you need. This is as close to complete outfitting as you can get without having them pack the food for you.

In the rare case where your outfitter cannot offer provisioning advice, get a good book on backpacking and use it as a guide. Meal planning considerations are about the same for backpackers as they are for canoeists.

Your Personal Gear

Your personal gear and clothes should be more substantial for a canoe trip than for a river-rafting expedition—better rain gear, more rugged clothes suited to the more active nature of the trip, and some additional equipment. As for any boating or wilderness trip, keep your personal gear to an absolute minimum and travel as light as possible.

Your outfitter will provide waterproof packs for your group's personal gear. You might also consider taking a *small* waterproof bag or box for your camera or anything else you want to keep both dry and readily available. It should either have a shoulder strap or (better) fit in one of the larger packs for portaging.

The following list contains everything you should need for a summer trip of about a week. Check off the items you want, use it as a shopping list, and then make sure everything is packed. If things on the list are supplied by your outfitter, just mark them as packed.

Personal Gear Checklist

WANT	BUY	PACKED	ITEM
☐	☐	☐	Bags (several, heavyweight plastic)
☐	☐	☐	Beverages (see below)
☐	☐	☐	Binoculars
☐	☐	☐	Books (paperback general reading)
☐	☐	☐	Camera and film
☐	☐	☐	Clothespins (just a few)
☐	☐	☐	Compasses (two)
☐	☐	☐	Eating utensils (see below)
☐	☐	☐	Eyeglasses and an extra pair
☐	☐	☐	First-aid kit
☐	☐	☐	Fishing tackle
☐	☐	☐	Flashlights (two, with extra batteries)

☐	☐	☐	Hat with strap
☐	☐	☐	Jacket (lightweight windbreaker)
☐	☐	☐	Jacket, warm but not heavy (or sweater)
☐	☐	☐	Knife (general purpose)
☐	☐	☐	Knife (small pocket type)
☐	☐	☐	Matches
☐	☐	☐	Medications
☐	☐	☐	Nylon cord, 50 feet of 1/8″ (misc. uses)
☐	☐	☐	Pants, one rugged pair (jeans)
☐	☐	☐	Pants (one light pair; quick drying)
☐	☐	☐	Pillow
☐	☐	☐	Rain gear (see below)
☐	☐	☐	Shirt, heavy long sleeve (wool is good)
☐	☐	☐	Shirts, two light ones (T-shirts are OK)
☐	☐	☐	Shoes (a rugged pair that can get wet)
☐	☐	☐	Shoes (lightweight tennis-shoe type)
☐	☐	☐	Shorts (one pair)
☐	☐	☐	Soap (biodegradable)
☐	☐	☐	Socks (several heavy pairs)
☐	☐	☐	Spices (your favorites)
☐	☐	☐	Suntan lotion/sunblock, also for the lips
☐	☐	☐	Sunglasses with safety strap
☐	☐	☐	Swimsuit
☐	☐	☐	Toilet kit
☐	☐	☐	Towel (small)
☐	☐	☐	Underwear (three changes)

☐	☐	☐	Washcloth
☐	☐	☐	Writing materials
☐	☐	☐	Miscellaneous (your list)
☐	☐	☐	_____
☐	☐	☐	_____
☐	☐	☐	_____

All complete outfitters will provide beverages during the day, usually powdered drink packages you mix with water. If you want beer or soft drinks, you may have to bring your own. Keep these heavy things to a minimum, and remember that cans and bottles are prohibited in some areas. If you take hard liquor, it is a good idea to transfer it to a plastic container (even in an area that permits bottles) to save weight and prevent breakage. The same goes for wine; either transfer it to a plastic bottle or buy the kind that comes in a soft plastic-lined box. Nearly all outfitters supply eating utensils, but there are a few exceptions. If it is not clear from the company's brochure, call and ask.

Your primary rain gear should be a rain suit, not a poncho. Paddling a canoe while wearing a poncho is not fun. Inexpensive rain suits are available in most sporting goods stores. I like to have a lightweight poncho in addition to my rain suit for backup and for wearing around camp.

Checkouts

On your arrival, the outfitter will go over your equipment with you, show you how to use it, and teach you the basics of paddling and carrying a canoe (see above), setting up a tent, and operating any special equipment (such as a stove or lantern) provided by the outfitter. You will then have an opportunity to practice what you have been shown. Take advantage of this time to make sure you are thoroughly familiar with everything. It will be too late to ask questions once you are in the wilderness.

Before arriving, you will have discussed your interests and plans with the outfitter, who will have done some preliminary planning and obtained any necessary permits. After your arrival, they will sit down with you and do the final "route planning," going over the map of the area in detail and working

An outfitter answers a few last-minute questions before the group starts out. Note the gear properly packed low down and in the center of the canoe. (Photo by Michael White)

out a proposed itinerary for the week. This route will be marked on the map, along with campsites along the way, fishing spots, portages, and other points of interest. You can make changes to the plan as you go along, but most people (particularly larger groups) find that a well-thought-out route makes for a better trip.

Plan to arrive at the outfitter's headquarters the day before your trip starts. As you can see, there is much to do after arriving; do not try to be out on the water the same day. If the outfitter is located on the water, this will give you a chance to try out the canoe and practice a little before leaving. There may be an additional charge if you take one out for more than a few minutes (remember, your rental does not start until the next day), but it will be worth it. Many outfitters have rooms or campsites available at their headquarters.

When you get up the next morning, you will be ready to go. The outfitter will transport your group and the equipment to your starting point and help you get the canoes in the water and loaded. Then it is up to you.

The Itinerary

The maximum speed of your canoe will be about 6 mph. A realistic cruising speed for most people will be between 2 and 3 mph. At this rate, if you paddle for 4 or 5 hours, you will travel between 8 and 15 miles a day. Mileage will vary among groups, depending on physical ability, number of portages, weather, and simple personal preference.

Most people plan on staying put at least one day during the trip (a "layover" day). This gives you a chance to just relax around camp, fish, do some hiking, or whatever you want, without having to bother with loading everything up and moving the camp.

A number of chores have to be done to make your camp livable: unloading gear, setting up tents, gathering firewood, cooking food, and so on. Each group divides up these duties differently. If you are lucky, each of your companions will like doing different things, and each person will just naturally do his or her "job." If not, you will have to work out some kind of camp routine. The only real rule is not to stick one or two people with all the work; this is a sure way to have problems.

Try to have your night camp selected by midafternoon. All too often, people pass a site to "just make another mile or two," then pass another because the next one might be better, then find the next one taken, and suddenly it is getting dark and they are still desperately paddling. It makes more sense to stop by 3:00 or 4:00 in the afternoon (or even earlier), which gives you a choice of sites and plenty of time to set up camp and relax before dark. It is far better to be the ones sitting around a fire, pitying that poor group still looking for a campsite.

Sources for Further Information

The American Canoe Association (ACA) operates a mail-order book service. They have an extensive catalog of books on canoeing, regional guides, and maps of canoeing areas.

American Canoe Association
Book Service
P.O. Box 248
Lorton, VA 22079
Telephone: 703-550-7523

A free publications catalog listing BWCA and related materials is available from:

Lake States Interpretive Association
P.O. Box 672
International Falls, MN 56649
Telephone: 218-283-9821

Canoe magazine has articles for the novice as well as the expert on canoe and kayak techniques, equipment, and areas. They also carry advertisements for outfitters.

Canoe Magazine
P.O. Box 3418
Kirkland, WA 98083
Telephone: 800-MY-CANOE

The local chamber of commerce or outfitter's association in many of the more popular canoe-tripping areas can provide information on their area and the outfitters in it. Some even have toll-free "800" numbers. Ely's is 800-522-9653; Grand Marais' is 800-328-3325.

The National Association of Canoe Liveries and Outfitters (NACLO) is the largest canoe-oriented trade association. They will send you a brochure listing their members which includes a brief description of the kinds of services each provides. The list of outfitters provided in chapter 10 is more complete (many outfitters are not NACLO members), but their membership list can be useful for finding a local livery to try a day or so of canoeing before committing to a longer trip. Many NACLO members only do day rentals and consequently are not on my list of outfitters.

National Association of Canoe Liveries and Outfitters
P.O. Box 88866
Atlanta, GA 30356
Telephone: 404-393-8625

10 Directory of River-Rafting and Canoeing Companies

There are two directories in this chapter, one for river-rafting companies and the other for canoe outfitters. Each is broken down by state for U.S. companies and by province for those in Canada. Companies are listed alphabetically within the state or province.

The rivers and areas used by the companies are shown; this will help you locate companies as well as the most popular rivers in a given area. Just scan the listings for the area and see which rivers come up most frequently.

For a specific river or area, look first for home companies in the state or province where it is located. But several large companies (particularly U.S. rafting companies) go to many different areas, so also check neighboring states. If you do not find the river or area listed, call some companies near it anyway; they may have added it to their list.

If you are interested in a more general area in the United States (such as the Southwest), you may need to look in several states to find all the companies operating there (most Canadian companies only work in one province). The following tips should help with locating river-rafting companies in some of the more popular areas.

Appalachians. Most of the companies running the rivers in the Appalachians are either in West Virginia or Tennessee. There are also a few in the Carolinas, and several that do some of the big rivers in the northern part of the area are in Pennsylvania.

Northeast. Maine has more companies than the other states put together. Also check New York, Pennsylvania, and New Hampshire.

Southwest. Pretty evenly divided among local companies in Texas, New Mexico, and Arizona and the big companies in Colorado. Also look at West Virginia; several of the Appalachian companies located there like to get down that way.

West Coast. As you would expect, almost all are in California, Oregon, or Washington.

High Desert. Colorado has the most, but Utah is close behind. Idaho also has quite a few. The rest are spread out among the adjoining states and California.

Grand Canyon. All but a few are evenly divided between Arizona, Utah, and California.

Canoe outfitters tend to operate in their base areas, making them a lot easier to find in the directory. Almost half of those listed are located in two major areas: the Northeast and BWCA/Quetico. For the Northeast, look in the appropriate state. All BWCA/Quetico outfitters are in Ontario or Minnesota.

The other half operate on a variety of waters throughout the United States and Canada and are usually located near them. The only exception is the South. The local companies are still there, but there are also some northern companies that like to go where it's warm during the winter.

River-Rafting Companies

The kind of services provided by the rafting companies are indicated in the "Trips" column: "**D**" for day trips; "**E**" for expeditions; and "**B**" if they are brokers for several companies.

ADDRESS/TELEPHONE	TRIPS/RIVERS	ADDRESS/TELEPHONE	TRIPS/RIVERS

United States
Arizona

ADDRESS/TELEPHONE	TRIPS/RIVERS
Adventure/Discovery Tours 319 N. Humphrey Flagstaff, AZ 86001 602-774-1926	E/San Juan
Arizona Raft Adventures 4050 E. Huntington-WA Flagstaff, AZ 86004 602-526-8200	E/Grand Canyon
Arizona River Runners P.O. Box 47788 Phoenix, AZ 85068 602-867-4866	E/Grand Canyon
Canyon Explorations P.O. Box 310 Flagstaff, AZ 86002 602-774-4559	E/Grand Canyon
Canyoneers, Inc. P.O. Box 2997 Flagstaff, AZ 86003 602-526-0924 800-525-0924	E/Grand Canyon
Descent River Expeditions P.O. Box 47788 Phoenix, AZ 85068 602-867-4960	E/Cataract and Westwater canyons
Expeditions, Inc. Route 4, Box 755 Flagstaff, AZ 86001 602-774-8176	E/Grand Canyon
Hualapai River Runners P.O. Box 246 Peach Springs, AZ 86434 602-769-2347	D-E/Grand Canyon
Rio Grande Rapid Transit P.O. Box 9053 Scottsdale, AZ 85252 602-998-RAFT 800-545-4020	D-E/Rio Grande, Rio Chama, Salt, Verde, Mexico rivers

ADDRESS/TELEPHONE	TRIPS/RIVERS
Saguaro Whitewater 3223 E. Lee St. Tucson, AZ 85716 602-326-6202	D/Salt
Wild and Scenic Expeditions P.O. Box 460 Flagstaff, AZ 86002 602-774-7343	E/Colorado, Green, San Juan, Rogue, Salmon, Snake
Wilderness River Adventures P.O. Box 717 Page, AZ 86040 602-645-3296	E/Grand Canyon
Wilderness World P.O. Box 310 Flagstaff, AZ 86002 602-774-6468	E/Grand Canyon, Rogue, Owyhee
Worldwide Explorations P.O. Box 3268 Flagstaff, AZ 86003 602-774-6462	D-E/Verde, Salt, Dolores, San Juan

California

ADDRESS/TELEPHONE	TRIPS/RIVERS
A.B.L.E. Rafting 4965 Little Rd. Coloma, CA 95613 916-626-6208	D-E/American, Giant Gap, Cal- Salmon, Scott, Carson, Klamath, Stanislaus
Action Adventures Wet 'N' Wild Box 1500 Woodland, CA 95695 916-662-5431	D-E/California and Oregon rivers
Adventure Connection Box 475 Coloma, CA 95613 916-626-7385 800-556-6060	E-B/Western rivers
Adventure River Tours P.O. Box 321 Yreka, CA 96097 503-482-0667	D-E/Klamath, Salmon, Owhyee, Cop- per, Stikine, Eel, Scott

Address/Telephone	Trips/Rivers
All Outdoors Adventures Trips 2151 San Miguel Dr. Walnut Creek, CA 94596 415-932-8993	D-E/American, Merced, Tuolumne, Salmon, Scott, Klamath, Carson
American River Recreation 11257 S. Bridge St. Rancho Cordova, CA 95670 916-635-4479	D-E/American, Carson
American River Touring Assn. Star Route 73 Groveland, CA 95321 209-962-7873 800-323-ARTA	D-E/Grand Canyon, Tuolumne, Merced, Kern, Cal-Salmon, Klamath, Rogue, Illinois, Salmon, Green, Yampa, American, Selway
California Adventures 2301 Bancroft Ave. Oakland, CA 94720 415-642-4000	D-E/American, Klamath, Carson
California River Trips P.O. Box CRT Lotus, CA 95651 916-626-8006	E/California rivers
Carlson River Touring 319 Lunada Ct. Los Altos, CA 94022 415-941-0394	D-E/American, Cal-Salmon, Klamath, Iceland rivers
Chili Bar Outdoor Center 1669 Chili Bar Court Placerville, CA 95667 916-622-6104	D-E/American
Chuck Richard's Whitewater Box W.W. Whitewater Lake Isabella, CA 93240 714-379-4685	D-E/Kern, California rivers, Alaska rivers
Earthtrek Expeditions & Travel 1534 E. Edinger #6 Santa Ana, CA 92705 714-547-5864	D-E-B/Western rivers
ECHO: The Wilderness Company 6529 Telegraph Ave. Oakland, CA 94609 415-652-1600	E/Salmon, Rogue, Tuolumne, American, Cal-Salmon
Friends of the River Building C, Fort Mason Center San Francisco, CA 94123 415-771-0400	D-E-B/Grand Canyon, Merced, Kings, Dolores, Kern, Cal-Salmon, Tuolumne, Klamath, American, Yuba
Grand Canyon Dories P.O. Box 7538 Menlo Park, CA 94026 415-854-6616	E/Grand Canyon, Green, Cataract Canyon, Owyhee, Grande Ronde, Salmon, Snake
Great Valley Canoe & Raft Trips 3213 Sierra Ave. Riverbanks, CA 95367 209-869-1235	D/California rivers
Jody Pullen's TI Bar Guide Service Somes Bar, CA 95568 916-469-3349	D-E/Cal-Salmon, Klamath
Kern River Tours Box 1884 Ridgecrest, CA 93555 619-375-5598	D-E/Kern, Merced, American, Carson, Klamath
Kings River Expeditions 93 E. Sierra Fresno, CA 93710 209-431-3416	D/Kings
Libra Whitewater Expeditions Box 4280 Sunland, CA 91040 818-352-3205	D-E/American, Rio Usumacinta

ADDRESS/TELEPHONE	TRIPS/RIVERS
Munroe's Wilderness Adventures P.O. Box 938 Redding, CA 96099 916-243-3091	E/Scott, Salmon, Wooley Creek, Klamath, Trinity, Sacramento Canyon
O.A.R.S. Inc. P.O. Box 67W Angels Camp, CA 95222 209-736-4677	D-E-B/Grand Canyon, American, Salmon, Merced, Rogue, Tuolumne, Klamath, Dolores, Carson, Snake, San Juan
Outdoor Adventures 3109 Fillmore St. San Francisco, CA 94123 415-346-8700	D-E/Salmon, Tuolumne, American, Carson, Kern, Merced
Outdoors Unlimited River Trips Box 854 Lotus, CA 95651 916-626-7668	E/Grand Canyon, Merced, Rogue, Klamath, Tuolumne
Riff Raft Drifters P.O. Box 15 Sacramento, CA 95801 916-441-4092	D-E/American, Klamath, Carson
River Travel Center P.O. Box 6-W Point Arena, CA 95468 707-882-2258 800-344-RAFT	D-E-B/Grand Canyon, Idaho, Alaska and California rivers
Sierra Club Sierra Club Outing 730 Polk St. San Francisco 94109 415-776-2211	E/Various—frequently combined with other activities and outings
Sierra Mac River Trips P.O. Box 366 Sonora, CA 95370 209-532-1327	D-E/Tuolumne
Sierra South Box Y Kernville, CA 93238 619-376-3745	D/Kern

ADDRESS/TELEPHONE	TRIPS/RIVERS
Sobek Expeditions Box 1089 Angels Camp, CA 95222 209-736-4524	O-E-B/Grand Canyon, all continents
Sunshine River Adventures P.O. Box 1445 9619 Jackson Rd. Oakdale, CA 95361 209-847-8908	D-E/Stanislaus, Mokelumne, American
Tributary Whitewater Tours 41 Sutter St. #1065 San Francisco, CA 94104 415-532-7238	D-E/Yuba, Trinity, American, Carson, Sacramento, Klamath, Salmon, Scott, Stanislaus
Trowbridge Recreation, Inc. 20 Healdsburg Avenue Healdsburg, CA 95448 707-433-7247	D-O-E/Russian, American
Turtle River Rafting Co. 507 McCloud Ave. Mt. Shasta, CA 96067 916-926-3223	D-E/Klamath, Owyhee, Sacramento, American, Eel, Smith, Salmon, Scott
W.E.T. P.O. Box 160024 Sacramento, CA 95816 916-451-3241	D-E/Grand Canyon, Klamath, Cal-Salmon, Merced, Tuolumne, Rogue, American, Carson
Whitewater Voyages P.O. Box 906 El Sobrante, CA 94803 415-222-5994	D-E/Kern, Merced, Carson, American, Cal-Salmon, Klamath, Scott, Rogue, Owyhee
Wild Water West P.O. Box 4833 Davis, CA 95617 916-758-9270	D-E/American, Yuba, Klamath, Cal-Salmon, Stanislaus, American, Tuolumne, Scott

Address/Telephone	Trips/Rivers	Address/Telephone	Trips/Rivers
Young's Ranch Somes Bar, CA 95568 916-469-3322	D-E/Klamath, Cal-Salmon	Bill Dvorak's Rafting Expeditions 17921 U.S. Hwy. 285 Nathrop, CO 81236 303-539-6851 800-824-3795	D-E/Colorado, Green, Dolores, Platte, Rio Grande, Arkan- sas, Gunnison
Zephyr River Expeditions P.O. Box 3607 Sonora, CA 95370 209-532-6249	D-E/Tuolumne, American, Kings, Eel, Klamath, Carson, Merced	Blazing Paddles Box 5929 Snowmass Village, CO 81615 303-923-4544	D-E/Colorado, Roaring Fork, Arkansas

Colorado

Address/Telephone	Trips/Rivers	Address/Telephone	Trips/Rivers
Adrift Adventures 1816 Orchard Place Fort Collins, CO 80521 303-493-4005	D-E/Yampa, Green, Dolores, Platte, Arkansas, Poudre	Boulder Outdoor Center 2510 N. 47th St. Boulder, CO 80301 303-444-8420	D-E/Colorado, Arkansas, Dolores, Rio Grande, Mexico rivers
Adventure Bound 649 25 Road Grand Junction, CO 81505 303-241-5633	E/Colorado, Green, Gunni- son, Yampa	Colorado Riff Raft Box 3681 Aspen, CO 81612 303-925-5404	D-E/Colorado, Roaring Fork, Arkansas, Gunnison
American Adventure Expeditions Box 25 Poncha Springs, CO 81242 303-395-2409	D-E/Arkansas, Dolores, Colo- rado, Rio Grande, Piedra, Gunni- son, Lake Fork, Roaring Fork	Colorado River Runs St. Rt. Box 32 Bond, CO 80423 303-653-4292	E/Colorado, Roaring Fork
American Wilderness Adventures 7600 E. Arapahoe Rd. #114 Englewood, CO 80112 303-771-0380 800-322-9453	D-E-B/All West- ern rivers, Alaska, Costa Rica	Colorado Whitewater Expe- ditions P.O. Box 187 Poncha Springs, CO 81242 303-539-6072	D-E/Arkansas, Dolores
Arkansas River Tours Box 20281 Denver, CO 80220 303-333-7831	D-E/Arkansas, Dolores, Green, Rio Grande	Echo Canyon River Expeditions Box 1002 Colorado Springs, CO 80901 303-632-3684	D-E/Arkansas, Dolores, Rio Rio Chama
Arkansas Valley Expeditions 944 East Hwy. 50 Salida, CO 81201 719-539-6669	D-E/Arkansas	Four Corners Expeditions P.O. Box 1032 Buena Vista, CO 81211 303-395-8949	D-E/Arkansas, Rio Grande, Gunnison, Dolores
Bighorn Expeditions Box 365 Bellvue, CO 80512 303-221-8110	E/Dolores, Green, Rio Grande	Joni Ellis River Tours P.O. Box 764 Dillon, CO 80435 303-468-1028	D/Colorado, Arkansas, Blue

ADDRESS/TELEPHONE	TRIPS/RIVERS	ADDRESS/TELEPHONE	TRIPS/RIVERS
Last Chance River Expeditions 2925 Jay St. Denver, CO 80214 303-233-6061	D/Arkansas	Roaring Fork River Company 6805 E. Arizona Ave. Denver, CO 80224 303-759-9599	D-E/Colorado, Roaring Fork, Arkansas, Dolores
Lazy J Resort and Rafting Co. P.O. Box W85 Coaldale, CO 81222 303-942-4274	D/Arkansas	Rock Gardens Rafting 1308 Road 129 Glenwood Springs, CO 81602 303-945-6737	D/Roaring Fork, Colorado
Mad River Rafting P.O. Box 5290 Winter Park, CO 80482 303-726-5290	D-E/Arkansas, Colorado, Dolores	Rocky Mountain Outpost 501 Camino Del Rio Durango, CO 81301 303-259-4783	E/Rio Grande, Animas, San Juan, Piedra, Guadalupe, Dolores, Mexico rivers
Mountain Waters Rafting Box 2681 Durango, CO 81301 303-259-4191	D/Animas	Rocky Mountain River Expeditions P.O. Box 427 Westminster, CO 80030 303-430-8333	E/Westwater and Desolation Gray canyons
Noah's Ark Box 850 Buena Vista, CO 81211 303-395-2158	D-E/Arkansas, Dolores		
Peregrine River Outfitters P.O. Box 808 Mancos, CO 81328 303-533-7235	D-E/Dolores, San Juan, Animas, Gunnison	Royal Gorge River Adventures P.O. Box 13 Texas Creek, CO 81250 303-269-3700	D-E/Arkansas
Raftmeister P.O. Box 1805 Vail, CO 81658 303-476-7238	D-E/Arkansas, Colorado, Eagle	Snowmass Whitewater Box 5929 Snowmass Village, CO 81615 303-923-4544	D-E/Colorado, Roaring Fork, Arkansas
River Rats Box 3231 Aspen, CO 81612 303-925-7648	D-E/Arkansas, Colorado, Dolores, Gunnison, Roaring Fork, San Juan, Rio Grande	Timber Rafting P.O. Box 403 Winter Park, CO 80482 303-670-0177	D-E/Colorado, Arkansas, Dolores
River Runners Ltd. 11150 U.S Hwy. 50, Dept. D Salida, CO 81201 719-539-2144 800-525-2081	D-E/Arkansas	Timberwolf Whitewater Expeditions Box 573 Salida, CO 81201 303-539-7508	D-E/Arkansas
		Whitewater Odyssey P.O. Box 2186 Evergreen, CO 80439 303-674-3637	E/Colorado, Platte, Rio Grande, Rio Chama

Address/Telephone	Trips/Rivers	Address/Telephone	Trips/Rivers
Wilderness Aware Box 1550 Buena Vista, CO 80211 Grande, Rio Chama	D-E/Dolores, Platte, Arkansas, Colorado, Rio	River Odysseys West P.O. Box 579 Coeur d'Alene, ID 83814 208-765-0841	D-E/Owyhee, Grande Ronde, Salmon, Snake, Lochsa
Delaware		Rocky Mountain River Tours P.O. Box 2552 Boise, ID 83701 208-756-4808	E/Salmon
Wilderness Canoe Trips Box 7125 Talleyville Wilmington, DE 19803 302-654-2227	D/Brandywine	ROW (River Odysseys West) P.O. Box 579 Coeur d'Alene, ID 83814 208-765-0841	D-E/Snake, Salmon, Lochsa, Moyie, St. Joe, Owyhee, Grande Ronde
Georgia			
Southeastern Expeditions 1955 Cliff Valley Way, N.E. Suite 220 Atlanta, GA 30329 404-329-0433	D-E/Chattooga, Ocoee, Rio Grande	Whitewater Adventures P.O. Box 184 Twin Falls, ID 83301 208-733-4548	E/Selway
Idaho		Whitewater Outfitters Salmon River Air Route Cascade, ID 83611 208-382-4336	E/Salmon
Epley's Idaho Outdoor Adventure P.O. Box 979 McCall, ID 83638 208-634-5173	D-E/Salmon, Clearwater, Payette	**Kentucky**	
Idaho Adventures P.O. Box 834-FV Salmon, ID 83467 208-756-2986	E/Salmon, Snake	Sheltowee Trace Outfitters 117 Hawkins Avenue Somerset, KY 42501 606-279-5026 800-541-RAFT	D/Rockcastle, Cumberland
Middle Fork River Company Box 54 Sun Valley, ID 83353 208-726-8888	E/Salmon, Owyhee, Bruneau	**Maine**	
Middle Fork River Expeditions Box 199 Stanley, ID 83278 208-774-3659	E/Salmon	Action River Adventures 10 Exchange St., Suite 304 Portland, ME 04101 207-775-2345	D/Kennebec, Penobscot, Dead
Northwest River Company P.O. Box 403 Boise, ID 83701 208-344-7119	E/Salmon, Selway	Adventure River Expeditions P.O. Box 101 The Forks, ME 04985 207-663-2249	D/Dead, Penob- scot, St. John, Rapid, St. Croix, Machias
		All Outdoors Lake Moxie Camps The Forks, ME 04985 207-663-2231	D/Kennebec, Dead, Penob- scot, Swift, Contoocook

ADDRESS/TELEPHONE	TRIPS/RIVERS	ADDRESS/TELEPHONE	TRIPS/RIVERS
Crab Apple Whitewater Crab Apple Acres Inn The Forks, ME 04985 207-663-2218	D/Kennebec, Penobscot, Dead	Wilderness Rafting Expeditions P.O. Box 41 Rockwood, ME 04478 207-534-2242	D/Kennebec, Penobscot, Dead, Hudson
Eastern River Expeditions P.O. Box 1173 Greenville, ME 04441 207-695-2411 800-634-RAFT	D/Penobscot, Kennebec, Dead, Hudson, Moose, Gauley	**Maryland**	
		Precision Rafting P.O. Box 185 Friendsville, MD 21531 301-746-5290	D/Yough- iogheny
Great Adventures P.O. Box 1 The Forks, ME 04985 207-663-2251	D/Swift, Kenne- bec, Penobscot, Dead		
Maine Whitewater Gadabout Gaddis Airport Bingham, ME 04920 207-672-4814	D/Kennebec, Penobscot, Dead	River and Trail Outfitters Rt. 2, Valley Rd., Box 246 Knoxville, MD 21758 301-695-5177	D/Shenandoah, Potomac
New England Whitewater Center 10 Exchange St., Suite 304 Portland, ME 04101 207-775-2345	D/Kennebec, Penobscot, Dead	**Minnesota**	
		Superior Whitewater 950 Chestnut Street Carlton, MN 55718 218-384-4637	D/St. Louis
North Country Outfitters P.O. Box 81-NA Rockwood, ME 04478 207-534-2242	D/Penobscot, Dead, Kennebec	**Montana**	
Northern Outdoors Box 100, Martin Pond The Forks, ME 04985 207-663-4466	D-E/Kennebec, Penobscot, Dead	Glacier Raft Company P.O. Box 264 West Glacier, MT 59936 406-888-5541	D-E/Flathead, Lochsa
Rolling Thunder River Company Box 70, Rt. 201 North The Forks, ME 04985 207-663-4441	D/Penobscot, Kennebec, Carra- bassett, Swift, Dead, Rapid	Great Northern Float Trips P.O. Box 82 West Glacier, MT 59936 406-387-5340	D-E/Flathead, Clark Fork, Kootenai, Yellowstone
Unicorn Expeditions P.O. Box T Brunswick, ME 04011 207-725-2255	D-E/Penobscot, Kennebec, Hudson, Dead, Moose	Montana River Outfitters 1524 10th Ave South Great Falls, MT 59405 406-761-1677	D-E/Smith, Missouri, Madison, Big Hole, Big Horn, Clark Fork, Black- foot, Yellowstone
Voyagers Whitewater P.O. Box 41-MP Rockwood, ME 04985 207-663-4423	D/Kennebec, Penobscot, Dead		

ADDRESS/TELEPHONE	TRIPS/RIVERS	ADDRESS/TELEPHONE	TRIPS/RIVERS
Wild Water Adventures Box 272 West Glacier, MT 59936 406-752-3801	D-E/Flathead	New Wave Rafting Co. 107 Washington Ave. Santa Fe, NM 87501 505-984-1444	D-E/Grand Canyon, Arkansas, Colo- rado, Salt, Rio Grande, Costa Rica
Wilderness Outfitters West Drawer A Lindbergh Lake, MT 59868 406-754-2422	D-E/Missouri, Blackfoot, Flat- head, Clark, Smith, Salmon, Snake	Rio Bravo River Tours 1412 Cerrillos Rd Santa Fe, NM 87501 505-988-1153 800-451-0708	D-E/Animas, San Juan, Dolores, Rio Grande
Yellowstone Raft Co. Box 46 Gardiner, MT 59030 406-848-7777	D/Yellowstone, Gallatin, Madison	Sierra Outfitters and Guides P.O. Box 2756 Taos, NM 87571 505-758-9556	D-E/Rio Grande, Gila, Rio Chama, Arkansas, Dolores
Nevada		Southwest Wilderness Center Box 2840 Santa Fe, NM 87504 505-982-3126	D/Rio Grande, Rio Chama, Big Bend, New Mexico rivers
Georgie's Royal River Rats P.O. Box 12057 Las Vegas, NV 89112 702-798-0602	E/Grand Canyon		
		New York	
New Hampshire		Adirondack River Outfitters P.O. Box 649 Old Forge, NY 13420 315-369-3536	D/Black, Hudson, Moose Scandaga
Downeast Whitewater Rafting Co. Box 119, Rt. 302 Center Conway, NH 03813 603-447-3002	D/Kennebec, Penobscot, Dead, Swift, Rapid	*North Carolina*	
Monadnock Whitewater Box 839 Henniker, NH 03242 603-888-4770	D-E/Contoocook, Batiscan, Rogue	Nantahala Outdoor Center U.S. 19W, Box 41 Bryson City, NC 28713 704-488-2175	D-E/Nantahala, French Broad, Ocoee, Noli- chucky, Chat- tooga, Costa Rica rivers
Saco Bound/Downeast Whitewater Route 302, Box 119 Center Conway, NH 03813 603-447-2177	D-O/Saco, Androscoggin, Penobscot, Kennebec, Dead	Nantahala Rafts U.S. 19 West, Box 45 Bryson City, NC 28713 704-488-2325	D/Ocoee
New Mexico		Wahoo's Outdoor Adventures P.O. Box 1915 Boone, NC 28607 704-262-5774	D/Nolichucky, Ocoee, French Broad, Watauga
Hawk, I'm Your Sister Box 9109 Santa Fe, NM 87504 505-984-2268	E/Green, Rio Grande, Missouri, San Juan, Allagash, Yukon		

Address/Telephone	Trips/Rivers	Address/Telephone	Trips/Rivers
Hudson River Rafting Co. Main Street North Creek, NY 12853 518-251-3215	D/Hudson, Moose, Black, Sacandaga	Oregon River Experiences 1935 Hayes St. Eugene, OR 97405 503-342-3293	E/Salmon, Rogue, Owyhee, Deschutes, John Day, Grande Ronde, Umpqua, McKenzie, Klamath

Oregon

Address/Telephone	Trips/Rivers	Address/Telephone	Trips/Rivers
All Seasons Guide Service 1360 Sunnyglen Way Sunny Valley, OR 97526 503-479-1081	D/Rogue	Otter River Trips P.O. Box 338 Merlin, OR 97532 503-476-8590	D/Rogue
Briggs Guide Service 2750 Cloverlawn Dr. Grants Pass, OR 97527 503-476-2941	D/Rogue	Pacific Crest Outward Bound 0110 S.W. Bancroft Portland, OR 97201 503-243-1993	E/Rogue, Des- chutes, John Day, Owyhee
Dave Helfrich River Outfitter 47555 McKenzie Hwy. Vida, OR 97488 503-896-3786	E/Owyhee, Rogue, McKenzie, Salmon	Paul Brooks' Raft Trips P.O. Box 638 Merlin, OR 97532 503-476-8051	D/Rogue
Eagle Creek Outfitters Rt. 1, Box 702 Summerville, OR 97876 503-534-4555	D/Owyhee, Grand Ronde	River Adventure Float Trips 2407 Merlin Rd. Grants Pass, OR 97526 503-476-6943	D/Rogue
Eagle Sun P.O. Box 873 Medford, OR 97501 503-772-9910	D-E/Rogue, Klamath	River Trips Unlimited 4140 Dry Creek Rd. Medford, OR 97504 503-779-3798	D-E/Rogue, Chetco, Illinois, Umpqua, Kla- math, Smith
Galice Resort 11744 Galice Rd. Merlin, OR 97532 503-476-3818	D/Rogue	Rogue Excursions Unlimited P.O. Box 855 Medford, OR 97501 503-773-5983	E/Rogue
Grants Pass Float Company Box 1111 Grants Pass, OR 97526 503-479-5061	D-E/Rogue	Rogue River Guide Service 1540 Savage Creek Rd. Grants Pass, OR 97527 503-582-0271	D/Rogue
Hells Canyon Adventures P.O. Box 159 Oxbow, OR 97840 503-785-3352 800-HCA-FLOT	D-E/Snake	Rogue River Raft Trips 8500 Galice Rd. Merlin, OR 97532 503-476-3825 800-826-1963	D/Rogue
Lute Jerstad Adventures P.O. Box 19537 Portland, OR 97219 503-244-4364	E/Deschutes, Rogue, Grande Ronde, Owyhee	Rogue Wilderness 3388 Merlin/Galice Rd. Grants Pass, OR 97526 503-479-9554	D-E/Rogue, Illinois, Owyhee

Address/Telephone	Trips/Rivers	Address/Telephone	Trips/Rivers
Sierra Whitewater Expeditions Box 1330 Springfield, OR 97477 503-741-2780	D-E/Rogue, Owyhee, Klamath, Cal-Salmon, Grande Ronde, American	Shawnee Canoe Trips Box 189 Shawnee-on-Delaware, PA 18356 717-424-6221 800-742-9633	D/Delaware
Sundance Expeditions 14894 Galice Rd. Merlin, OR 97532 503-479-8508	D/Rogue	Whitewater Adventurers Box 31 Ohiopyle, PA 15470 412-329-8850 800-WWA-RAFT	D/Yough-iogheny, Cheat
Tag Two Guide Service 606 Templin Grants Pass, OR 97526 503-476-7962	D/Rogue	Whitewater Challengers P.O. Box 8 White Haven, PA 18661 714-443-9532	D/Lehigh, Hudson, Moose
White Water Cowboys 209 Merlin Rd. Merlin, OR 97532 503-479-0132	D/Rogue	Whitewater Rafting Adventures Box 88, Rt. 534 Albrightsville, PA 18210 717-722-0285	D/Lehigh

Pennsylvania

Address/Telephone	Trips/Rivers	Address/Telephone	Trips/Rivers
Jim Thorpe River Adventures P.O. Box 4066 Jim Thorpe, PA 18229 717-325-2570	D/Lehigh	Wilderness Voyagers P.O. Box 97 Ohiopyle, PA 15470 412-329-4752	D/Youghiogheny

South Carolina

Address/Telephone	Trips/Rivers	Address/Telephone	Trips/Rivers
Laurel Highland River Tours P.O. Box 107 Ohiopyle, PA 15470 412-329-8531 800-4-RAFTIN	D-E/Yough-iogheny, Cheat	Wildwater, Ltd. Box 100-E Long Creek, SC 29658 803-647-9587	D-E/Ocoee, Chattooga, Nan-tahela, Costa Rica rivers
Lehigh River Rafting P.O. Box 66 White Haven, PA 18661 717-443-9777	D/Lehigh		

Tennessee

Address/Telephone	Trips/Rivers	Address/Telephone	Trips/Rivers
Mountain Streams Outfitters Box 106 Ohiopyle, PA 15470 412-329-8810 800-245-4090 PA	D-E/Yough-iogheny, Cheat, Gauley, Tygart, Big Sandy	Cherokee Adventures Route 1, Box E-605 Erwin, TN 37650 615-743-8666	D/Nolichucky, Gauley, French Broad, Ocoee
Pocono Whitewater Rafting Rt. 903 Jim Thorpe, PA 18229 717-325-3656	D/Lehigh, Hudson, Moose, Rouge, Batiscan, Cheat	Cherokee Rafting P.O. Box 111 Ocoee, TN 37361 615-338-5124	D/Ocoee

ADDRESS/TELEPHONE	TRIPS/RIVERS	ADDRESS/TELEPHONE	TRIPS/RIVERS
Cripple Creek Expeditions P.O. Box 98 Ocoee, TN 37361 615-338-8841 800-338-RAFT	D/Ocoee, French Broad	Texas River Expeditions P.O. Box 770485 Houston, TX 77215 713-242-1525	D-E/Rio Grande, Guadalupe, Salmon
Ocoee Inn Rafting Hwy. 64 Benton, TN 37307 615-338-2064 800-272-RAFT	D/Ocoee	*Utah* Adrift Adventure in Canyonlands P.O. Box 81032 Salt Lake City, UT 84108 801-259-8594	D-E/Colorado, Green, Lochsa, Flathead, Kootenay, Kick- ing Horse
Ocoee Outdoors P.O. Box 72 Ocoee, TN 37361 615-338-2438	D/Ocoee, Hiwassee, Obed, Big South Fork	Adventure River Expeditions P.O. Box 96 Green River, UT 84525 801-564-3648	E/Green, Colorado
Ocoee Rafting P.O. Box 461 Ducktown, TN 37326 615-496-3388 800-251-4800	D/Ocoee	Colorado Outward Bound School Box 111 Jensen, UT 84035 801-789-4952	E/Colorado, Roaring Fork, Arkansas, Gun- nison
Quest Expeditions P.O. Box 499 Benton, TN 37307 615-338-2979	D-E/Ocoee, Mexico rivers	Colorado River and Trail Expeditions P.O. Box 7575 Salt Lake City, UT 84107 801-261-1789	D-E/Grand Canyon, Cataract and Westwater canyons, Tatshen- shini, Noatak, Koyokuk
Sunburst Adventures P.O. Box 329E Benton, TN 37307 615-338-8388	D/Ocoee	Cross Tours and Expeditions 274 West 1400 South Orem, UT 84058 801-225-0849	E/Grand Canyon
Texas Big Bend River Tours P.O. Box 317 Lajitas, TX 79852 915-424-3219	D-E/Rio Grande	Don Hatch River Expeditions P.O. Box C Vernal, UT 84078 801-789-4316	E/Salmon, Selway, Green, Yampa, Colorado
Far Flung Adventures P.O. Box 31 Terlingua, TX 79852 915-371-2489	E/Rio Grande, New Mexico, Mexico, and Alaska rivers	Don Neff River Company 2121 W. White Cr. Salt Lake City, UT 84109 801-467-5356	E/Dolores, Green, Yampa
Gruene River Company 1495 Gruene Loop Rd. New Braunfels, TX 78130 512-625-2800	D/Guadalupe	Grand Canyon Expeditions P.O. Box O Kanab, UT 84741 801-644-5735	E/Grand Canyon

Address/Telephone	Trips/Rivers	Address/Telephone	Trips/Rivers
High Desert Adventures 818 East South Temple P.O. Box 8514 Salt Lake City, UT 84108 801-355-5550 800-345-RAFT	E-B/Grand Canyon, Cataract, Westwater and Desolation canyons, San Juan, Yampa, Animas, Salmon, Green, Snake	Sheri Griffith River Expeditions Box 1324 Moab, UT 84532 801-259-8229	E/Green, Colorado, Dolores
Holiday River Expeditions 544 E. 3900 S. Salt Lake City, UT 84107 801-266-2087 800-624-6323	E/Colorado, Green, Yampa, San Juan, Dolores, Salmon, Lochsa, Snake	Sierra Western River Guides P.O. Box 1634 Provo, UT 84603 801-377-9750 800-453-1482	E/Grand Canyon, Salmon, American, Tuolumne, Colorado, Arkansas
Hondoo River and Trails P.O. Box 306 Torrey, UT 84775 801-425-3519	E/Desolation-Gray canyons	Sleight Expeditions P.O. Box 40 St. George, UT 84770 801-673-1200	E/Grand Canyon
Lake Powell Tours P.O. Box 40 St. George, UT 84770 801-673-1733	E/San Juan	S'Plore 255 E. 400 S. 107 Salt Lake City, UT 84111 801-363-7130	E/Colorado, Carson
Moki Mac River Expeditions P.O. Box 21242 Salt Lake City, UT 84121 801-943-6707	D-E/Grand Canyon, Cataract, Westwater and Desolation canyons, Green, Dolores, Colorado, San Juan	Steve Curry Expeditions Box 1574 Provo, UT 84603 801-224-6797	E/Salmon, Selway, Mexico rivers
North American Rive Expeditions P.O. Box 1107-W Moab, UT 84532 801-259-5865	E/Colorado	Tag-A-Long Expeditions 452 North Main Street Moab, UT 84530 801-259-8946	D-E/Cataract, Westwater and Desolation-Gray canyons
Peregrine River Outfitters P.O. Box 158 Mexican Hat, UT 84531 801-683-2206	D-E/San Juan	Tex's River Expeditions Box 67 Moab, UT 84532 801-259-5101	D-E/Cataract and Desolation-Gray canyons, Green, Colorado
Red Rock River Company 2144 Highland Dr. Salt Lake City, UT 84105 801-484-9022	E/Green, San Rafael	Tour West P.O. Box 333 Orem, UT 84057 801-942-6669 800-453-7450	E/Grand Canyon, Salmon
		Western River Expeditions 7258 Racquet Club Dr. Salt Lake City, UT 84121 801-942-6669 800-453-7450	E/Grand Canyon, Cataract and Westwater canyons, Green, Salmon
		Wild Rivers Expeditions P.O. Box 118 Bluff, UT 84512 801-672-2244	D-E/San Juan

ADDRESS/TELEPHONE	TRIPS/RIVERS	ADDRESS/TELEPHONE	TRIPS/RIVERS
World Wide River Expeditions 1275 E. Ft. Union Blvd. Midvale, UT 84047 801-566-2662	E/Colorado, Green, Yampa, Salmon	Pacific NW Float Trips P.O. Box 736 Sedro Woolley, WA 98284 206-855-0535	D-E/Sauk, Skagit, Suiattle, Nooksack, Wenatchee, Methow, Yakima, Toutle, Hoh, Queets

Virginia

Richmond Raft Company 4400 E. Main Street Richmond, VA 23231 804-222-7238	D/James	River Recreation Rafting 13-211 PI SE Redmond, WA 98052 206-392-5899	D-E/Green, Snoqualmie

Washington

		River Runners Northwest P.O. Box 678 Darrington, WA 98241 206-676-4099	D-E/Sauk, Sui- attle, Skagit, Sky- komish, Wenatchee
Cascade Whitewater 5665 Tigner Rd. Cashmere, WA 98815 509-662-4488	D/Wenatchee, Methow, Tieton	Wenatchee Whitewater Trips P.O. Box 12 Cashmere, WA 98815 509-782-2254	D-E/Wenatchee, Methow, Tieton
Downstream River Runners 12112 NE 195th Bothell, WA 98011 206-483-0335	D-E/Skykomish, Wenatchee, Methow, Grande Ronde, Owyhee, Sauk, Suiattle, Skagit, Tieton, Green		

West Virginia

		American Whitewater Tours P.O. Box 277 Rowlesburg, WV 26425 304-454-2475 800-624-8060	D/Youghiogheny, Cheat, New, Noli- chucky, Gauley
Four Seasons Outfitters P.O. Box 1778 Chelan, WA 98816 509-682-5032	D-E/Nooksack, Methow, Stehe- kin, Tieton		
Northern Wilderness River Riders P.O. Box 369 Leavenworth, WA 98826 509-548-4583	D/Wenatchee, Methow, Suiattle, Skykomish	American-Canadian Expeditions P.O. Box 249 Glen Jean, WV 25846 304-469-2651 800-ACE-2641	D-E/New, Gauley, Tygart, Rio Grande, Ivanhoe
Orion Expeditions 17218-30th Ave. N.E. Seattle, WA 98155 206-364-9860	D/Wenatchee, Methow, Sauk, Suiattle, Skyko- mish, Tieton, Klickitat, Deschutes, Owyhee	Appalachian Wildwaters, Inc. P.O. Box 277 Rowlesburg, WV 26425 304-454-2475 800-624-8060	D-E/Yough- iogheny, Cheat, New, Gauley, Tygart, Ocoee, Nolichucky, French Broad
		Cheat River Outfitters, Inc. P.O. Box 134 Albright, WV 26519 304-2024	D/Potomac, Cheat

ADDRESS/TELEPHONE	TRIPS/RIVERS	ADDRESS/TELEPHONE	TRIPS/RIVERS
Class VI River Runners Ames Heights Rd., P.O. Box 78 Lansing, WV 25862 304-574-0704	D-E/New, Gauley, Green- briar, Rio Grande	Rough Run Expeditions, Inc. P.O. Box 277 Rowlesburg, WV 26425 304-454-2475 800-624-8060	D-E/Cheat, Tygart, Rio Grande
Drift-A-Bit Box 885 Fayetteville, WV 25840 304-574-3282	D/New, Gauley	Songer Whitewater Box 27 A Saturday Rd. Victo, WV 25938 304-658-4207 800-356-RAFT	D/New, Gauley, Meadow, Blue- stone
Expeditions, Inc. P.O. Box 277 Rowlesburg, WV 26425 304-454-2474 800-624-8060	D/Cheat, Gauley, Nolichucky, French Broad, Nantahala, Ocoee	The Rivermen Box 360 Fayetteville, WV 25840 304-574-0515 800-422-7238	D/New, Gauley
Mountain River Tours P.O. Box 88 Sunday Rd. Hico, WV 25854 304-658-5266 800-822-1FUN	D/New, Gauley, French Broad, Nolichucky, Laurel, Cheat, Youghiogheny	USA Whitewater P.O. Box 277 Rowlesburg, WV 26425 304-454-2475 800-USA-RAFT	D-E-B/New, Gauley, Cheat, Tygart, Youghio- gheny, Noli- chucky, French
New River Scenic Whitewater Box 637 Hinton By-Pass Hinton, WV 25951 304-466-2288 800-292-0880	D/New, Gauley, Bluestone		Broad, Ocoee, Nantahala, Rio Grande
		West Virginia River Adventures P.O. Box 95 Hico, WV 25854 304-658-5277	D/New, Gauley
New/Gauley Expeditions Box 264 Fayetteville, WV 25840 304-574-3679 800-472-RAFT	D/New, Gauley	Wildwater Expeditions Unlimited P.O. Box 55, Dept. E Thurmond, WV 25936 304-459-2551 800-WVA-RAFT	D-E/Grand Canyon, Rio Grande, Salmon, New, Gauley, Cheat, Costa Rica rivers
North American River Runners Box 81 Hico, WV 25854 304-658-5276	D/New, Gauley, Cheat, Meadow, Youghiogheny		
Passages to Adventure, Inc. P.O. Box 71 Fayetteville, WV 25840 304-574-0137	D/New, Gauley, Cheat, Yough- iogheny	*Wisconsin* Kosir's Rapid Rafts Star Route Box 72A Athelstane, WI 54104 715-757-3431	D/Peshtigo, Menominee
Rivers II P.O. Drawer 39 Lansing, WV 25862 304-574-3834	D/New, Gauley, Cheat		

ADDRESS/TELEPHONE	TRIPS/RIVERS	ADDRESS/TELEPHONE	TRIPS/RIVERS

Wyoming

Barker-Ewing Float Trips
P.O. Box 1243
Jackson, WY 83001
307-733-1000
D-E/Snake, Salmon

Triangle X Float Trips
Box 120
Moose, WY 83012
307-733-5500
D/Snake

Wyoming River Trips
Box 1541
Cody, WY 82414
307-587-6661
D-E/Shoshone

Canada
Alberta

Chinook River Sports
93 Lorelei Close
Edmonton, Alberta T5X 2E7
403-454-3878
D-E/Red Deer, Highwood, Great Slave

Clearwater Rafting
Adventures
Box 597
Midnapore, Alberta T0L 1J0
403-256-2484
D/Red Deer

Hunter Valley Recreational
Box 1620
Canmore, Alberta T0L 0M0
403-678-2000
D-E/Red Deer, Kananaskis

Mad Rafter River Tours
5004 Stanley Rd. S.W.
Calgary, Alberta T2S 2R5
403-282-1324
D-E/Red Deer, Old Man, Castle

Mukwah Adventure Tours
1216 16 Avenue N.W.
Calgary, Alberta T2M 0K9
403-282-0509
D/Red Deer

River Adventure Float Trips
5678 Brenner Crescent N.W.
Calgary, Alberta T2L 1Z4
403-282-7238
D-E/Red Deer

WB Adventures Ltd.
215 Parkvalley Dr., S.E.
Calgary, Alberta T2J 4V1
403-271-9384
D-E/Red Deer

British Columbia

Action River Expeditions
5389 S.E. Marine Dr.
Burnaby, B.C. V5J 3G7
604-437-6679
D-E/Chilliwack, Babine, Skeena, Chilko, Chilcotin

B.C. Wilderness Outfitters
7137 Kennedy Crescent
Prince George, B.C. V2K 2P9
604-962-6438
D/Bowron, Quesnel

Bighorn River Excursions
2717 Roseberry Ave.
Victoria, B.C. V8R 3V1
604-595-3464
D/Thompson

Canadian River Expeditions
#401-845 Chilco St.
Vancouver, B.C. V6G 2R2
604-738-4449
E/Chilcotin, Fraser

Clearwater Expeditions
R.R. #2, Box 2506
Clearwater, B.C. V0E 1N0
604-674-3354
D-E/Clearwater

Fraser River Raft Expeditions
P.O. Box 10
Yale, B.C. V0K 2S0
604-863-2336
D-E/Fraser, Chilliwack, Thompson, Lillooet

Frontier River Adventures
927 Fairfield Rd.
North Vancouver, B.C.
V7H 2J4
604-929-7612
D-E/Thompson, Fraser

Glacier Raft Company
Box 219
Radium Hot Springs, B.C.
V0A 1M0
604-347-9218
D-E/Kicking Horse, White

Golden Valley Rafting
Box 2566
Golden, B.C. V0A 1H0
604-344-2182
D-E/Kicking Horse

ADDRESS/TELEPHONE	TRIPS/RIVERS	ADDRESS/TELEPHONE	TRIPS/RIVERS
Highwater Expeditions 917 Sprice Ave. Coquitlam, B.C. V3J 7M2 604-939-4842	D-E/Chilliwack, Elaho, Squamish, Thompson, Chilko, Chilcotin	River Rogues Adventure Box 115 Spences Bridge, B.C. V0K 2L0 694-458-2252	D/Thompson
HYAK River Expeditions 1698 W. 4th Avenue Vancouver, B.C. V6J 1L9 604-734-8622	D-E/Thompson, Chilko, Chilli- wack, Firth	River Runners 2151 West 4th Ave. Vancouver, B.C. V6J 1L9 604-984-2958	D-E/Lillooet, Thompson, Fraser
Interior Whitewater Exp. General Delivery Celista, B.C. V0E 1L0 604-955-2448	D-E/Clearwater, Babine, Skeena	Shuswap Whitewater Expeditions General Delivery Celista, B.C. V0E 1L0 604-955-2447	D-E/Adams, Clearwater, Babine, Skeena
Iskut River Adventures General Delivery Iskut, B.C. V0J 1K0 604-234-3331	E/Stikine, Klappan	Thompson Guiding Ltd. Riske Creek, B.C. V0L 1T0 604-659-5635	D-E/Chilko, Chilcotin, Fraser, Taseko, Cariboo, Quesnel
Kicking Horse Rafting Box 1890 Golden, B.C. V0A 1H0 604-344-5729	D-E/Kicking Horse, Blaeberry	Whistler River Adventures Box 202 Whistler, B.C. V0N 1B0 604-932-3532	D-E/Lillooet
Kootenay River Runners P.O. Box 81 Edgewater, B.C. V0A 1E0 604-347-9210	D-E/Kootenay, Kicking Horse	Whitewater Adventures 1616 Duranleau Street Granville Island Vancouver, B.C. V6H 3S4 604-669-1100	D-E/Chilliwack, Thompson, Fraser, Chilko Nahanni, Cop- permine, Tat- shenshini
Kumsheen Raft Adventures 281 Main Street Lytton, B.C. V0K 1Z0 604-455-2296	D-E/Thompson, Fraser, Chilcotin		
Nikaia River Holidays P.O. Box 6 Lytton, B.C. V0K 1Z0 604-455-2419	D-E/Fraser, Thompson	*Manitoba* Northern Manitoba Outfitters Berens River, Manitoba R0B 0A0 204-382-2379	E/Hayes, Blood- vein, Pigeon
R.A.F.T. Ranch Box 34051, Stn. D Vancouver, B.C. V6J 4M1 604-684-RAFT 800-663-RAFT	D-E/Chilliwack	*Ontario*	
REO Rafting Adventures 1199 W. Pender St., Suite 411 Vancouver, B.C. V6E 2R1 604-684-4438	D-E/Chilliwack, Chehalis, Elaho, Nahatlatch, Chilko, Similkameen	Algonquin Canoe Routes Box 187 Whitney, Ontario K0J 2M0 613-637-2699	D-E/Madawaska

ADDRESS/TELEPHONE	TRIPS/RIVERS	ADDRESS/TELEPHONE	TRIPS/RIVERS
C.A.T. Rafting Box 531, Station "B" Sudbury, Ontario P3E 4P8 705-522-3439	D-E/Spanish Sudbury	*Quebec*	
		Excursions Jacques-Cartier 835 Avenue Jacques-Cartier Nord Tewkesbury, Quebec G0A 4P0 418-848-7238	D/Jacques- Cartier
Madawaska River Rafting Box 635 Barry's Bay, Ontario K0J 1V0 613-756-3620	D/Madawaska		
		New World River Expeditions 5475 Pare, Suite 221 Montreal, Quebec H4P 1P7 514-733-7166	D/Rogue, Batis- can, Jacques- Cartier
O.W.L. Rafting Box 29 Foresters Falls, Ontario K0J 1V0 613-646-2263	D-E/Ottawa, Madawaska		
		Wilderness Tours Outdoor Centre 105 rue de la Commune ouest Montreal, Quebec H2Y 2C7 514-284-9607	D-E/Ottawa, Rogue
Ottawa Whitewater Rafting P.O. Box 179 Beachburg, Ontario K0J 1C0 613-646-2501	D-E/Ottawa		
Parry Sound Rafting Tours P.O. Box 515 Parry Sound, Ontario P2A 2X5 705-389-2011	D-E/Magne- tawan	*Saskatchewan*	
		Clearwater Raft Tours Box 290 Kerrobert, Saskatchewan S0L 1A0 306-834-5444	Canada rivers
River Run P.O. Box 179 Beachburg, Ontario K0J 1C0 613-646-2501	D-E/Magne- tawan		
		Paull River Wilderness Camp Holbein, Saskatchewan S0J 1G0 306-747-2862	Canada rivers
Wilderness Tours Box 89 Beachburg, Ontario K0J 1C0 613-646-2291	D-E/Ottawa		

Canoe Outfitters

Most of the companies on this list are strictly outfitters; they provide every-thing necessary for you to do it yourself. But a number of them do tours or expeditions (remember, an expedition is where you join a group that will be doing a trip with a guide on fixed dates). I have listed a company as an out-fitter if it can provide a trip that includes at least one night camping out; liv-eries that do only day rentals are not included.

The kinds of services provided are indicated in the "Trips" column: "**O**" for outfitters, "**T**" for tours, and "**E**" for expeditions. I have not included a "**D**" for day rental because almost all outfitters do them.

ADDRESS/TELEPHONE	TRIPS/RIVERS	ADDRESS/TELEPHONE	TRIPS/RIVERS
United States		Sobek Expeditions	O-E/All
Alaska		Box 1089	continents
		The Angels Camp, CA 95222	
		209-736-4524	
ABEC's Alaska Adventures	O/Alaska and		
1304-CL Westwick Dr.	Arctic rivers	Trowbridge Recreation, Inc.	O-E/Russian,
Fairbanks, AL 99712		20 Healdsburg Ave.	American
907-457-8907		Healdsburg, CA 95448	
		707-433-7247	
Alaska River Tours	O/Alaska rivers		
1831 Kuskokwim, Suite 4		*Colorado*	
Anchorage, AL 99508			
907-276-3418		Colorado Canoe Adventures	O/Arkansas,
		P.O. Box 202	Colorado, Dolo-
Sourdough Outfitters	O/Alaska and	Cotopaxi, CO 81223	res, Champa,
P.O. Box 90	Arctic rivers	719-942-4362	Gunnison
Brooks Bettles, AL 99726			
907-692-5252		Dvorak's Expeditions	O/Southwest
		Hwy. 285	rivers, Mexico
Arizona		Nathrop, CO 81236	rivers
		303-539-6851	
Jerkwater Canoe Co.	O-E-T/Colorado		
P.O. Box 800		*Connecticut*	
Topack, AZ 86436			
602-768-7753		Down River Canoes	O/Connecticut
		P.O. Box 283	
California		Haddam, CT 06438	
		203-345-8355	
Cactus Canoes	O/Colorado		
121½ Midway Place		High Adventure	O/Farmington
Blythe, CA 92225		Box 771	
619-922-8752		Simsbury, CT 06070	
		203-651-3989	
California Canoe and	O/California		
Kayak, Inc.		Main Stream Canoe	O/Farmington
249 Tewksbury Ave.		P.O. Box 448	
Pt. Richmond, CA 94801		New Hartford, CT 06057	
415-234-0929		203-379-6657	
Driftwood Resort	O/Sacramento	North American Canoe Tours	O-E/Connecti-
24630 Tehama-Vina Rd.		65 Black Point Rd.	cut, Everglades
Los Molinos, CA 96055		Niantic, CT 06357	
916-384-2851		203-739-0791	
Sierra Club Outing	E/Many areas	River Running Expeditions,	O/Housatonic,
Department		Ltd.	Shepaug
730 Polk St.		Main Street	
San Francisco, CA 94109		Falls Village, CT 06031	
415-776-2211		203-824-5579	

ADDRESS/TELEPHONE	TRIPS/RIVERS	ADDRESS/TELEPHONE	TRIPS/RIVERS
The Mountain Workshop P.O. Box 625 Ridgefield, CT 06877 203-438-3640	O/Housatonic, Naugatuck	*Idaho*	
		Canyons, Inc. P.O. Box 823 McCall, ID 83638 208-634-4303	O/Salmon
White Creek Expeditions 99 Myanos Rd. New Canaan, CT 06840 203-966-0040	O/Saugatuck, Farmington, Housatonic, Shepaug	*Illinois*	
Florida		Chicago Canoe Base 4019 N. Narragansett Chicago, IL 60634 312-777-1489	O/Illinois rivers
Adventures Unlimited, Inc. Rt. 6, Box 283 Milton, FL 32570 904-623-6197	O/Coldwater, Blackwater, Sweetwater, Juniper	Fox River Canoes Rental Rt. 2, Box 32 Sheridan, IL 60551 815-496-9285	O/Fox, Vermil- lion, Mazon
Canoe Outfitters of Florida 16346 N. 106th Terrace Jupiter, FL 33478 407-746-7053	E/Canada rivers	Freeman Sports, Inc. 129 E. Hydraulic Yorkville, IL 60560 312-553-9515	O/Fox
Canoe Outpost-Peace River Route 7, Box 301 Arcadia, FL 33821 813-494-1215	O-E/Everglades, Peace	Reed's Canoe Trips 907 N. Indiana Ave. Kankakee, IL 60901 815-932-2663	O/Kankakee, Iroquois
Canoe Outpost- Withlacoochee P.O. Box 188, S.R. 476 Nobleton, FL 34263 904-796-4343	O/South Withla- coochee	*Indiana*	
Georgia		Blue's Canoe Livery 6700 W. Lowell Rd. Columbus, IN 47201 812-526-9851	O/Sugar Creek, Driftwood
Broad River Outpost Route 3, Box 3449 Danielsville, GA 30633 404-795-3242	O/Broad, Ogeechee, Oke- fenokee swamp	Cave County Canoes Box 145 Milltown, IN 47145 812-633-4993	O/Blue
Flint River Outdoor Center 4429 Woodland Rd. Thomaston, GA 30286 404-674-2633	O/Flint	Morgan's Brookville Canoe Center 7040 Whitewater River Lane Brookville, IN 47012 317-647-4904	O/Whitewater
Wilderness Southeast 711 Sandtown Rd. Savannah, GA 31410 912-897-5108	E/Everglades, Okefenokee, Florida Springs, St. John's		

ADDRESS/TELEPHONE	TRIPS/RIVERS	ADDRESS/TELEPHONE	TRIPS/RIVERS
Wapitiland, Inc. P.O. Box 153 Sumava Resorts, IN 46379 219-992-3795	O/Kankakee	Moosehead Country Outfitters P.O. Box D, Squaw Mountain Greenville, ME 04441 207-695-2272	O/Penobscot, St. John, Allagash
Kentucky		North Country Outfitters P.O. Box 81-NA Rockwood, ME 04478 207-534-2242	O/Moosehead Lake, Kennebec, Dead, Penobscot
Sheltowee Trace Outfitters 117 Hawkins Avenue Somerset, KY 42501 606-279-5026 800-541-RAFT	O/Rockcastle, Cumberland	Sunrise County Canoe Expeditions Cathance Lake Grove Post, ME 04638 207-454-7708	O-E/Maine, Canada, Alaska, Newfoundland, Labrador, Rio Grande
Thaxton's Canoe Trails Rt. 2, Box 391 Falmouth, KY 41040 606-654-5111	O/Licking		
Maine		*Massachusetts*	
Allagash Canoe Trips Box 713M Greenville, ME 04441 207-695-3668	E/Allagash, Penobscot, St. John	Charles River Canoe Service 2401 Commonwealth Avenue Newton, MA 02166 617-965-5110	O/Charles
Allagash Wilderness Outfitters 620, SR #76 Greenville, ME 04441 207-695-2821	O/Allagash, Penobscot, Box, St. John	*Michigan*	
Katahdin Outfitters P.O. Box 34 Millinocket, ME 04462 207-723-5700	O/Allagash, St. John	Carlisle Canoe Livery 110 State St. Grayling, MI 49738 517-348-2301	O/Au Sable
Maine Canoe Adventures Box 105-Route 161 Allagash, ME 04774 207-398-3191	O/Allagash, St. John	Carl's Canoe Livery 10499 S. 15 Mile Rd. Cadillac, MI 49601 616-862-3402	O/Pine
Maine Wilderness Canoe Basin Box 100P Springfield, ME 04487 207-796-2843	O/Washington County Wilder- ness Waterways, Grand Chain of Lakes	Chippewa Landing 3241 W. Houghton Lake Rd. Lake City, MI 49651 616-839-5511	O/Manistee
		Famous Jarolim Canoe Rental M-37 Wellston, MI 49689 616-862-3475	O/Pine
		Float Trips 5355 Croton Dr. Croton Dam, MI 49337 616-652-6037	O/Muskegon

Address/Telephone	Trips/Rivers	Address/Telephone	Trips/Rivers
Horina Canoe Rental Highway M-37 Wellston, MI 49689 616-862-3470	O/Pine	Beland's Wilderness Canoe Trips Box 808 Ely, MN 55731 2218-365-5811	O/BWCA, Quetico
Penrods Au Sable Canoe Trips 100 Maple St., P.O. Box 432 Grayling, MI 49738 517-348-2910	O/Au Sable	Bill Rom's Canoe Outfitters Box 30-EM, 629 E. Sheridan St Ely, MN 55731 218-365-4046	O/BWCA, Quetico
Pines Canoe Rental Rt. 3, Box 3217A Baldwin, MI 49304 616-745-4138	O/Pere Marquette	Bob Anderson's Canoe Outfitters Rt. 3, Box 126EM Crane Lake, MN 55725 218-993-2287	O/BWCA, Quetico, Voya- geurs National Park
Sawmill Canoe Livery 230 Baldwin Big Rapids, MI 49307 616-796-6408	O/Muskegon	Boundary Waters Canoe Outfitters Box 447, 1323 E. Sheridan St. Ely, MN 55731 218-365-3201	O/BWCA, Quetico
Sawyer Canoe Company 234 S. State St. Oscoda, MI 48750 517-739-9181	O/Au Sable	Canadian Border Outfitters Box 117 Ely, MN 55731 218-365-5847 800-247-7530	O/BWCA, Quetico
Shel-Haven Canoe Livery P.O. Box 268 Grayling, MI 49738 517-348-5384	O/Manistee	Canadian Waters 111 East Sheridan St. Ely, MN 55731 218-365-3202 800-ALL-BWCA	O/BWCA, Quetico
U-Rent-Em Canoe Livery 522 W. Grand St. Hastings, MI 49058 616-345-3191	O/Thornapple	Canoe Country Escapes 5422 Lake Elmo Ave. Lake Elmo, MN 55042 612-439-3766	O-T-E/BWCA, Quetico
Uncommon Adventures P.O. Box 6066 East Lansing, MI 48823 517-332-3609	O-E/Michigan rivers, Alaska rivers, Everglades	Canoe Country Outfitters 629 E. Sheridan St. Ely, MN 55731 218-365-4046	O/BWCA

Minnesota

| Arrowhead Outfitters
St. Rt. 1, Box 3299
Ely, MN 55731
218-365-5614 | O/BWCA,
Quetico | Clearwater Canoe Outfitters
C.R. 31-0 Gunflint Trail
Grand Marais, MN 55604
218-388-2254 | O/BWCA,
Quetico |
| Bear Track Outfitting Co.
Box 51, Hwy. 61
Grand Marais, MN 55604
218-387-1162 | O/BWCA,
Quetico, Isle
Royale | | |

ADDRESS/TELEPHONE	TRIPS/RIVERS	ADDRESS/TELEPHONE	TRIPS/RIVERS
Cliff Wold's Canoe Outfitting 1731 E. Sheridan Ely, MN 55731 218-365-3267	O/BWCA, Quetico	Lake of the Woods Outfitters Box 16MD Warroad, MN 56763 218-386-1436	O/Lake of the Woods
Duane's Outfitters Hwy. 21 Babbitt, MN 55706 218-827-2710 800-223-2774	O/BWCA, Quetico	Mississippi Headwaters Canoe General Delivery Lake Itasca, MN 56460 218-266-3445	O/Mississippi
Gunflint Northwoods Outfitters Box 100 GT Grand Marais, MN 55604 218-388-2296	O-T/BWCA, Quetico	North Country Canoe Outfitters Star Rt. 1, Box White Iron Lake Ely, MN 55731 218-365-5581 800-552-5581	O/BWCA, Quetico
Hungry Jack Canoe Outfitters Box HJ-18, Gunflint Trail Grand Marais, MN 55604 218-388-2275	O/BWCA, Quetico	Northern Waters Canoe Rental 3030 Isleview Rd. Grand Rapids, MN 55744 218-326-6764	O/Mississippi
Irv Funk Canoe Outfitters Rt. 2, Box 51 Sebeka, MN 56477 218-472-3272	O/Crow Wing	Northwind Canoe Outfitters Box 690, Fernberg Rd. Ely, MN 55731 218-365-5489	O/BWCA, Quetico
Fall Lake Canoe Trips Box 780-EM88 Ely, MN 55731 218-365-3788	O/BWCA, Quetico	Olson's Borderland Outfitters Box M-89 Crane Lake, MN 55725 218-993-2233	O/BWCA, Quetico, Voya- geurs National Park
John Herrick's Moose Bay Co. Box 697 Ely, MN 55731 218-365-6285	O/Quetico, Crooked Lake	Outdoor Adventure Outfitters Box 576 Ely, MN 55731 218-365-3466 800-522-9653	O/BWCA, Quetico
Johnson's Wilderness Canoe Trips Box 658 Ely, MN 55731 218-365-3559	O/BWCA, Quetico	Papoose Bay Outfitters HC06, Box 397A Park Rapids, MN 56470 218-732-3065	O/Mississippi
Kawishiwi Lodge and Outfitters Box 480, on Lake One Ely, MN 55731 218-365-5487	O/BWCA, Quetico	Portage Seagull Canoe Outfitters Box 126, Gunflint Trail Grand Marais, MN 55604 218-388-2216	O/BWCA, Quetico

Address/Telephone	Trips/Rivers	Address/Telephone	Trips/Rivers
Rockwood Outfitters 75 Gunflint Trail Grand Marais, MN 55604 218-388-2242	O/BWCA, Quetico	Voyageur North Outfitters 1829 E. Sheridan St. Ely, MN 55731 218-365-3251	O/BWCA, Quetico
Root River Canoe and Outfitters 210 Burr Oak St. Chatfield, MN 55923 507-867-3234	O/Root, Mississippi	Way of the Wilderness Box 131, Gunflint Trail Grand Marais, MN 55604 218-388-2212	O/BWCA, Quetico
Sandy Point Outfitters Kabetogama (Rt. 122) Ray, MN 56669 218-875-2615 800-223-2774	O/Voyageurs National Lake Park	Wilderness Adventures 943 E. Sheridan St. Ely, MN 55731 218-365-3416	O/BWCA, Quetico
Sawbill Canoe Outfitters Box 2127, Sawbill Trail Tofte, MN 55615 218-387-1360	O/BWCA	Wilderness Outfitters One E. Camp St. Ely, MN 55731 218-365-3211	O/BWCA, Quetico
Sawtooth Outfitters Highway 61, Box 2214 Tofte, MN 55615 218-663-7643	O/BWCA, Isle Royale	Wilderness Waters Outfitters Box 1007-M, W. Hwy. 61 Grand Marais, MN 55604 218-387-2525	O/BWCA, Quetico, Isle Royale
Superior North Canoe Outfitters Box 141-E, Gunflint Trail Grand Marais, MN 55604 218-388-4416	O/BWCA, Quetico	*Missouri*	
		Doniphan Canoe Rental 204 West Jefferson Doniphan, MO 63935 314-996-7861	O/Current
Tom and Woods' Moose Lake Canoe Trips P.O. Box 358 Ely, MN 55731 218-422-9654	O/BWCA, Quetico	Eminence Canoe Rental P.O. Box 276 Eminence, MO 65466 314-226-3642	O/Ozark rivers, Jacks Fork, Current
Top of the Trail Outfitters Rt. 2, Box 197, Gunflint Trail Grand Marais, MN 55604 218-388-2255 800-328-3325	O-BWCA, Quetico	Twin Bridges Canoe Rental HCR 64, Box 230 West Plains, MO 65775 417-256-7507	O/North Fork, Bryant
		Montana	
Tuscarora Canoe Outfitters Box 110, Gunflint Trail Grand Marais, MN 55604 218-388-2221	O/BWCA, Quetico	Missouri River Outfitters P.O. Box 1212 Fort Benton, MT 59442 406-622-3295	O-E/Missouri

ADDRESS/TELEPHONE	TRIPS/RIVERS	ADDRESS/TELEPHONE	TRIPS/RIVERS
Nebraska		**New Mexico**	
Dryland Aquatics HC-13, Box 33A Sparks, NE 69220 402-376-3119	O/Niobrara	Hawk, I'm Your Sister P.O. Box 9109 Santa Fe, NM 87504 505-984-2268	E/Green, Rio Grande, San Juan, Missouri, Yukon, Allagash, Everglades, Puget Sound
Graham Canoe Outfitters HC-13, Box 16AA Valentine, NE 69201 402-376-3708	O/Niobrara		
Rocky Ford Canoe Base Box 3 Valentine, NE 69201 402-497-3479	O/Niobrara	**New York** Battenkill Sportsquarters Rd. 1, Box 313 Cambridge, NY 12816 518-677-8868	O/Battenkill
Sunny Brook Camp HC-13, Box 36A Sparks, NE 69220 402-376-1887	O/Niobrara	C.R.K. Rentals, Inc. Kent St. Palmyra, NY 14522 315-597-9294	O/Erie Barge Canal, Ganargue, Finger Lakes
New Hampshire North Star Canoe Rentals R.R. #2, Rt. 12A Cornish, NH 03745 603-542-5802	O/Connecticut	Champaign Canoeing c/o LeClair Brayton Park Ossining, NY 10562 914-762-5121	O/Farmington, Salmon, Housa- tonic, Shepaug
Saco Bound/Downeast Whitewater Route 302, Box 119 Center Conway, NH 03813 603-447-2177	O/Saco, Andro- scoggin, Penob- scot, Kennebec, Dead	Lander's Delaware River Trips R.D. 2, Box 376 Narrowsburg, NY 12764 914-252-3925	O/Delaware
		Adirondack Challenges P.O. Box 855 Saranac Lake, NY 12983 518-891-1176	E-T/Adirondacks
New Jersey Bel Haven Lake RFD 2, Box 107 Green Bank Egg Harbor, NJ 08215 609-965-2205	O/Mullica, Batsto, Wading, Oswego	Raquette River Outfitters P.O., NY Box 653 Tupper Lake, NY 12986 518-359-3228	O-T/Adirondacks
Pineland Canoes, Inc. R.D. 2, Box 212, Route 527 Jackson, NJ 98527 201-364-0389	O/Toms	Rivett's Boat Livery Lake Trail Old Forge, NY 13420 315-369-3123	O/Adirondacks
		St. Regis Canoe Outfitters P.O. Box 318 Lake Clear, NY 12945 518-891-1838	O-E-T/Adiron- dacks, Ever- glades, Telos Lake, St. John

ADDRESS/TELEPHONE	TRIPS/RIVERS	ADDRESS/TELEPHONE	TRIPS/RIVERS
Tickner's Moose River Outfitters Riverside Dr. Old Forge, NY 13420 315-369-6286	O/Adirondacks	*Pennsylvania*	
		Adventures Tours, Inc. P.O. Box 175 Marshall's Creek, PA 18335 717-223-0505	O-E/Delaware
White Water Canoe and Raft Rental Route 97 Barryville, NY 12732 914-557-8178	O/Delaware	Belltown Canoe Rental R.D. #1, Box 98F Sigel, PA 15860 814-752-2561	O/Clarion
Ohio		Cook Forest Canoe Livery Rt. 36, Cook Forest State Park Cooksburg, PA 16217 814-744-8094	O/Clarion
Bob Evans Farm Canoe Livery Box 330 Rio Grande, OH 45674 614-245-5304	O/Racoon Creek		
Casey's Recreational Center 22951 SR. 83 N. Lake Park Rd. Coshocton, OH 43812 614-622-4080	O/Walhonding	Doe Hollow Canoe Rentals Rd. #2, Dept. BA Bangor, PA 18013 215-498-5103	O/Delaware
Hocking Valley Canoe Livery 31251 Chieftain Dr. Logan, OH 43136 614-385-8685	O/Hocking Hills	*Rhode Island*	
		Quaker Lane Bait and Tackle 4019 Quaker Lane, Rt. 2 North Kingstown, RI 02852 401-294-9642	O/Wood
Mohican Canoe Livery P.O. Box 263, State Route 3 Loudonville, OH 44842 419-994-4097	O/Mohican	*Tennessee*	
Morgan's Mad River Outpost 5605 Lower Valley Pike Springfield, OH 45506 513-882-6925	O/Mad	Canoe the Sequatchie Box 211 Dunlap, TN 37327 615-949-4400	O/Sequatchie
Pleasant Hill Canoe Livery P.O. Box 10, State Route 39 Perrysville, OH 44864 419-938-7777	O/Black Fork, Mohican, Wal-honding, Markingum	Quest Expeditions P.O. Box 499 Benton, TN 37307 615-338-2979	O/Mexico rivers
Oregon		*Texas*	
Leierer's Outdoors, Ltd. 934 Hylo Rd., S.E. Salem, OR 97306 503-581-2803	O-E/Willamette, Santiam, Deschutes, John Day, Owyhee	San Bernard River Canoe Rental Rt. 1, Box 659A Sweeny, TX 773480 409-345-2732	O/San Bernard

Address/Telephone	Trips/Rivers	Address/Telephone	Trips/Rivers
Utah		New River Canoe Livery P.O. Box 100 Pembroke, VA 24136 703-626-7189	O/New
Tex's Riverways P.O. Box 67 Moab, UT 84532 801-259-5101	O/Colorado, Green	Shenandoah River Outfitters R.F.D. #3 Luray, VA 22835 703-743-4159	O/Shenandoah
Vermont		**Washington**	
Battenkill Canoe, Ltd. P.O. Box 65 River Rd. Arlington, VT 05250 802-375-9559	T-E/All Vermont rivers, New England rivers, Rio Grande, Ever- glades, Dumoine	Northwest Outdoor Center 2100 Westlake Ave. N. Seattle, WA 98109 206-281-9684	O/Pacific North- west, Costa Rica, Mexico
Canoe USA Box 610 Waitsfield, VT 05673	T-E/Vermont rivers, New England rivers, Everglades	Pacific Water Sports 16205 Pacific Hwy. South Seattle, WA 98188 206-246-9385	O/Pacific North- west and Cana- dian rivers
Connecticut River Safari Putney Rd., Rte. 5 Brattleboro, VT 05301 802-257-5008	T/Vermont rivers	**West Virginia**	
Outdoor Tours Unlimited P.O. Box 97, Maple Corner Calais, VT 05648 802-229-4570	T/Vermont rivers	American Canadian Ltd. P.O. Box 265 Glen Jean, WV 25846 304-465-0820	E/New, Gauley, Cheat
Vermont Canoe Trippers, VT (owned by Battenkill Canoe, Ltd.—see above)		Wildwater Expeditions Unlimited P.O. Box 55, Dept. E Thurmond, WV 25936 304-459-2551 800-WVA-RAFT	E/Rio Grande, Salmon, Costa Rica rivers
Vermont Voyageur Expeditions Route 242 Montgomery Ctr., VT 05471 802-326-4789	T/Vermont rivers	**Wisconsin**	
Virginia		Kickapoo River Canoe Rental Rt. 2, Box 210A La Farge, WI 54639 608-625-2252	O/Kickapoo
Downriver Canoe Company P.O. Box 10 Bentonville, VA 22610 703-635-5526	O/Shenandoah	Quest Canoe and Boat Rental Box 2, Cascade St. Osceola, WI 54020 715-755-2692	O/St. Croix
James River Runners, Inc. Rt. 4, Box 106 Scottsville, VA 24590 804-286-2338	O/James	Wolf River Lodge White Lake, WI 54491 715-882-2182	O/Wolf, Peshtigo

ADDRESS/TELEPHONE	TRIPS/RIVERS	ADDRESS/TELEPHONE	TRIPS/RIVERS
Canada		Strathcona Lodge Box 2160 Campbell River, B.C. V9W 5C9	O/Campbell and Buttle Lakes
Alberta			
Nahanni River Adventures P.O. Box 8368, Stn. "F" Edmonton, Alberta T6H 4W6 403-435-6417	O/Nahanni	*Manitoba*	
		Day Spring Outfitting 6 Athlone Cr. Pinawa, Manitoba R0E 1L0 204-753-2478	O/Manitoba rivers
British Columbia			
Becker's Canoe Outfitters Bowron Lake Box 129 Wells, B.C. V0K 2R0 604-492-2390	O/Bowron Lakes	Dymond Lake Outfitters Box 304 Churchill, Manitoba R0B 0E0 204-675-2583	O/Manitoba rivers
Ecosummer Expeditions 1516 Duranleau St. Vancouver, B.C. V6H 3S4 604-669-7741	E/Pacific Northwest, Canadian, Arctic, and Antarctic rivers	Einarsson's Guide Service Box 149 Gypsumville, Manitoba R0C 1J0 204-659-4573	O/Manitoba rivers
Gold River Infocentre Box 39 Gold River, B.C. V0P 1G0 604-283-7123	O/Campbell and Buttle Lakes	North Country River Trips Berens River, Manitoba R0B 0A0 204-382-2284	O-E/Bloodvien, Berens, Poplar, Hayes, Gods
Helmcken Falls Lodge P.O. Box 239 Clearwater, B.C. V0E 1N0 604-674-3657	O/Clearwater Lake	Northern Manitoba Outfitters Berens River, Manitoba R0B 0A0 204-382-2379	O-E/Hayes, Bloodvein, Pigeon
Liard Tours P.O. Box 3190 Fort Nelson, B.C. V0C 1R0 604-774-2909	O/Nahanni, Kwadacha Wilderness Area	Saskoba Outfitters 321 Prince Charles Place Flin Flon, Manitoba R8A 1R3 204-687-4098	O/Manitoba rivers
Okanagan Canoe Holidays S1-C6, R.R. #1 Glenmore Rd. Kelowna, B.C. V1Y 7P9 604-762-8156	O/British Columbia rivers, Bowron Lakes	Saskwin Outfitters Grand Rapids, Manitoba R0C 1E0 204-687-4098	O/Manitoba rivers
On The Loose Expeditions 18359 63A Ave. Surrey, B.C. V3S 5M1 604-263-1476	O/British Columbia and Yukon rivers	Seal River Outfitters Box 999 Lynn Lake, Manitoba R0B 0W0	O/Manitoba rivers
Pathways Tours 5915 West Boulevard Vancouver, B.C. V6M 3X1 604-263-1476	E/Bowron Lakes	Spence's Mantario Outfitters General Delivery Bissett, Manitoba R0E 0J0 204-277-5232	O/Manitoba rivers

ADDRESS/TELEPHONE	TRIPS/RIVERS	ADDRESS/TELEPHONE	TRIPS/RIVERS
Tan Lake Outfitters Box 123 Gypsumville, Manitoba R0C 1J0 204-659-5284	O/Manitoba rivers	Canoe Canada Outfitters 300 O'Brien St. Atikokan, Ontario P0T 1C0 807-597-6418	O/Quetico
Ontario		Canoe Kawartha R.R. #3 Lakefield, Ontario K0L 2H0 705-652-8470	O/Kawartha Lakes
Algonquin Canoe Routes Box 187 Whitney, Ontario K0J 2M0 613-637-2699	E-O/Madawaska	Canoeing Canadian Waters 5651 Gordon St., Box 608 Osgoode, Ontario K0A 2W0 613-826-3094	O/Algonquin Park
Algonquin Outfitters R.R. #1, Oxtongue Lake Dwight, Ontario P0A 1H0 705-635-2243	O/Algonquin Park, Temagami, Killarny	Clayton's General Store Box 159 Dorset, Ontario P0A 1E0 705-766-2271	O/Ontario rivers
Black Feather Wilderness Adventures 1341 Wellington St. Ottawa, Ontario K1Y 3B8 613-722-4229	O/Magnetawan, Spanish, Pukaskwa National Park	Don Smith Box 1115 Deep River, Ontario K0J 1P0 613-584-3973	O/Algonquin Park, Petawawa, Fildergrand, Dumoine, Pukaskwa
Camp Catchacoma R.R. #1 Buckhorn, Ontario K0L 1J0 705-657-8432	O/Cavendish, Burleigh, Anstruth, Kawartha Highlands	Equinox Adventures 5334 Yonge St., Box 609 Toronto, Ontario M2N 6M2 416-222-2223	O/Ottawa, Madawaska, Elora Gorge
Camp Quetico Box 1087 Atikokan, Ontario P0T 1C0 807-929-2266	O/Quetico	Grundy Lake Supply Post R.R. #1 Britt, Ontario P0G 1A0 705-383-2251	O/Wolf, Pickerel, French, Magnatewan
Canadian Nature Tours 355 Lesmill Rd. Don Mills, Ontario M3B 2W8 416-444-8419	O/Spanish, Chapleau, Kinogama, Wenebegon, Missinaibi, Pickerel, Tatachikapika	Haliburton Forest Reserve R.R. #1 Haliburton, Ontario K0M 1S0 705-754-2198	O/Kennisis Lake
		Indian River Lodge P.O. Box 29 Keene, Ontario K0L 2G0 705-295-6867	O/Indian River
Canadian Quetico Outfitters Box 910 Atikokan, Ontario P0T 1C0 807-929-2177	O/Quetico		
Canadian Wilderness Trips 187 College St. Toronto, Ontario M5T 1P7 416-977-3703	O/Algonquin Park, Killarney, Temagami, Dumoine, Missinaibi	Kandalore Outdoor Recreation Centre R.R. #2 Minden, Ontario K0M 2K0 705-489-2419	O/Algonquin Park

ADDRESS/TELEPHONE	TRIPS/RIVERS	ADDRESS/TELEPHONE	TRIPS/RIVERS
Killarney Outfitters Hwy. 637 Killarney, Ontario P0M 2A0 705-287-2828	O/Killarney Provincial Park	Perch Lake Outfitters Box 907 Atikokan, Ontario P0T 1C0 807-597-2828	O/Quetico, White Otter Wilderness Area
Killbear Park Mall R.R. #1 Park Nobel, Ontario P0G 1G0 705-342-5715	O/Killbear Provincial	Pine Grove Port Loring, Ontario P0H 1Y0 705-757-5221	O/Wolf, Smokey Lake, Dollars Lake, Parry Sound Wildlands
Maple Leaf Canoe Outfitters P.O. Box 247 Nestor Falls, Ontario P0X 1K0 807-484-2167	O/Nestor Falls	Polar Bear Sports Box 396, 22 5th St. Cochrane, Ontario P0L 1C0	O/Missinaibi, Groundhog, Mat- tagami, Abitibi, Horning
Multi-Trek Canadian Explorers 1180 Tawney Rd. Ottawa, Ontario K1G 1B7 613-748-6165	O/Petawawa, Missinaibi, Mississippi	Powell Lake Resort Box 206 Thunder Bay, Ontario P7C 4V8 807-597-2891	O/Quetico
Niobe Environmental Trips P.O. Box 550 Atikokan, Ontario P0T 1C0 807-929-2341	O/Quetico	Quetico North Tourist Services Box 100 Atikokan, Ontario P0T 1C0 807-929-3561	O/Quetico
Northern Wilderness Outfitters Box 89 South River, Ontario P0A 1X0 705-386-0466	O/Algonquin Park	Ranger Lake Lodge General Delivery Searchmont, Ontario P0S 1J0 705-841-2553	O/Wenebagon, Mississabi, Megison
Northland Outfitters Cordingly Lake Rd. Nakina, Ontario P0T 2H0 807-329-5253	O/Cordingley Lake	Roland Hill Moose Crossing Farm Hwy. 66 Larder Lake, Ontario P0K 1L0 705-643-2677	O/Misema, Magusi, Raven
Opeongo Outfitters Box 123 Whitney, Ontario K0J 2M0 613-637-5470	O/Algonquin Park	Seine River Canada Campgrounds Box 546 Atikokan, Ontario P0T 1C0 807-947-2391	O/Quetico
Oskar's Heyden Crafts Co. R.R. #2 Sault Ste. Marie, Ontario P6A 5K7 705-777-2426	O/Lake Huron	Smoothwater Wilderness Outfitters and Tours P.O. Box 100, Dept. 1 Temagami, Ontario P0H 2H0 705-569-3539	O-E/Temagami, Lady Evelyn, Makobe, Wana- pitei, Dumoine, Kipawa, Sturgeon
Pelican Lake Marina P.O. Box 1209 Sioux Lookout, Ontario P0V 2T0 807-737-1244	O/English, Pipe Stone, Lac Seul, Sturgeon		

Address/Telephone	Trips/Rivers	Address/Telephone	Trips/Rivers
Sobek Expeditions Canada 159 Main St. Unionville, Ontario L3R 2GB 416-479-2600	E/Canada rivers	Wanapitei Wilderness Centre Sandy Inlet Temagami, Ontario P0H 2H0 705-237-8830	O-E/Temagami, Magnetawan, Spanish, Lady Evelyn, Copper- mine, Kat- tawagami
Sunset View Camps Box 1090 Chapleau, Ontario P0M 1K0 705-864-1748	O/Unegam Lake	Wayland Marine Outfitter 1115 W. Gore St. Thunder Bay, Ontario P7E 3T4 807-577-5812	O/Quetico, Graham, Armstrong, Kenora, Rainy, Thunder Bay
Temagami Canoe Trip Outfitters Box 444 Temagami, Ontario P0H 2H0 705-569-3872	O/Temagami	White Squall Wilderness Shop R.R. #1 Nobel, Ontario P0G 1G0 705-342-5324	O/Georgian Bay
Temagami Wilderness Centre R.R. #1 Temagami, Ontario P0H 2H0 705-569-3733	O/Temagami, Algonquin Park, Kipawa Park, Sturgeon, Dumoine, Noir, Coulonge	Whitefish Lodge Box 368 Wawa, Ontario P0S 1K0 705-889-2054	O/Manitowik Lake, Whitefish Lake, Michipico- ten, Shikwamkwa
Thunderhouse Outfitters P.O. Box 112 Pointe au Baril, Ontario P0G 1K0 705-366-2755	O/Magnetawan, Naiscoot, French, Georgian Bay, Harris Lake	Wildwater Nature Tours Expeditions 119 N. Cumberland St. Thunder Bay, Ontario P7A 4M3 807-345-0111	O/Ogoki-Albany and Wilderness Area
Tumblehome Lodge R.R. #1 Clarendon, Ontario K0H 1J0 613-279-2414	O/Mississippi	Young's General Store P.O. Box 524 Wawa, Ontario P0S 1K0 705-856-2626	O/Whitefish Lake
Valley Ventures Box 1115 Deep River, Ontario K0J 1P0 613-584-3973	O/Dumoine, Petawawa	*Saskatchewan*	
Voyageur Outfitting Box 346, Station K Toronto, Ontario M4P 2G7 416-488-6175	O/Algonquin Park	Churchill River Canoe Outfitters Box 1110 LaRonge, Saskatchewan S0J 1L0 306-635-4440	O/Saskatchewan, Manitoba, Arctic rivers
Voyageurs North P.O. Box 507 Sioux Lookout, Ontario P0V 2T0 807-737-1809	O/Severn, Winisk, Attawa- piskat, Albany	Horizons Wilderness Tours Box 202 LaRonge, Saskatchewan S0J 1L0	O/Churchill, Clearwater, Fond du Lac, Kazan, Seal

ADDRESS/TELEPHONE	TRIPS/RIVERS
Jan Lake Canoe Outfitters Box 1017 Canora, Saskatchewan S0A 0L0 306-563-5527	O/Saskatchewan rivers
Sportsmen's Adventures 94 Empress Dr. Regina, Saskatchewan S4T 6M6 306-522-6381	O/Saskatchewan rivers

III
Yachts

11 Luxury Afloat

The early-morning sun is just starting to touch the tops of the lush green hills behind your anchorage. Your gaze wanders over the sleek lines of the yacht and then is drawn to a squadron of pelicans flying slowly into view, wings barely moving as they search the shallow water along the shoreline for their breakfast. You recognize the slight cocking of the leader's wings as a school of minnows is spotted, and, in a second, all seven of the big birds have started their dives. The splashes as they hit the water from fifty feet up briefly shatter the stillness of the cove, and then the birds bob back to the surface. You lean back in the cockpit and take another sip of coffee. The unmistakable aroma of frying bacon wafting up from the galley tells you that your breakfast should be ready soon.

The captain comes on deck, smiles a good morning, and takes a glance around the anchorage. ''Nice weather,'' he says while turning on the cockpit instruments. ''Should be a fine sail today. Ready for another cup of coffee?''

''Wonderful,'' you say, handing him the cup. Your thoughts drift back to the last few days floating around the islands. A medley of images passes through your mind. Beautiful white sand beaches, warm sun on your back, brilliant blue water teeming with every color of fish imaginable, the feel of the yacht as it glides effortlessly along under full sail, dinner at anchor under the stars, the sound of the reggae band at the beach party last. . .what day was it? ''Yes, it really is wonderful.''

A fantasy of the rich? Not anymore. For many people, the word "yacht" still conjures up images of Commodore Vanderbilt, resplendent in white ducks and blue blazer, lounging in a deck chair while his uniformed steward serves cocktails. There are certainly yachts like this—and many of them are available for charter—but most of today's charter yachts are much less formal and much less ostentatious. And you don't have to be the descendant of a Vanderbilt to afford a vacation on one.

The Yachts

The word "yacht" is difficult to define. I have been sailing them for years, and I'm still not sure what it takes for a boat to reach the elevated status of yacht. It is clearly not size alone (a 24-foot sailboat might properly be called a yacht but not a 60-foot houseboat); it is more a matter of design and intended use. Basically, a yacht is a sailing or power vessel used for pleasure purposes, either cruising or racing. Some would say it has to have sleeping and dining accommodations to be a yacht (this was true a few decades ago), and others would add to the definition that it be capable of use in open water. Any way you look at it, a yacht is a large, expensive toy.

Charter yachts range from under 40 feet to over 100 feet in length. How large a yacht to charter depends on the number of people in your group and the amount of money you want to spend. Generally speaking, two people will charter a yacht of about 40 feet; four, a yacht between 40 and 55 feet; and six or more, a yacht over 55 feet. But there are a lot of variations (see chap. 13).

Today, many yachts are designed specifically for charters. Built for comfort and extravagantly equipped, they provide every amenity that can be packed into a boat. Not surprisingly, they are among the most popular yachts available. But just about every type of vessel imaginable can be found for charter.

Do you dream of the days of "wooden ships and iron men," or are creature comforts more your style? Both traditional sailing crafts and luxury motor yachts are available. Perhaps watching the America's Cup made you wonder what it felt like to be at the helm of a sleek modern racing yacht; charter one and find out. Have you ever had the urge to sail across an ocean? You can spend a week on a boat that did and learn what it was like from the crew. Would you like to do some scuba diving? There are yachts that have all the equipment and certified instructors to teach you how to use it. Time for a romantic getaway? Some yachts specialize in making that honeymoon (first or second) one to remember.

Regardless of your activity, when you take a vacation on the finest of them—the fully crewed charter yachts—you can expect a true "yacht," attractively appointed, impeccably maintained, and professionally operated by a crew devoted to providing you with the best vacation experience ever.

Yachting Areas

Charter boats are available in virtually every decent-size port in the world, although some areas are better than others for yacht vacations. A good charter yachting area should have pleasant weather and sailing conditions, a good selection of inviting anchorages close enough together to allow each day's sail to be as long or as short as you want, and a variety of interesting things to do and places to explore ashore. Not all yacht areas have all three. San Francisco Bay, for instance, has great sailing conditions and many fascinating places to explore ashore, but there are not enough anchorages to make it a good area for the usual week-long charter.

Unlike other floating vacations in this book, there are not hundreds of different yachting locations easily accessible to U.S. residents. There are not even a dozen. But a variety of places meet all three criteria, so you should be able to find one that is right for you.

Most first-time charterers choose a major charter yacht area, and rightfully so. Not only do they offer booking convenience and a large choice of yachts but the areas themselves—places like Newport and the Virgin Islands—are superb. Before looking at the major chartering areas, there are some others worth considering. If your main interest is getting away from the crowds or going someplace different, one of these might be perfect.

For instance, a number of interesting islands are located right off the coast of southern California. Santa Catalina is only 26 miles from Los Angeles, and about 60 miles north are the Channel Islands. Noted for their rugged beauty, the Channel Islands provide excellent offshore sailing and a true "get-away-from-it-all" feeling, despite being located only a few miles from the urban sprawl of the mainland.

This is not a major chartering area. The Pacific Ocean is cold, there is an almost constant swell, and the weather can be unpredictable (the Santa Ana winds). But if you want a charter vacation that is a little more challenging, or if you live in this area and have always wanted to see these islands, a cruise here can be fascinating. You will probably want to have the yacht "deadhead" to Santa Barbara and join it there. (A yacht deadheads when it travels to other than its home port to pick up guests; usually, there will be a "deadhead fee" for this.) That way, you can make it a one-way trip, going with the prevailing winds and current and ending the cruise back in the Los Angeles area.

There is no charter yacht fleet located in southern California. Even a good local broker might have trouble finding you an appropriate yacht. But if you want to do it, it can be arranged.

The Chesapeake Bay is another delightful cruising place that does not have a large crewed charter fleet. I particularly like the Chesapeake in the fall, when the weather is starting to turn crisp and the geese are returning from their summer up north. Terry and I spent a *month* cruising there a few years back and had an unforgettable time. The eastern shore has lots of creeks, inlets, and coves to explore, and the friendliness and hospitality of the small towns and villages there is unsurpassed. On the other side of the bay, you can visit Baltimore's historic inner harbor or enjoy the traditional nautical atmosphere of Annapolis.

A large number of "bareboats" (a boat you charter but on which you do everything yourself) are based here, but, again, crewed charter yachts are in short supply (most of them are probably attracted to the more glamorous Newport area to the north). Having the services of a broker with good local knowledge is important if you want to find the right yacht.

The Bahama Islands offer exceptional cruising. This group of over 700 low-lying islands and cays off the southeast coast of Florida has long been a favorite of fishermen, divers, and those who just wanted to get away from it all without having to sail to the South Pacific to do it. Unfortunately, the options for a crewed yacht charter are quite limited. In the early 1980s, the dangers caused by drug running in the area, coupled with restrictions imposed by the Bahamian government, kept crewed chartering from developing in the area. The major problem now is that charter yachts other than those carrying the Bahamian flag are for practical purposes prohibited from picking up or dropping off guests in the Bahamas.

There are U.S. flag yachts that operate legally in the Bahamas by leaving from and returning to ports in the Miami/Fort Lauderdale area, but that means crossing the Gulf Stream at the start and end of the charter. This is a fairly long passage—about fifty miles to get across the stream and considerably more to get to the best cruising areas—and the seas can be rough outside the protection of the islands. A few sailing yachts make the trip, but your best choice would be one of the larger (50- to 75-foot) motor yachts. It is also better to plan for a longer trip in order to have more time after you get there.

Several bareboat fleets operate in the Bahamas, so the best alternative if you want to charter a smaller sailing yacht is to get a "bareboat with crew." This option will be explained in the next chapter.

Outside of the swamps, the southern coast of Florida and the Florida Keys are heavily built up and offer few good crewed charter possibilities. An exception would be a cruise to the Dry Tortugas. This small group of islands sixty miles west of Key West offers good snorkeling, fishing, and bird-watching. This is also the site of Fort Jefferson, the "Gibraltar of the West," an impressive edifice well worth exploring.

THE SEA OF CORTEZ

The Sea of Cortez (called the Gulf of California on some U.S. maps) is the first of our "major" chartering areas, but I include it here mainly because it has the potential for becoming one. The Sea of Cortez has everything a major char-ter area should have, but until the mid-1980s (when the Mexican government began easing the regulations for chartering foreign vessels), there were vir-tually no charter yachts available there.

This huge body of water is bordered by Baja California to the west, the Mexican mainland to the east, and the Pacific Ocean at its southern end. It's over 700 miles long and about 150 miles across where it joins the Pacific. The home port for most of the crewed charter yachts is La Paz ("City of Peace"), located about 100 miles south of Puerto Escondido and about the same dis-tance from Cabo San Lucas at the tip of the Baja Peninsula.

This is an impressive region of stark natural beauty that has been little touched by the hand of man and is still relatively undiscovered. There are many remote coves where you are more likely to run across a local fishing camp than another yacht—places where you can anchor for the night and find true solitude, your yacht sitting like an oasis amid the rugged rocks and steep hills rising out of the desert shoreline.

During the day, you will be sailing on some of the most beautiful cobalt-blue water found anywhere and exploring the many coves, beaches, and uninhabited islands in the area. There is also an incredible variety and quan-tity of marine life in that water. The Sea of Cortez has been likened to a nat-ural aquarium, in part because it is considerably warmer than the adjoining Pacific Ocean. It is home to more than 600 different species of fish and water mammals. Understandably, one of the main attractions here is the excellent fishing.

Do not expect to be covering this entire area in a one-week charter. Most

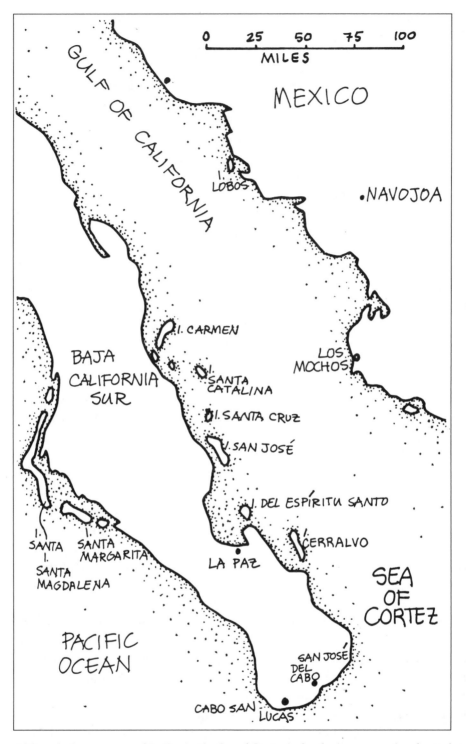

Although the area around La Paz in the Sea of Cortez is developing as a major chartering area, it still provides a true get-away-from-it-all cruising opportunity.

cruises out of La Paz range up or down the coast fifty or sixty miles and enjoy leisurely visits to four or five of the closer islands. On a longer charter—or if you have either chartered a motor yacht or want to do a lot of sailing—you can head north toward Puerto Escondido, where resort development is slowly taking place and there are some fascinating islands to explore. If you want to stretch your sea legs even more than that, discuss it with your broker. Some yachts do extended cruises that can include overnight sails.

Cruising the Sea of Cortez is more of an adventure than many charter areas. Shore facilities are limited or nonexistent once you leave La Paz, and you will find little of the shopping, nightlife, and other "benefits" of civilization. This is a place to get away from it all.

There are only about twenty yachts chartering out of La Paz, but they vary sufficiently to provide you with a reasonably good selection. Although most are motor yachts (including some large sportfishers), there are a number of different sailing yachts from which to choose. Excellent fresh seafood and a good selection of produce are available here, but other provisions are considerably more limited. Expect your cook to do some improvising. Although the yacht will probably stock regular sodas and possibly local alcoholic beverages, you will usually be charged extra for diet sodas and any imported brands (both are expensive).

Air connections are easily made to La Paz through Los Angeles or Mexico City. A short, inexpensive cab ride will take you to the marina where your yacht is waiting. If you are arriving late or just want to spend a night ashore before boarding your yacht, there is a good selection of reasonably priced hotels in La Paz. This is an idea well worth considering. Although La Paz is a good-sized city (the population is around 100,000) and is developing as a popular seaside resort, it still retains that slow, easy quality that the area is noted for. A number of good restaurants specialize in seafood and (surprise!) Mexican food. Nightlife is casual. Local bars featuring live music provide the most popular evening entertainment.

The best time to charter in the Sea of Cortez is the spring or fall, when the weather is mild and temperatures hover in the 70s and 80s. During the winter, although the air temperature will still usually be warm, the water is going to be too cold for comfortable swimming, and the northerly winds can cause some unpleasant swells. In the summer, the temperature can get way up there—over 100 degrees—and local squalls and thunderstorms (called "Chubascos") are common. Also, many charter yachts go back to the States during the summer, so you will have less of a selection.

THE PACIFIC NORTHWEST

When most people think of charter yacht places, they have in mind white sand beaches lined with palm trees, coral reefs, and the hot tropical sun. But there are other kinds of areas where chartering can be a delight. One place that is growing in popularity is the magnificent Pacific Northwest.

The most popular cruising area in the Pacific Northwest is the San Juan and Gulf islands, located on the border between the province of British Columbia and the state of Washington. There are hundreds of islands in this group stretching over an area about 65 miles long between Anacortes, Washington, and Nanaimo, on Vancouver Island in British Columbia. Although these islands are talked about as if they were two archipelagoes, the distinction is primarily political; the San Juan Islands are on the U.S. side of the border, and the Gulf Islands are in Canada.

A charter trip here combines the joys of a vacation in the northern woods with the pleasure and convenience of your own yacht. Most of the islands are uninhabited (frequently protected park areas), mountainous, and heavily wooded. Some even have lakes and meadows that would be at home in the High Sierras. This contrast between the mountains and the sea makes these islands unique and, somehow, improbable. (One usually does not think about going yachting in the mountains.)

A few of the larger islands have shopping or dining opportunities, but a voyage here is not for people who want to spend their time in towns. Whether exploring the fjordlike inlets, walking in the woods, observing and photographing wildlife, salmon fishing, or simply relaxing and enjoying the peace and beauty, a voyage to the islands is one of discovery.

For the more adventurous, north of the Gulf Islands is the isolation of Desolation Sound. Farther north, and with charter yachts available, is Alaska.

The largest fleet of crewed charter yachts on the West Coast is in the Pacific Northwest. You will be able to select from more than 60 vessels, ranging from modest sailing yachts of 40 feet or so up to luxurious, 100-foot motor yachts. Most operate around the San Juan and Gulf islands, but making arrangements for a charter farther north is not difficult.

Because of the nature of the area, motor yachts outnumber sailing yachts. Although the wind is frequently good for sailing here, the number and height of the islands means you will seldom have steady, undisturbed breezes. This does not mean you should rule out a sailing yacht, just that you will likely encounter less-than-ideal sailing conditions.

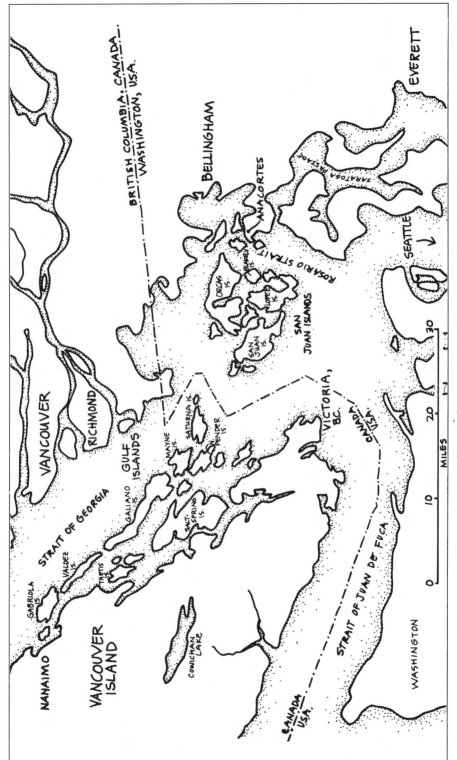

A cruise of the San Juan and Gulf islands combines a charter yacht vacation with a visit to the grandeur of the Pacific Northwest.

With major metropolitan areas nearby, provisioning for a cruise in the San Juan or Gulf Islands is easy, and the selections are virtually unlimited. Fresh seafood, such as the famous Pacific king salmon, is abundant and figures prominently in most cooks' planning. The meals served on many of the yachts reflect the rugged Northwest, with an emphasis on good substantial food rather than "gourmet" offerings. Make sure your broker knows what kind of food you prefer.

Your destination will probably be Seattle or Vancouver, although Victoria is a pleasant alternative. The northern Gulf Islands are about 25 miles from Vancouver, and the southern San Juans are about 40 miles from Seattle. If you choose a sailing yacht, this makes the islands a fairly long (but pleasant in good weather) day's sail from Vancouver and a long one from Seattle. But you can easily start and stop your cruise wherever you want. Most yachts do not charge a deadhead fee for pick-ups anywhere in the San Juan or Gulf Islands, and there is excellent ferry service to the major islands. If you want a convenient way to get there that also adds a little extra adventure to your trip, charter a float plane in Seattle and take a short, scenic flight that ends beside your yacht in the San Juans. The cost is fairly reasonable, and your broker can make all the arrangements.

The chartering season in the Pacific Northwest is basically the summer months of June, July, and August. The winds are better for sailing in the spring, although the weather can still be chilly; September is pleasant, but there is a good chance of fog. Summer temperatures are generally in the 70s and 80s during the daytime and the 60s at night. You will want to pack a sweater and a comfortable jacket regardless of the time you choose.

NEW ENGLAND

There are two main chartering areas in New England: Newport, the most famous yachting center in North America, and the coast of Maine.

The Newport area, which includes Nantucket Island, Martha's Vineyard, Block Island, and Cape Cod, is the historic playground of the rich. This is where the Vanderbilts and many other immensely rich industrialists of the Gilded Age kept their yachts and built their summer "cottages." (Cornelius Vanderbilt's "The Breakers" is probably the most incredible and most famous. This magnificent mansion of 70 rooms—designed to resemble a sixteenth-century Northern Italian palace—and others only slightly less majestic are now open for public tours.) The opulence of this period of Newport's history ended during the Great Depression, but Newport retains the flavor of the era.

Hammersmith Farm, a 28-room cottage on Narragansett Bay, was the Kennedy Summer White House. Many such ''cottages'' are found along the shores in the Newport area. (Photo by John T. Hopf, courtesy of Newport County Chamber of Commerce)

It is still the summer escape for many of today's "rich and famous," but the rest of us can now escape there, too.

The rich chose this area for good reasons: the sailing conditions are excellent, the offshore islands are fascinating, there are many good anchorages, and the weather in the summertime is splendid. Activities center around shore excursions (water sports are limited here because of the cold water). You will probably spend many hours exploring the islands, the history of the area—its architecture and museums—and visiting the charming shops found near the waterfront of most harbors. Although a number of good anchorages offer real escape, most nights you will either anchor near towns or stay at one of the many marinas. Although you can explore on foot, bicycling is also very popular, providing a good way to see sights up close (very few yachts carry their own bicycles, but rentals are available everywhere). As you would expect, there are many excellent restaurants and a variety of nightlife.

A typical Newport cruise will cover more distance than one in most other yachting areas. It is a great area for people primarily interested in sailing; they

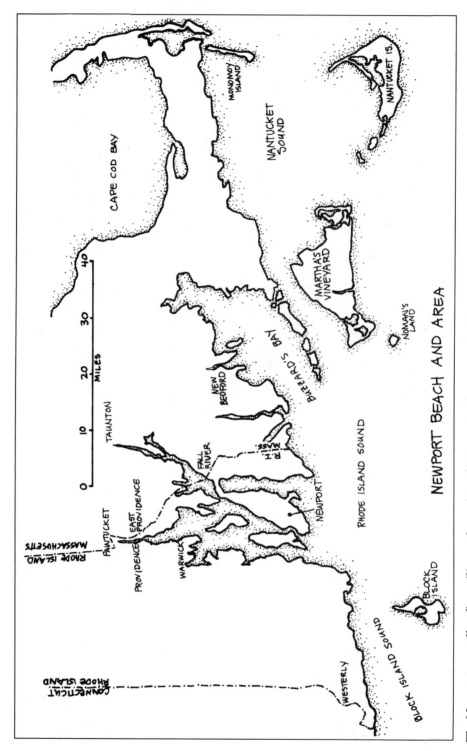

The Newport area offers fine sailing and a variety of interesting places to explore.

will get lots of it. At times, most of the day will be spent sailing from one island to the next, with the following day spent exploring ashore. If you prefer to spend less time on the water, choose either a larger (therefore faster) sailing yacht or a motor yacht.

The coast of Maine offers a considerably different sort of yacht vacation than does Newport. This dramatic coastline has hundreds of uninhabited offshore islands to explore and hundreds of anchorages to use as bases to explore them. This is also a rustic area, where wildlife is more common than nightlife and the crowds found farther south have been left behind.

Although a good number of bareboats operate in Maine, few crewed charter yachts are actually based there. Most likely, you will have to book a Newport-based yacht and pay a deadhead fee for it to meet you in Maine. One way to avoid the deadhead fee (particularly if your dates are fairly flexible) is to call a local broker well ahead of time and inquire about any yachts that might be coming into the area for other charters. If a broker can arrange several charters in a row for a yacht, the captain will usually waive the deadhead fee.

About 150 crewed yachts are available for charter in New England during the summer (the only larger fleet is in the Virgin Islands during the wintertime). Many of them are large, luxurious (and expensive) motor yachts. But with a fleet this size, there will be a yacht to meet just about anyone's taste and budget. The yachting season is fairly short in New England, from about mid-June to mid-September. It can still be cool in June, and fog is more likely to be a problem early or late in the summer. August is the most popular month. If you plan to go then, book your cruise well ahead of time.

THE VIRGIN ISLANDS
The Virgin Islands, located in the northeast corner of the Caribbean about 1,100 miles southeast of Miami, consist of nearly 100 islands (some large, some barely big enough to have a name) so close together that you are never out of sight of land and seldom more than a few miles from a good anchorage. The sea surrounding the Virgins is crystal clear, warm (about 80° year-round), and generally calm. It is also home to an incredible variety of tropical fish. The weather is ideal for sailing, with average temperatures ranging from 78 degrees in January to 83 degrees in July and consistent trade winds in the 10- to 15-knot range.

Add to these blessings the ambience of the West Indies and easy accessibility from North America, and it is not difficult to see why the Virgin

Islands are by far the most popular chartering destination in the world. There are probably more charters taken there each year than in the rest of the world combined. The Virgin Islands are also home to the largest fleet of crewed charter yachts in the world—about 300 yachts from which to choose. The good selection is due to the ideal sailing conditions, which attract every type and size of yacht imaginable.

Politically, these islands are two different entities—the U.S. Virgin Islands (USVI) and the British Virgin Islands (BVI)—but customs and immigration formalities are minimal, and charterers regularly visit both. It only takes about half an hour to get from the north side of St. John in the USVI to the BVI customs house on the west end of Tortola. You will be required to pay a tourist tax in the BVI based on the number of days you will be there (not included in your charter fee).

The area where you will spend most (if not all) of your time on a charter in the Virgin Islands is only about 40 miles long. But this area offers such a variety of coves, beaches, reefs to snorkel, and islands to explore that you could easily spend a month here and not see it all. I have drawn anchors on a chart to show places where we have spent the night on *Esprit*; at last count, there were 34 of them. I know of many others that would be fine for an overnight anchorage. That's a lot of choices.

The most popular starting place for a Virgin Islands charter is the Yacht Haven Marina in the bustling main harbor of Charlotte Amalie. It is about 15 minutes from the airport, near the duty-free downtown shopping, and is easily the busiest chartering center in the world. From there, you will sail up the south side of St. Thomas and probably spend a night or two near St. John (USVI) before checking into the BVI. Most charterers spend four or five days there before heading back to U.S. waters for the last night. Although the USVI has the larger—and more populated—islands, and the north coast of St. John has several of the best spots to be found anywhere, more time is usually spent in the BVI because of the large number of interesting anchorages available on its small, relatively unpopulated islands.

The other major departure points are Red Hook, on the east end of St. Thomas, and Road Town, on Tortola in the BVI. These have the advantage of being closer to the center of the main cruising area (Road Town is the center), but they are somewhat less convenient than a Yacht Haven departure.

Yachts chartering from Tortola (about 25 are based there) nearly always stay in the BVI for the entire week. Virtually all of them will include stops on the U.S. side if you want, but the captains believe (rightfully so) that there is

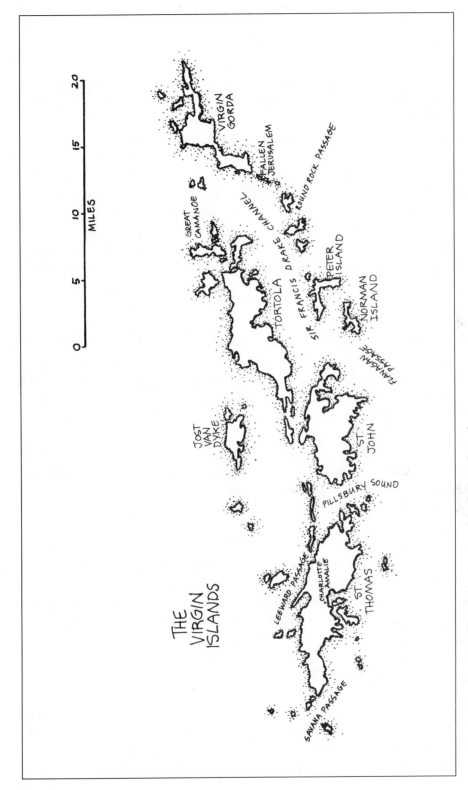

The Virgin Islands are the first choice for most North American charterers.

202 Part III Yachts

plenty to do in the BVI without taking the time and going through the hassle of sailing around to Cruz Bay (the closest U.S. customs and immigration office) in order to spend a night or two in the USVI. If you want to include some time in the USVI, you are better off with a boat based there.

Yacht vacationers frequently spend a few days or a week at one of the many resorts in the Virgin Islands. Often, the yacht can pick you up at the resort's beach at the end of your stay there (most yachts do not charge deadhead fees for pickups anywhere in the main cruising area of the Virgins). If you do this, plan to take the resort portion *before* the cruise. Otherwise, after a week of freedom on a yacht, you may find the resort a little boring. I know one captain who was offered a substantial bribe to fake mechanical problems, terminate the charter he was on, and "rescue" a couple from a resort. (He did not do it.)

One advantage to chartering in the Virgin Islands is that you can do as much or as little sailing as you want. If you would like to spend a lot of time sailing, just do it. If not, the islands are so close together that short cruises are easily planned for. On a typical charter aboard my yacht *Esprit*, we sail between 90 and 120 miles in a week. This works out to three or four hours under way on an average day. On some days, we will do a lot more than that, and on others—when the guests decide it is time for a lazy day—we don't sail at all. On many occasions, we have had "sailing days" that amounted to pulling up the anchor and powering for less than an hour just to go over to the next island, see a new cove, snorkel a different reef, or all three.

Activities in the Virgin Islands center around the water. Swimming—off the beaches or the yacht—is delightful, and the consistently clear water makes for superb snorkeling and diving on the many coral reefs. Those same consistent trade winds that make this such a good sailing area are also great for windsurfing.

One of the most popular shoreside activities in the islands is visiting the local beach bars and restaurants. Many are well worth a visit. The food is frequently very good, and some of the beach bars are island traditions. Dress is casual (you usually will not even bother with shoes). You will go in by dinghy, probably just beach it in front of the bar, and kick back in a *very* casual setting. More elegant dining is available for those who prefer it.

The high season in the Virgin Islands is from mid-December to mid-April, but the weather is fairly consistent and charters are done year-round. The reason for there being a season at all is the weather in North America: people want to escape the winter ice and snow for a week in the tropics.

Christmas and New Year's are easily the busiest charter times of the year. Plan on booking these dates *at least* four months ahead of time. An off-season cruise is well worth considering. The anchorages will be less crowded then, and as a bonus, some yachts offer a discount of 10 percent or so.

Weather variations might affect your choice of season. In late December, the trade winds pick up and can blow in the 25-knot range for days at a time (or weeks, as they did during the 1987-88 season). These "Christmas Trades" usually settle back down by the end of January. If you want some exciting sailing, this is the time to go. The summer is warmer and usually has less wind than during the winter. In the fall, there is the chance of a hurricane interrupting your vacation. Although this is not dangerous to you, your captain will have to make arrangements to take care of the yacht—and put you ashore—if a hurricane is forecasted.

DOWN ISLAND

When you leave the Virgin Islands and head south, you are going "down island." This chain of Caribbean islands, extending east and then curving south to Grenada, offers some excellent charter opportunities.

Chartering down island is in many ways quite different from chartering in the Virgins. This is a much larger area (about 600 miles from St. Thomas to Grenada along the island chain), the distances between islands are frequently must greater, and there is much more diversity in the islands here. Some are large (much larger than the largest of the Virgins) and well developed; others are relatively small and retain native customs and ways of life. Most of the island nations have been under several different flags during their histories, and although many are now independent countries, they still reflect this diverse heritage in their language and traditions.

Given the size of this area, you will undoubtedly be limiting your cruise to one part of it (unless you can go for several weeks). The Grenadines, a group of smaller islands located between St. Vincent and Grenada, are a good choice.

Chartering down island is for the adventurous. You will make long, sometimes rough passages and visit primitive places that are less convenient —both in getting there and ashore—than other areas. If these things do not bother you and you want more in the way of adventure, you'll find it down island. But the Virgin Islands are a far more popular (and probably better) first choice for most people, particularly those who have never sailed before.

The captain on your crewed charter yacht will help you find those special places.
(Photo by Michael White)

A large fleet of charter yachts operates down island. Most work out of Antigua (at least that is where they congregate for the annual charter yacht show), but they tend to range farther and travel more than yachts in any other area. They are liable to be found home-ported, temporarily or permanently, just about anywhere. Many of the yachts in the Virgin Islands also do charters down island (make sure the crew has experience down island if you choose one of these).

Seasonal considerations are the same as for the Virgins, with the exception that hurricanes are seldom a threat south of St. Lucia.

12 Choosing a Yacht Vacation

Putting together a compatible group for a charter yacht vacation is easier than for most other boating vacations, because no one in the group has to do any work or take any responsibility. The crew does it all. Without the potential for friction that having "jobs" can cause, most groups have very few problems.

A professional crew is used to living for extended periods of time on a boat with strangers. They are quick to adapt to new people and experienced in avoiding potential problems. For instance, if one member of the group keeps getting outvoted on what to do next, the crew will solve that problem simply by making separate arrangements (if at all possible) for that person. As long as each person in the group acts with reasonable consideration for his fellow shipmates, problems seldom arise. This usually means selecting—as you would for any vacation—a group made up of close friends or family.

Bring the children along if you want. Most kids love being on a yacht, adapt quickly to it, and have a great time exploring the new world it opens up. Children of sufficient age and maturity to understand and follow rules of basic boating safety are welcome on most yachts. Nearly all yachts, however, have a minimum age requirement. Be sure to check with boats you are considering. (This is one of the many things that your broker can do for you.)

Fully Crewed Charter Yachts

There are several different ways to charter a yacht. For most people who don't have boating experience (and many of those who do), the best choice is called a "fully crewed" charter yacht. These are private yachts (not part of a fleet) that are staffed with a professional crew, including a licensed captain. In some cases, the yacht may even be "owner operated" (the captain, or captain and mate, owns the yacht and runs it personally).

On a fully crewed yacht, the captain and crew take care of everything. They will do the preparation and provisioning for the cruise, handle the operation of the yacht, and serve as your group's personal tour guides, chauffeurs, waiters, bartenders, and—if you want to try something new, such as windsurfing or snorkeling—instructors. There will also be a cook to prepare all the meals and clean up afterward. And what meals they will be! Yacht cooks take great pride in their culinary excellence. The food served on most charter yachts is equal, and frequently superior, to what you would get in a better restaurant ashore.

Based on prearrival requests, the cook will select a variety of meals for your cruise and stock the yacht with everything necessary to prepare them. If you specified breakfasts fit for a hungry lumberjack, that's what you will get. If your taste runs more to a light continental affair with fresh fruit and rolls, it will be there. You can request any sort of lunches—large or small, hot or cold, salads, quiches, sandwiches (even bologna if you really want it). Snacks will be available throughout the day, and hors d'oeuvres are regularly served during cocktails. Dinner will be the cook's finest hour. The quality, variety, and creativity of the dinners will delight and astonish you. Dessert? Do I need to say it? If you want it, it will be there. All you have to do is relax and wait in anticipation for the next delectable creation to come out of the galley. The only thing to worry about is facing your bathroom scale when you get home.

Some people are concerned about spending a week on a boat with a crew. They wonder who these people will be, whether they will like them, and how it will be to spend that much time that close to strangers. This should be no cause for worry. Although crew members on charter yachts are as varied as the yachts themselves, all of them have one thing in common: they want you to have the best vacation ever. And they will bend over backward to see that it happens. Most of them are outgoing, fun-loving folks who like yachts and like people. You will probably feel at ease with them within the first few minutes.

You can take a vacation on a fully crewed yacht without knowing the slightest thing about boats and without having to do anything except lay back and enjoy the good life. These are the true yacht vacations, the kind we will be primarily concerned with. Some other alternatives will be discussed below (including "bareboating," where you charter the boat only and run it yourself, an option available only to groups that include someone with substantial boating experience).

On most fully crewed yachts, you will be able to get involved in the operation of the boat if you want to. If you are a novice, the captain and crew will be happy to teach you what you need to know and let you try your hand at it. In many cases, particularly on sailboats, this is one of the major attractions—an excellent opportunity to learn new skills while also having a great vacation.

In nearly all cases, fully crewed yachts are chartered on an "exclusive" basis. This means that you and your group (whether two people or a dozen) charter the entire yacht and are the only guests on board, an arrangement that lets you go where you want and do what you want without a fixed itinerary and without a concern for what some strangers on board want to do. This flexibility of pace and schedule is one of the main appeals of a yacht vacation.

Yacht charters are arranged by "charter brokers" (people who specialize in providing the information and advice you need to choose a yacht and then take care of booking it). Selecting and working with a broker will be discussed in detail below.

The cost of a crewed charter yacht vacation varies, depending on the location, the yacht, and the size of your group. Yacht cruises are not cheap, but they are surprisingly less than you would assume. A fully crewed yacht can be chartered for under $1,000 per person per week; only the most expensive will cost over $1,500 per person.

Of course, it is possible to spend a lot more on a charter. Some huge luxury yachts go for over $70,000 a week *plus* the considerable operating expenses (a motor yacht this size can easily burn several hundred gallons of fuel an hour). But one of these will probably accommodate ten guests, so that is only a measly $1,000 plus per person per *day*. Fortunately, the majority of the crewed charter yachts are priced between $1,100 and $1,600 per person per week, and if you get into the $2,000 range, there are some fantastic choices.

These figures include sumptuous meals (complete with wine), a full bar (with a bartender ready to concoct those special tropical drinks), as well as unlimited use of the yacht's complement of "toys" (always including snorkeling gear in tropical waters, usually a windsurfer, maybe scuba diving gear, water skis, jet skis, and even a sailing dinghy) and instruction in how to use them if you need it. You will not have to reach for your wallet every time you want to play or have another beer. You can stow that wallet—and your watch—in your cabin below and start relaxing.

The only other cost you should anticipate (besides travel cost to the yacht and shopping) is gratuities for the crew. And while the decision about whether to leave a tip is yours, of course, the service on a crewed charter yacht is among the best you will get anywhere: diverse, complete, and available 24 hours a day. It is appropriate to express your appreciation with a gratuity and to simply assume from the start that this will be part of your trip's cost. Ten to 15 percent of the charter cost, distributed among the crew, is customary. (Since it is likely you will be thinking of the crew as friends by then, leaving a tip may seem awkward. The simplest approach is to put it in an envelope, with a note of thanks, and give it to the captain to distribute among the crew.)

If you realistically look at what you would spend on a land-based vacation at a nice resort (including all those unanticipated little extras that make opening the next month's credit card statements such a shock), you will find that for about the same, or less, you can be on your own yacht. Considering what you get for your money, a crewed charter yacht vacation is a real bargain.

Some Other Options

It is possible to book a single cabin on a crewed charter yacht in much the same way you would on a cruise ship. This kind of arrangement (on what is called in the chartering business a "head" boat) is most commonly found on larger boats catering to a dozen or more people, but a few smaller yachts also offer the option. This is primarily of interest if you want to go on a larger yacht with other people but cannot put together your own group or don't want to. It is usually cheaper for two people to go on a head boat than to charter their own two-person yacht.

Another idea is to charter a yacht "captain only" (no other crew). But you will be expected to help with the actual running of the boat and to do all the other jobs (including cooking and cleaning) yourself. Several very large sailing vessels offer an attractive vacation package—commonly called "windjammer" or "barefoot" cruises—at an affordable price. These are popular, particularly among singles, as an alternative to conventional cruise ships, but they are not really yacht vacations.

If you or a member of your group have substantial boating experience, you can charter a "bareboat." You do it yourself— everything from the actual navigation and operation of the boat to the cooking and cleanup. Doing this is called "bareboating," and the people who do it are "bareboaters."

Most people seem to select this option because they want the challenge of "doing it themselves" or because they believe they will save money. They probably will save a little money, but nowhere near as much as they think. As far as the challenge goes, think about it. I'd be the first to admit that there is a strong appeal to the idea of sailing off on your own vessel to explore the unknown. There are few memories I treasure more than the thrill I had when Terry and I sailed my 34-foot sloop *Vivamus* under San Francisco's Golden Gate on our first great sailing adventure. The destination was Baltimore, Maryland, by way of the Panama Canal. We planned to be gone a year.

But I have never found the challenge of doing dishes very rewarding. And if I am going to sail in strange waters for a week on vacation, I like having someone along who knows the area and can tell me where everything from the best snorkeling to the wildest party spots can be found. I want to be the one lounging about with a cold drink in my hand while someone else hauls the garbage off the boat. I want to sit in the cockpit at sundown and look forward to a gourmet meal without having to lift a finger or feel guilty because someone who is supposed to be on vacation is down below cooking. Most of all, I want to be able to roll over and go back to sleep when that sudden squall hits at three in the morning instead of having to scramble up on deck to make sure nothing is going wrong.

A guest on *Esprit*, a man with considerable sailing experience, said it best. "I like sailing on crewed yachts for the same reason I like playing with my grandchildren. You can play with them when you want and let somebody else take care of them the rest of the time; you get all of the fun and none of the responsibility."

There are big differences between bareboating and chartering a professionally crewed yacht. People without substantial boating experience (and those with it) should think carefully about these differences before deciding to bareboat.

One major difference is the yachts themselves. As I said above, there are a tremendous number of crewed yachts from which to choose. Each is unique, and many are truly magnificent vessels. Bareboat companies, however, may have large fleets but only a few types of boats. You pick the kind you want (usually a question of size; the largest available are about 50 feet), and one boat of that type will be reserved for you.

Although a bareboat will probably be as clean and well maintained as a crewed yacht, it will have none of the niceties of decor or personal touches a permanent crew adds. Nor will it usually be equipped as well as a crewed yacht. Most bareboats have the personality of a rental car.

It is possible to charter a bareboat *with* a crew. Many of the larger bareboat companies provide boats complete with captain and cook. There is still a big difference between doing this and taking a true crewed charter yacht. Besides the boat differences already mentioned, the bareboat crew will usually not be permanently assigned to a yacht, so they are unlikely to have the same personal stake or pride in it that a permanent crew would. (This is not to say that the crew won't be competent or that they won't be working hard to show you a good time; they almost certainly will be.) In addition, it is usually more expensive than a crewed charter yacht. In 1986, I did a comparative study of prices as part of a project for the Virgin Islands Charteryacht League. The average cost—with a crew and with provisioning added at the companies' published prices—for the larger boats of the major bareboat companies operating in the Virgin Islands was 27.3 percent *higher* than that of a crewed charter yacht of the same size.

A couple of circumstances may warrant your choosing a bareboat, with or without crew. The first is if you have no choice. Some areas with few crewed charter yachts *do* have bareboat fleets, which may be the best alternative. Or if you have a large group and want to charter two or more identical boats (to do some match racing or just to avoid one group having a "better boat"), it may be easier for the large bareboat company to accommodate you.

Selecting a Charter Yacht Broker

Selecting a broker is one of the most important decisions you make in planning a yacht vacation. It is the job of the crewed charter yacht broker to know every yacht and crew she recommends (I will say "she," because, for reasons I have never figured out, the great majority of charter brokers are women). Your broker will ask lots of questions about your group, send you information on yachts that meet your requirements, discuss the strong and weak points of each with you, and answer all those questions not answered in brochures. If you have any unusual requests or special requirements, your broker will check with the yacht to find out if they will be a problem. Most important, she will try to learn enough about your group to help find the best yacht and crew for you. Good brokers think of themselves as matchmakers; they work at least as hard to find the right crew for you as they do the right yacht.

Your broker does more than help you select the yacht. She arranges the dates for the charter, ensures they are blocked out on the yacht's master calendar, takes care of the contract between you and the captain, makes sure your deposit is in the yacht's trust account, provides you with a food and drink preference questionnaire, and forwards your completed copy to the captain. In most cases, your broker will also (through travel agents) be able to help you with travel and hotel accommodations.

But charter brokers are not travel agents. Although some people do both jobs, they are the exception. Charter brokers are in a very specialized line of work. If you go to your local travel agent to book a yacht charter, he or she will start by contacting a charter broker (assuming they do not talk you into a cruise ship instead; few travel agents know much about yacht chartering).

If you do use a travel agent, insist on talking to the charter broker directly concerning your choice of yachts. Occasionally, a travel agent will want to be the exclusive intermediary between you and the broker. Apparently, they are concerned about the charter broker "stealing" you as a client or not paying them their entitled commission (unfounded fears, since most brokers want to establish good working relationships with travel agents). At any rate, booking a yacht is not the same as booking a hotel room; you need to discuss everything with the broker. You probably will want a travel agent to assist you with your travel to the yacht and any hotel accommodations before or after the cruise; few charter brokers do this directly.

Your decision about what yacht to book will be heavily based on information, suggestions, and advice given you by your broker. After this decision, there is still the booking procedure to complete. Problems can arise here if the broker does not fully understand the system. It is essential that you choose a broker who is qualified and experienced.

There are more than 200 charter brokers in North America. Unfortunately, the majority of them are hobbyists who work part-time (probably out of their home), book a few charters each year, and get to write off an annual trip to the Caribbean to look at the yachts. The true professionals spend most of their waking time thinking about yachts and clients. They will have a greater knowledge of the yachts and crews, the latest information, the largest number of clients, and they will command the attention of the captains. If a captain gets a message from somebody at a place called "Happy Hobby Yacht Charters," the first reaction will probably be, "Who's that?" If the call comes from a major broker (who could book a third of the yacht's calendar each year), it will be, "Where's the nearest telephone?" It takes considerable time, money, and effort to keep up on the many charter yachts; this is the real difference between a hobbyist and a professional broker.

If you know someone who has chartered before, ask about their broker. A personal recommendation from a friend is a good way to find a good broker. Or call several brokers and request their information package (many have toll-free numbers). Chapter 14 is a directory of professional charter brokers. The material you receive from them will include information on their brokerage, the chartering area or areas you are interested in, and the charter yacht vacation in general. You can write instead of call, but calling lets you find out a little more about the broker and how easy she would be to work with.

When you contact the brokers, try to provide them with some basic information about your proposed charter. The things they would like to know, in approximate order of importance, are:

1. The area where you want to charter.
2. The number of people in your party.
3. Whether you want a sailing or motor yacht.
4. When you want to go.
5. The length of the charter.
6. Your approximate price range.

If you do not know the answers to all those questions, answer what you can and guess at the rest. Right now, you are mainly interested in getting information on *brokers*. Have them send you information on their brokerage and some yacht brochures. The only advantage to giving them specific information now is that they will be more likely to send you the information you're really looking for (which could save a little time).

Notice that I put price at the bottom of the list. At this point, you can be vague about it if you want. People frequently change their price range after they begin seriously looking for a yacht.

All good brokers will be very familiar with chartering in Newport, the Virgin Islands, and (probably) down island, and the yachts available at these locations. They might not know less-popular charter areas quite as well. For these other areas, be sure to contact any brokers located nearby. Their local knowledge will usually be to your advantage.

Brokers work on a commission basis (the fee is paid by the yacht) in what is called an "open" listing system. That is, any one of them can book any yacht available for charter. **Warning**: the promotional literature and advertising of some brokers—even a few of the best—implies otherwise, proclaiming that they "have" a fleet of hundreds of yachts for you to choose from. True, but so does every other broker—it is the same fleet. Do not choose a broker because you erroneously believe they "have" the most yachts and, therefore, the best selection.

Most brokers will send you half a dozen or more individual yacht brochures with their information packages (brochures are produced and supplied to the brokers by the yacht owners). After looking the yacht's brochures over, daydreaming for a while, and getting a better idea of what is generally available, put them aside. At this point, your primary concern should be selecting a broker. Don't be shy about discussing their qualifications with them. The broker you select is going to work for you, and you have the right to know if she can do the job. The good ones will be happy to answer your questions, and the others will give themselves away immediately by their unwillingness to do so.

A simple "tell me about your brokerage" should suffice. Ask them when was the last time they attended a boat show or otherwise visited the yachts in the area you are considering (anytime within a year is fine); how many yachts they have booked there (a dozen in the last year is a good minimum number for a fairly busy area); and, generally, how much experience they have.

How long a broker has been in business is something to consider, but it does not necessarily indicate competence. Many hobbyists have been in business for years, and a few new brokers work hard to know the boats and do an excellent job.

Aside from these questions, how professional do they seem? If a kid answers the phone and shouts, "Mom, it's for you," you probably haven't reached a true professional. The information they send you should be complete and thoughtfully presented. They should return your calls promptly and have the answers to your questions when they do.

If you wrote for information initially, do not hesitate to call the brokers you are considering. There is nothing wrong with simply telling them you are trying to decide which broker to use; they will probably appreciate your candor and be more than happy to tell you why it should be them.

Carefully review all the information, call them back if you need more, then choose your broker. There is no reason to work with more than one broker. Remember, all the brokers can book all the yachts. If you want more brochures to look at, your broker will be happy to send them. If you are interested in a particular yacht, your broker can get its brochure for you. If a particular time is closed out on a yacht's calendar, it is closed out; calling another broker is not going to help.

Also, no broker can get you a better price on a particular yacht than another broker; charter fees established by the yachts are the same for everybody. If two brokers quote different rates for the same yacht, something is wrong. Either the lower price is for a "six-night" week (this is occasionally, and improperly, done) or one of them has bad information; ask for clarification. Another possibility is that a broker is offering a slight savings by discounting the commission, a practice frowned on by most brokers because it encourages unnecessary confusion and "broker shopping."

Some people choose a broker by first choosing a yacht and then simply calling the broker who sent them that particular yacht's brochure. Although this is a somewhat backward way of doing it, it can work if one yacht just jumps out at you and says "Me!"—and if you are comfortable with that broker.

The most important thing is to choose a knowledgeable professional whom you feel comfortable working with. Once you have a broker, it's time to get on with the fun part—choosing a yacht.

Selecting a Yacht

Yachts are a matter of personal taste. One that would be perfect for your group might not be right for another. In fact, few things I can think of are more a matter of individual taste than yachts (maybe spouses?).

The process of choosing your yacht probably started the first time you saw one. Yachts do that to people. Who has not watched one go by and thought, "Someday. . .," or walked down a dock, looking at the yachts and dreaming? Even if all you know about yachts is what you learned wandering around a dock, you undoubtedly have some idea of what kind you'd like. The goal now is to find the one that best matches this idea.

NARROWING THE CHOICES

Almost without exception, every one of the hundreds of yachts available for crewed charter is individually owned and independently operated. The crew is responsible for everything: maintenance and cleaning, provisioning, boat handling and safety, caring for the guests, and normal business matters such as bookkeeping and publicity. Each yacht is a small, autonomous business, and as with most small businesses, each will be unique and operated with a great deal of concern for the patrons. Given the wide variety of distinctive yachts available, how do you decide (with some degree of confidence) which is the right one for you?

Fortunately, this is not a big problem. By looking at the basic requirements and desires of your group, you should be able to narrow the choices considerably. Once you have done this, your chances of making a *bad* choice are small, simply because your chances of finding a lousy yacht trip are small. A few are not up to the quality of the rest, but these quickly become known to the brokers, and their brochures are not sent out. The issue, therefore, is not one of making a bad choice but of making the *best* choice.

Now get out that pile of brochures you set aside earlier. First, answer the basic questions listed in the last chapter (area, number of people, sail or power, when, how long, and price range). Then decide—as a group—what specific features are essential for your yacht, which are desirable, and which are strictly extras. It might help to make a list of these features, both to organize your thoughts and to be sure that everyone in the group agrees. The list will also be useful later when talking to your broker. Remember that, in general, the more you want in a yacht, the more you will be paying. Following are some of the features to consider.

Cabin size. The size of the cabin (bedroom) varies tremendously with the yacht's size and design. Except on the largest and most expensive yachts, do not expect to have a cabin the size of your bedroom at home. The cabins on most yachts are comfortable and functional, but if you want a really large one, it will cost you.

Equal cabins. Yacht cabins are rarely identical; more often, they are "comparable," and on some yachts, the cabins will be quite different. If you fear a "you-got-the-best-cabin" problem, specify at least comparable cabins.

Many yachts carry windsurfers; make sure yours is one of them if you want to try this exciting sport. (Photo by Rick Friese)

Your bedroom on a yacht can equal the one in a luxury resort if you charter a large enough yacht. (Photo by Rick Friese)

At least, make sure it is understood ahead of time who gets which cabin.

Berths. Take a look at the berths themselves. Some yachts have doubles in every cabin; others have a variety of berthing arrangements that could include cabins with single berths or bunk beds. Even if the kind of bed is not important to you, it is still a good idea to decide ahead of time (if berths are different) who gets which cabin.

Crew's quarters. On some yachts (usually smaller ones), the crew sleeps in the main salon. If so, you will still have full use of it, but it may be awkward. Crew members who sleep in the main salon will have to wait for that late-night card game to finish before going to bed, and if you get up to walk on deck at night, you will be walking through their bedroom. If you think this would be a problem for your group, specify separate crew's quarters.

Performance. This is something you may want to consider. If one of your major interests is the actual sailing, you will want a yacht with good sailing ability. Performance can also be important if you will be making long passages.

Air-conditioning. Most of the larger, more expensive yachts (and virtually all motor yachts) have air-conditioning. The question is whether you need it. Yachts are generally well designed to let the breeze circulate below. In most areas and seasons, this is all you really need. Remember, to turn it on (unless you are at dock), the generator must be on, and generators can be noisy.

Cockpit dining. Nearly all yachts have good-size dining areas on deck as well as down below. If being able to have dinner under the stars is one of your priorities, make sure yours is not one of the exceptions.

Tender. A "tender" is an auxiliary boat (usually called a dinghy) used to get back and forth from the beach, snorkeling and diving trips, and water sports. All charter yachts have one, but they vary in size and power. Having a large, fast tender is essential if you want to water ski, and it can be an advantage for making longer side trips.

Windsurfers. Most yachts have one. Yachts that carry a windsurfer usually have a crew member who can give instruction. If you are serious about learning to windsurf, check with your broker and make sure your choice has an instructor.

Scuba gear. Some yachts carry complete scuba diving gear (including compressors). Frequently, there is a separate "per dive" charge. Some only offer it for certified divers; others will teach novices. Scuba dives can be arranged at an extra cost—even if the yacht does not carry its own equipment—in most good diving areas.

Fishing tackle. Most yachts carry a limited supply of fishing gear. But remember, most of these are not primarily fishing vessels. Any fishing you do will probably be quite casual unless you charter a sportfisher or a yacht with sportfishing capability.

TV, VHS, movies. Some yachts carry video cameras and extensive collections of movie tapes. Movies might be of particular importance if you have children along.

Underwater camera. Many yachts carry simple underwater cameras that anyone can easily learn how to use. This is a small item but one that can add a lot of fun to exploring the reefs. If you decide one is "essential," and your yacht does not have one aboard, you can usually rent one for a slight additional charge.

Pets. A few yachts have pets aboard. You should ask about this if they might be a problem, such as if a member of your group has an allergy. You will not be able to bring your own pet unless the captain agrees to it ahead of time—something few captains will do.

Smoking. Most yacht captains allow smoking above deck but not below. Some do not allow it at all, and others allow it anywhere (unless it will bother nonsmoking guests). This will not be covered in the brochure, so ask your broker about the yacht's smoking policy if it is important to you.

All proper charter yachts have marine radios and full safety equipment. Virtually all have snorkeling equipment (in snorkeling areas), sun awnings, a barbecue grill, and a stereo tape player (bring your own tapes or use theirs). If any of these things are important to you, double-check them with your broker.

Some yachts carry water skis, jet skis, underwater scooters, a sailing dinghy, or all of them. Some yachts even have hot tubs. And a few of those $70,000-a-week jobs have a helicopter on the aft deck. The search for better toys continues.

Despite my glowing descriptions of the sybaritic pleasures of vacationing on your own floating resort, keep one important fact in mind: although these yachts are among the finest in the world, they are still boats. Only on the largest yachts will the accommodations equal those of a resort on land. You will have a comfortable cabin, but since space is limited, it will not be anywhere near as large as a resort room. Marine toilets can be cantankerous devices, and the showers frequently resemble a telephone booth in which you hold the receiver over your head to get wet. And it may be necessary to be a little conservative with water, electricity, ice, and privacy; the supplies of each can run low on all but the largest boats.

If you need the optimum in creature comforts to be happy, you should either charter a very large yacht or forget the whole idea. But if your sense of adventure is relatively intact, you will see these yacht characteristics as the minor inconveniences they are.

THE FINAL SELECTION

If after refining your yacht ideas with your broker, you find that one yacht in the brochures seems right for you, call and tell her that's your choice. Again, it does not matter if you received the brochure from a different broker; your broker can book it for you. She will give you some more information about it and its crew and probably offer her opinion—now that she knows you better—about the yacht's suitability for your group. If she does not raise any questions that could affect your decision, book it. You do not want to delay once your choice is made (see Booking the Yacht, below).

If none of the yachts seem quite right, discuss the features you consider essential or desirable with your broker and request additional brochures. With this new batch of brochures in hand, you should be able to find the one you want.

Usually the problem is one of choosing among several yachts that look great. When you narrow the choices down to two or three, call your broker and discuss them with her. She will be able to offer additional insights and information. If she has booked a particular yacht before, she may also have the comments of past guests to pass on to you.

Throughout this selection process, feel free to ask your broker any questions about the yacht or the crew, but do not expect her to have all the answers off the top of her head. With hundreds of yachts out there, it would be unrealistic to expect anyone to know everything about each of them *and* their crews. If she does not have the answer, she can probably get it.

A final thing to keep in mind: you might not want a yacht. Tandem or flotilla charters—where a larger group takes two or more yachts—have several advantages over one boat. One is versatility: with two or more yachts it is easy to split up the group, so people who want to pursue different activities during the day can do so and then rendezvous later at that night's anchorage. With sailing yachts, it is fun (if they are similar boats) to have races from one bay to the next. Separate yachts can also provide more privacy, and they will probably be cheaper. The per-person per-day rate for eight people on one yacht, for example, is usually higher (bigger yachts are more expensive) than for the same group on two four-person yachts.

CHARTER YACHT CREWS
You will spend a good deal of time talking to your broker about the crews. Matching you with the right crew is an important part of her job. Moderate-size yachts (under 60 feet) carrying less than six passengers will, in most cases, have a crew of two: the captain and the cook/first mate. If there are six guests, there will usually be a crew of three. The size of the crew goes up as the size of the yacht and the number of passengers increase; in general, the ratio remains one crew member for every two guests.

On most yachts, the relationship between guests and crew is fairly casual. Even on a yacht of 60 or 70 feet, the close contact makes excessive formality awkward. It is a little difficult to be formal when you're both sitting around the cockpit in your swimming suits after a snorkeling trip. Besides, the idea is to have a good time, and most people find that easier to do in a relaxed atmosphere. The degree of formality usually increases as the size of the yacht goes up, with the very largest yachts being quite formal.

There are as many kinds of crews as there are people, and the style and specialties of the crews on the yachts you are considering can be an important consideration. By "style" I mean who they are and how they run the boat—their personalities. "Specialties" could include anything from favorite pursuits or skills (scuba diving, fishing, sailing instruction, windsurfing, etc.) to special knowledge of a subject such as astronomy or marine biology. Your broker should be aware of these differences and help you select a yacht crew that matches your style and interests.

Style can be a bit subtler consideration. For example, I know the captain of a 68-foot sailing yacht who has strict rules governing his crew's conduct: proper uniform at all times, no unnecessary socializing with guests, and so on. This captain believes a certain formality should be maintained on a yacht. Another friend of mine—the captain of a 73-footer—is so laid back and relaxed that you wouldn't know he was the captain unless someone told you. His yacht has a well-deserved reputation for being the place to party, and the only rule he has for his crew is, "Have fun."

Both of these captains are very experienced, both are very competent, and their yachts are among the most popular in the Virgin Islands. A week on either yacht would be an unforgettable experience. They just have different styles, and, as a result, there would be differences in the two vacations. Your broker should be fully aware of these differences, and the first things she will tell you about a crew will probably have to do with their style.

Because of the large number of yachts chartering, there are a fairly large number of new crews each season. Assuming your broker has met the crew and has confidence in their professionalism, you should not reject a yacht just because it is the crew's first season. The enthusiasm that a first-year crew brings to their new business may well outweigh any lack of chartering experience. A lower price is also possible, because the new crew wants to build business.

A final note on the crew: they're human beings. Despite this, they have to be constantly "up" and on duty, ready to do whatever is necessary to ensure your comfort and happiness. No human being can do this full-time without occasionally being alone to recharge his batteries. Try to ignore crew members if they walk out to the bow alone or sneak off to their cabin for a few minutes. You might also take a walk ashore occasionally to give them—and you—some time alone. It will be appreciated and help keep the smiles on their faces.

YACHT PRICING

For uniformity's sake, nearly all yachts quote their prices based on a one-week cruise, but you can charter one for any length of time you want. Your fee is simply adjusted on a pro rata basis based on the number of nights you will be aboard. Most yachts do have a surcharge (usually 10 percent of the charter fee) for charters of five nights or less.

The charter fee is based on the number of people on board. Prices will be listed starting with a single couple and going up to the maximum that the yacht will accommodate. The price *per person* is invariably less for a particular yacht as the number of guests goes up. For example, a yacht might list prices of $6,000 for two, $6,900 for four, and $7,500 for six. This means that two people chartering that yacht would pay a per-person rate of $3,000, with four it would be down to $1,725, and for the maximum of six it would be $1,250. It is always more economical to charter a yacht whose maximum number of guests is the same number as your group's.

Usually, this is your goal: to book a boat for its maximum number of guests. A few boats advertise a price for groups larger than they can comfortably accommodate, but they are the exception. Unless saving money is your primary concern, avoid such "deals" by surveying the sleeping arrangements. On most yachts, each couple has a private cabin, but occasionally, cabins will have to be shared if the maximum number of guests are aboard.

As a rule, the larger the yacht, the more expensive it will be. "Larger" does not refer only to length, although that is what you will primarily be looking at. It means the actual room on board. Yachts of about the same length can have drastically different actual space aboard, depending on their type and design. Because of their design, motor yachts almost always have more room than conventional sailing yachts of the same length. Multihulled yachts (catamarans and trimarans) have tremendous beams for their length and are therefore larger than single-hulled vessels of the same length. Even among single-hulled sailing yachts, there is frequently a big difference in actual room because of differences in design and layout.

When comparing yacht prices, the old maxim "you get what you pay for" still applies, but not in every instance. There are simply too many variables for that to always be true. And the question really is a subjective one: is the price being asked for the yacht one you are willing to pay? As for the objective question of value ("Is the price being asked a fair one for that yacht?"), your broker can answer it for you.

CHARTER CONTRACTS

The charter fee your group pays will either be "all-inclusive" or "cost plus." All-inclusive means that everything—the yacht, the crew, full provisioning, fuel, and all onboard activities—is included in the charter fee. Wine and an open bar stocked to your specifications are included in the provisioning; the only separate charge you might have is if you make "extraordinary" requests (particularly expensive wines or liquors). If your charter fee is cost plus, you will be paying for certain expenses in addition to the initial charter fee. These can range from an additional charge for scuba diving (fairly common) to a "plus all" charter, where you pay separately for food and drink, fuel, and other incidentals. On a cost-plus charter, you may have to pay an estimate of costs up front and then either get a refund or pay an additional amount at the end of the charter based on the actual costs.

You will not generally get a choice as to which type of charter arrangement to use. It will depend on your choice of yacht (each yacht establishes its own pricing policy) and, to a certain extent, on the charter area. Most yachts in the Virgin Islands operate on an all-inclusive basis; those on the East Coast and the southern Caribbean are usually cost plus. Other areas vary, but cost plus is by far the most common. Motor yachts are nearly always cost plus.

Now, if you are suitably confused, the good news: as a practical matter, these different pricing schemes are not that important. All that is done on an all-inclusive yacht is to estimate the average expenses for a charter and add them to the base fee. The only difference to you is whether you pay an estimated amount for expenses up front or an actual amount by way of a bill at the end of the charter. Since the estimates are usually pretty accurate, the actual cost is going to be about the same regardless of payment method.

One clause that should be in every contract (regardless of where you charter) prohibits you from bringing any controlled substance not covered by prescription aboard the yacht. If you do, the charter will be terminated at the nearest port, and there will be no refund of charter fees. The captains are deadly serious about this. In U.S. waters, the "Zero Tolerance" drug enforcement program mandates the confiscation of the vessel if drugs (no matter how small an amount) are found aboard. Similar laws are in effect in most countries. No sensible captain is going to risk the loss of his yacht. Even if the clause is not in the contract, anyone found with drugs on board a charter yacht (this includes bareboats) can expect to be taken to the nearest dock and turned over to the police.

The rest of the charter contract is fairly straightforward. It will lay out the terms of payment, the amounts, the dates, and the charter area. The duties of the master (captain) will be described in terms such as "handle clearance and the normal running of the yacht and be responsible for the safe navigation of the vessel." If, as a result of some major catastrophe not caused by you, the vessel becomes "unfit for the use or purpose of the charter," the charter is terminated. There will also be a section dealing with "mechanical breakdowns" which allows you to cancel, with a pro rata refund, if the boat is not fixed within 24 hours. You agree to be responsible for any damage you cause.

You can start your trip on any day of the week you want. The charter usually begins at noon on the day you arrive and ends at noon the last day.

Booking the Yacht

After you have selected a yacht and the vacation dates, you will be required to pay, through your broker, a deposit of 50 percent of the charter fee to confirm the booking. Should you cancel the charter—for any reason—the deposit is forfeited. If the yacht is rebooked for any or all of the time period you had booked, a refund will be made based on the number of days that were rebooked. Some brokers offer "trip insurance" that will pay you the amount of the deposit if you have to cancel because of a death, illness, or injury in your group. The deposit will be refunded if for any reason the yacht becomes unfit for service or if you and the captain agree to cancel the booking.

Your deposit will be held in a trust fund and disbursed to the captain shortly before your arrival date. You will generally pay the balance of the charter fee directly to the captain, in cash or traveler's checks, at the time you board. In some areas, you will also have to make this final payment ahead of time.

Note that I said that the deposit was necessary to confirm the booking. This is important. Calling your broker and saying that you have made your decision is not enough. You must have the money there to confirm the booking. This is a policy established by the yachts, not your broker; your broker cannot make an exception to it. Remember, the yachts work on an open system. This means that there could be several brokers working on booking the same yacht for the time slot you want. And there is no way to find out if that's happening. Nothing is more disappointing than finally deciding which yacht to book, telling your broker, and then getting a call back that someone else booked it the day before your check arrived. The broker can confirm that the yacht is still available with a telephone call; if it is, get the money there as fast as possible. Many people use a wire transfer of funds to get instantaneous confirmation.

13 Getting Under Way

I once watched a big celebrity arrive at a hotel. The manager, his assistant, and a porter were standing out front to meet him and to assure his secretary that everything had been prepared to his specifications. I heard them say that the kitchen had been stocked according to his requirements and his personal bar had been furnished with his favorite brands of liquor. Arrangements had been made for some special services he had requested. The staff, I was later told, had been thinking of nothing else but his arrival for days. My arrival had been somewhat less auspicious.

Not used to having people go to this kind of trouble for your visit? Well, get ready. Long before you step aboard the yacht, the crew will have been hard at work making preparations. And after you arrive, they will continue to provide the same personal service. This is what makes a crewed charter yacht vacation so special: it is a custom vacation designed specially for you. You are the celebrity.

The Preference Sheet

In order for the crew to roll out the red carpet, they have to know what you want. This is done by way of a "preference sheet," an information form sent by your broker after you book the yacht. On it, you will answer a variety of questions designed to help the crew plan for your trip, and then your broker will pass it on to them. The preference sheet should be complete and accurately reflect the tastes of *all* the guests. If possible, try to get everybody together to fill it out (it's a good excuse for a party). At least let everybody see it and have the chance to make changes before sending it in. More problems result from incomplete or inaccurate preference sheets than from any other cause.

You will be asked to list everyone's name, age, citizenship, arrival time and flight, and hotel information. Make sure this is complete and accurate. Provide at least one daytime telephone number at home, even if it is not specifically requested. If there is some kind of delay or problem on either end (such as a delayed flight), the captain will use this information to track you down.

There will be a section asking for a general description of yourselves, any prior sailing or chartering experience you might have, and the activities you like most. This gives the crew some idea of who you are. It is easier to prepare for a group knowing something more about them than the name on the contract.

The most important questions concern food and drink preferences. This section will ask for your group's likes and dislikes regarding particular food (chicken, fish, pork, etc.), your general eating habits, and the soft drinks and liquors you prefer. You will only be giving a general description, not ordering specific breakfasts, lunches, and dinners for each day of the trip. Any allergies or special dietary requirements also go in this section.

The important thing about this is to understand that your statements on the preference sheet will be taken literally and believed. State your preferences as preferences; reserve the absolutes for when you really mean it. For instance, if you say you dislike chicken because you are thinking about the stuff that comes out of a fast-food restaurant, the cook's prize-winning Chicken Almondine will be taken off the menu. The more you say "no" to, the more you limit the variety of your menu and the cook's creativity.

The cook will try to plan meals that appeal to everyone in your group. This "please everybody" approach can cause difficulties if one person hates a dish that everybody else likes. If you put down that "one person doesn't like veal," the cook will probably just eliminate veal from that week's menu. The best solution is to ask if a substitution can be made for the person with that specific dislike. It is fairly easy for the cook to do this in many recipes. In addition, some adapting for kids can be done if the cook knows what to expect.

Try to be flexible concerning soft drink and liquor requests. Do not list a brand name unless it is really important to you. Most yachts stock the standard "house" brands, and although they will do everything possible to get specific requests, sometimes—particularly in the islands—that is not easy to do (remember, too, that you will be charged extra for extraordinary requests, even if your charter fee is all-inclusive). The wine section should contain a general statement of your preferences and whether you want it only with dinner or also during the day. An appropriate wine will be selected for each dinner. If you prefer Beaujolais, for instance, to other red wines, say so. If you like Riesling, mention it. But do not get too specific unless you really mean it.

Trip Planning

One of the nice things about a yacht vacation is that once your booking is confirmed and the preference sheet is completed, your planning is pretty much done. You will need to arrange transportation to the yacht and a few other matters, but basically, everything else will be taken care of. Just pack a few clothes, your camera, sunglasses, an ample supply of suntan lotion, and be on your way. Most, if not all, of the cruise itself will be planned after you get on board.

Ask your broker for clothing suggestions. Simple, comfortable clothes are the rule on most yachts. The only time you might need to "dress up" is for evenings ashore, but even this is rare in most chartering areas. In the Caribbean, you need very little in the way of clothes. Island life is pretty casual: all you really need are a couple of pairs of shorts, a couple of swimsuits, some casual shirts, two pairs of shoes (one suitable for getting wet on the beach), one pair of lightweight pants, a sweater or lightweight jacket, a hat, and your personal items. "Island formal" for men is a pair of long pants and a shirt with buttons on it; for women, a casual lightweight dress or a skirt (or long pants) and a top.

Avoid hard luggage (it has to be stowed on board) and pack light. You should be able to get everything you really need in an airline carryon bag. One of our charter guests arrived with no luggage at all; the airline had lost it on the trip down. Rather than delay the trip, the woman walked up to one of the marina shops, bought a few things, and stepped back aboard a half-hour later with a small shopping bag. For the entire week, she amazed us with the variety of her outfits, created by cleverly combining basic items in different ways. That little bag contained everything needed for a week aboard.

Staying at a hotel the night before your charter is a good idea, particularly if you are traveling a long distance. That way, you can start your adventure fresh instead of having to scurry straight from an airport to the dock. Any delays (a late arrival or lost luggage) will be of far less importance if you are staying at a hotel. Also, if your flight is not scheduled to arrive until late, you will not be losing the first afternoon aboard (remember, most charters start at noon). Consider staying at a hotel the day *after* the cruise, too. This gives you a chance to see some of the local land-based sights, do some shopping, and enjoy a smooth transition back to life ashore.

Prior to leaving home, you will have made arrangements, either through your broker or directly with the captain, as to where and when you will meet the yacht. Usually, this will be at a marina regularly used by the crew.

If you have any last-minute questions, call your broker. If she cannot answer them directly, she'll call the captain and either get the answers or have the captain call you. On many yachts, it is standard procedure for the captain or the first mate/cook to call the guests shortly before the charter to discuss final arrangements, answer any questions, and confirm the meeting time and place.

The Itinerary

When you charter a yacht, you become in many ways its surrogate owner. The captain is responsible for operating the yacht and for the passengers' safety, but virtually everything else is up to you. You will decide where to go, what to do, and when to do it. This does not mean you can immediately set sail for Tahiti, but as long as your requests are not too outrageous, they will be complied with.

Early on in your cruise, the captain will sit down with you and discuss the week's plans. He or she will show you a chart of the area, point out the major attractions and options, and ask what you are interested in doing. Any matters of boating safety or procedures that have not previously been mentioned will also be covered.

The purpose of this session is not to design a hard-and-fast schedule. Schedules are for people on cruise ships. You will be making some tentative plans that will form the basis for a rough itinerary. Usually, the only plans that have to be fairly firm (so the cook can plan meals) are the next day's.

It is a bad idea to plan an itinerary ahead of time. Wait until you get on board and can take advantage of the captain's expertise and suggestions. I had one group show up on *Esprit* with a typed schedule prepared by their broker (who was fairly new to the business) which was several pages long and showed our activities on an hourly basis for the entire charter. When I first saw it, I thought about penciling in something like, "Saturday: 1425 to 1430: Relax." But one has to be polite. The schedule was hectic beyond belief, completely unworkable (if *Esprit* had been a helicopter, we might have been able to stick to it), and quickly discarded. The only good purpose it served was giving the guests a few hearty laughs when, near the end of the charter, they happened to take another look at it.

If you've read about things in the area that you think you might like to see or do or if you've had friends who have been there tell you about places that "you just have to see," this is the time to bring them up. Your captain will probably be very familiar with them and able to pass on all kinds of information to help you decide if you want to include them in your plans for the cruise. This is also a good time to mention any special physical problems (or such things as lack of swimming ability) that might be important from a safety standpoint. One of my guests, who was practically blind at any distance over ten feet, lost the group while snorkeling and struck out at flank speed on a course toward Venezuela to catch up. I managed to intercept him, but a potentially bad situation could have been avoided if I had been told ahead of time about the problem.

The amount of sailing you do each day depends on the area, the speed of your boat, and how much you *want* to do. An average of three or four hours a day will let you see a great deal of most areas and still leave plenty of time for other activities. A sailing yacht, depending on its size and with good wind, will usually make from 5 to 10 mph. The speed of a motor yacht depends on its size, design, and power; it is not unusual for one to cruise at 20 mph or more.

Safety

Yacht vacations are extremely safe. Your boat will not sail off the edge of the earth or be attacked by a great white shark, and the only pirates are found in the gift shops. If you wear shoes when walking in the water and take proper precautions to avoid sunburn, your chances of injury are slight. If there are any hazards peculiar to your particular area or vessel, your captain will warn you about them.

Yacht vacations are also physically undemanding. Activities such as windsurfing can be fairly rigorous, but your participation in these is not required. If age or other factors seriously limit your mobility, choose a motor yacht or a larger sailing yacht. Smaller sailing yachts tend to be a little more difficult to get around on.

Seasickness is rarely a problem. Of the few who do initially experience it, nearly all get their "sea legs" within a short time. In five years of chartering, I can think of only a half-dozen times when anybody had a serious problem with it after the first day.

If you are particularly prone to motion sickness, talk to your doctor about getting a prescription for Transderm-scop (usually called "patches"). These are small medicated adhesive pads worn behind the ear to prevent motion sickness. You put one on the day before the trip and wear one continuously thereafter. Patches do have some side effects, and many doctors are reluctant to prescribe them except under extreme circumstances. If you plan to use patches, put one on several days before the charter to find out if they are going to bother you.

An over-the-counter remedy such as Dramamine or Bonine is generally effective for occasional use. A single dosage of Bonine (available generically as meclizine) lasts for twelve hours or more; Dramamine lasts for three or four. I recommend to guests on *Esprit* that they use no medication the first afternoon unless certain they are going to have a problem. In most cases, they are fine. If they do have difficulties, a Bonine taken that evening will usually settle things down, provide a good night's sleep, and take care of any problems for the next day and probably the rest of the cruise.

Activities

Frequently, people do not know how they'll want to spend their time until they try a few things. Some might become enchanted with snorkeling and want to plan the rest of the trip around going to the best diving spots; others might decide that sailing is for them or decide to spend most of their time lazing about in a quiet cove, playing with the yacht's toys and exploring ashore. No problem; there is no schedule. Generally speaking, the more flexible your plans, the better. Just relax and take each day as it comes.

SAILING

Sailing itself is the activity that sets this vacation apart from all others. Even on a motor yacht, the romance of the water and the feeling of freedom you get from being able to set your own course and schedule are exhilarating. On a sailing yacht, the exhilaration is even greater. There is no feeling quite like that you get on a clear, blue morning as the wind fills the sails and the yacht heels slightly, begins to pick up speed, and quietly leaves last night's anchorage behind.

On a sailing yacht, you also have the option of learning how to sail. A charter can be a great introduction to the sport; you can learn a lot in a week while still having a relaxing vacation. Tell the captain how much you want and how you want to handle it. If sailing instruction is one of the major reasons you are going on the trip, make sure your broker knows it. Obviously, all captains on sailing yachts can sail, but there are differences both in their experience and in how they feel about giving sailing instruction. Some enjoy teaching and are very good at it; others will do it if requested but would prefer to run the boat themselves and not to have the guests involved.

SNORKELING

Snorkeling is one of the most popular activities in tropical waters. There is something almost mystical about gliding silently above the extraordinary world of the coral reefs, watching its inhabitants—usually oblivious to you— going about their business. Forests of staghorn and elkhorn coral rise from the sand and cast strangely beautiful, flickering shadows on the smaller corals below. Fragile-looking plants, sea fans, and other soft corals wave gently with the ebb and flow of the water. Brightly colored fish constantly drift through this incredible scene: fairy basslets, angelfish, hamlets, butterflyfish, parrot-fish, wrasses, the ever-present and ever-curious sergeant major, the spectacular queen triggerfish, and many more. It is a panorama that many, including myself, never tire of.

Snorkeling is easy and safe. If you haven't done it before, a crew member will show you everything you need to know in one short lesson. Even if you cannot swim, you can still enjoy snorkeling, simply by wearing one of the yacht's life vests (swim fins make it easy to propel yourself). Few things on the reef could hurt you even if they wanted to (your captain will warn you about any "look but don't touch" things). There are a few varieties of coral that can cause a burnlike rash, but these are easy to identify and avoid. As I have

Snorkeling is fun, easy, and adds a whole new dimension to your charter yacht vacation.
(Photo by James Ulik)

mentioned, underwater cameras usually can be rented for a small extra
charge if your boat does not have one.

WINDSURFING

Windsurfing is not quite as easy as snorkeling, but if you have not tried it
before, you will never get a better opportunity to learn than on a crewed charter. The board is right there, the water is just a few feet away, and your instruction is readily available and already paid for.

No other sport or skill prepares one for learning to windsurf. It is just one
of those sports you have to *do* to learn. After spending hundreds of hours
with every type of windsurfing student imaginable, I have concluded that the
most important trait a person needs is tenacity. If you spend enough time on
the board and don't get discouraged, you will probably be sailing it reasonably well by the end of the week. Whatever your skill level, windsurfing can
be a real thrill.

FISHING

Fishing, either from the yacht while under way or at anchor, will be a major
part of your trip only if you choose an area and boat with that in mind. You
will usually be able to do some casual fishing, but most yachts are not set up

for serious fishing, nor are their owners interested in using them for that purpose. If fishing is important to you, make this known to your broker, and if you want big-league fishing, tell your broker you want a "sportfisher" or something very much like one. A sportfisher is a boat designed specifically for big game fishing. It will have all the necessary equipment—such as fighting chairs—and will seldom be found except in good sportfishing areas. Sportfishers available for week-long charters usually have all the amenities of yachts. You might also consider a yacht that has "sportfishing capability," meaning that it is not really a sportfisher but can serve as such.

On Shore

The kind of shore activities available depends on where you are chartering; most areas have places to take a walk, explore, or go shopping. St. Thomas has its famous duty-free port, for example, and Newport has dozens of quaint shops. In places, you will be able to anchor or dock your yacht right next to the major shoreside attractions and mingle with the land-based tourists.

When you go ashore, you will need to dig out that wallet you stowed away earlier. The charter fee covers all meals and activities on board, but, unless special arrangements have been made, any off-boat expenses are your responsibility.

Many chartering areas have unique restaurants that can be a fascinating experience. Your captain will be glad to offer suggestions and make all the arrangements, but remember that this shore leave will be at your expense, and no adjustment will be made to your charter fee (even if it was all-inclusive). If you want to invite the crew along, feel free to do so. They will probably be delighted to have a night off, and they will definitely appreciate the offer.

All popular chartering areas have a variety of safe, comfortable overnight anchorages, ranging from small secluded coves to large bays dotted with dozens of other boats. You will spend most nights at anchor rather than going to a dock. Sometimes you will be anchoring off towns or villages, with the lights ashore supplying the backdrop for your evening. Often, the shore of your anchorage will be uninhabited, with other yachts as your only neighbors. Regardless, you can look forward to that most popular of all charter activities—relaxing as the sunset fades and the yacht becomes your own private world.

Sources for Further Information

Some of the best sources for current information on chartering are the major boating magazines. Buy a copy of one of them and browse through the advertisements for charter brokers. Having an advertisement in one of these magazines does not guarantee that a brokerage is staffed with experts, but it does mean they are serious enough about their business (and probably doing well enough in it) to afford a fairly expensive advertisement. This is also a good way to get more information about the brokers listed in chapter 14.

Cruising World, Sail, and *Yachting* usually have the most information on chartering. Each also has a special fall issue devoted to chartering, which will have more broker advertisements than usual, articles on chartering, and also individual boat advertisements. These popular magazines are available at most well-stocked magazine stands. Or write:

Cruising World
524 Thames St.
Newport, RI 02840
401-847-1588

Sail
Charlestown Navy Yard
100 First Ave.
Charlestown, MA 02129
617-241-9500

Yachting
2 Park Ave.
New York, NY 10016
212-779-5000

Yacht Vacations is a magazine strictly about chartering. Because of its smaller circulation and narrower focus, you probably will not find it on the stands.

Yacht Vacations
P.O. Box 1657
Palm Harbor, FL 34628
813-785-3101

The Virgin Islands Charteryacht League is the largest organization of professional yacht captains in the world. They will send you a free information package on chartering in the Virgin Islands at your request. This package includes a catalog with the pictures and descriptions of some of their member yachts.

Virgin Islands Charteryacht League
The Flagship
St. Thomas, USVI 00802
800-524-2061

The local tourism office or chamber of commerce at your charter destination can be a source of good information, both with regard to chartering and the area in general.

14 Directory of Crewed Charter Yacht Brokers

S ince this directory deals with brokers who can book charters in any area (rather than individual companies at particular locations), the listing is simply alphabetical by company name. It should be easy to find brokers in a particular area because this list is short.

Each year, the Virgin Islands Charteryacht League hosts a show of its members' yachts. This nine-day event is the biggest charter yacht show in the world and is attended by crewed charter yacht brokers from around the world. Of the 130 or so brokers attending each year, about a third are designated by the league—based on the broker's professional experience and performance—as "Honored Guests." This directory, with a few additions of my own, is the list of Honored Guests who attended the show at the start of the 1989 season.

Since the Virgin Islands is the most active chartering area in the world, most professional brokers attend this show each year. This directory, therefore, contains virtually every professional broker booking charters in North America.

Crewed Charter Yacht Brokers

Avery's Boathouse
P.O. Box 5248
St. Thomas,
Virgin Islands 00803
809-776-0113

Blue Water Cruises
P.O. Box 758
St. Thomas,
Virgin Islands 00801
800-776-2029
800-524-2020

Blue Water Yacht Charters
2500 Westlake Ave. N.
Seattle, WA 98109
206-286-3618
800-732-7245

Boat/U.S. Travel
890 S. Pickett St.
Alexandria, VA 2230
703-651-6456
800-262-8872

Brayne Charters
3808 W. 57th St.
Edina, MN 55410
612-920-4867

Camper & Nicholsons
31 Berkeley St.
Mayfair Ltd.
London, UK W1X 5FA
01-491-2950

Caribbean Adventures
Yacht Charters
P.O. Box 9997
St. Thomas,
Virgin Islands 00801
809-776-7245

Caribbean Sailing Charters
3883 Andrews Crossing
Roswell, GA 30075
404-641-9640
800-824-1331

Caribbean Yacht Cruises
7310 Blanco Road
San Antonio, TX 78216
512-340-4444
800-982-4000

Comsail Yacht Charters
Red Hook, Box 32
St. Thomas,
Virgin Islands 00802
809-776-3382
800-522-3085

Crewed Charters
6 Long Bay Road
St. Thomas,
Virgin Islands 00802
809-776-4811

Easy Adventures
The Anchorage
Est. Nazareth, Rt. 6
St. Thomas,
Virgin Islands 00802
809-775-7870
800-524-2027

Ed Hamilton, Inc.
Box 430
N. Whitefield, ME 04353
207-549-7855

Fairwind Yacht Charters
P.O. Box 7332
St. Thomas,
Virgin Islands 00801
809-776-3650
800-524-2028

Fraser Yacht Charters
2353 Shelter Island Dr.
San Diego, CA 92106
619-225-0588

Fraser Yacht Charters
3471 Via Lido
Suite 202A
Newport Beach, CA 92663
714-675-6960

Global Yacht Vacations
P.O. Box 814786
Irving, TX 75062
214-869-9055

International Charter Association
278 Glenneyre, #127
Laguna Beach, CA 92651
714-494-3411

Jody Lexow Yacht Charters
5 Brook St.
Darien, CT 06820
203-655-8668
800-662-2628

Jubilee Yacht Charters
P.O. Box 1637
Darien, CT 06820
203-966-1868

Judy Whitney, Inc.
P.O. Box 1721
Englewood Cliffs, NJ 07632
201-592-0100
800-227-0791

Kathy Fay Yacht Charters
1550 S.E. 17th St.
Ft. Lauderdale, FL 33316
305-467-8876

Kiko Toro, Inc.
2165 General del Valle
Santurce, Puerto Rico 00916
809-726-1870

Lynhollen Yacht Charters
601 University Ave.
Suite 150
Sacramento, CA 95825
916-920-0820

Lynn Jachney Charters
P.O. Box 302
Marblehead, MA 01945
617-639-0787
800-223-2050

Nicholson Yacht Charters
432 Columbia St.
21A
Cambridge, MA 02141
617-661-8174
800-662-6066

Ocean Escapes
P.O. Box 6009
Newburyport, MA 01950
508-465-7116
800-227-863

Preferred Yachting Vacations
4544 Post Oak Place
Suite 112
Houston, TX 77027
713-622-7245
800-999-2248

Regency International Yacht Charters
Long Bay Road
P.O. Box 997
St. Thomas,
Virgin Islands 00802
809-776-5950
800-524-7676

Regency Yacht Vacations
Mariner's Marina
13605 Fiji Way
Marina del Rey, CA 90292
213-823-6669

Ricci Davis, Inc.
1323 S.E. 17th St.
Suite 209
Ft. Lauderdale, FL 33316
305-761-3237

Richard Heath & Associates
9744 Wilshire Blvd.
#200
Beverly Hills, CA 90212
213-275-1194

Russell Yacht Charters
2750 Black Rock Turnpike
Fairfield, CT 06430
203-372-6633

Sailaway Yacht Charter Consultants
P.O. Box 016933
Miami, FL 33101
305-757-5115

Sparkman & Stephens
79 Madison Ave.
Suite 1207
New York, NY 10016
212-689-9292

Tom Collins Yacht Charter Service
400 S. Hibiscus Dr.
Miami Beach, FL 33139
305-255-2222

Virgin Island Sailing Ltd.
P.O. Box 146
Road Town
Tortola,
British Virgin Islands
809-494-2774
800-624-1839

Whitney Yacht Charters
2209 North Halsted
Chicago, IL 60614
312-929-8989
800-223-1426

Windward Leeward Yacht Charters
1212 A Union St.
San Francisco, CA 94109
415-441-1334
800-922-4874

Windward Mark
P.O. Box 307
Camden, ME 04843
207-236-4300
800-633-7900

Yacht Vacations Worldwide
Upper Havensight Mall
St. Thomas,
Virgin Islands 00802
809-776-1666
800-524-5008

Index

Other Books from John Muir Publications

Asia Through the Back Door, Rick Steves and John Gottberg (65-48-3) 336 pp. $15.95

Buddhist America: Centers, Retreats, Practices, Don Morreale (28-94-X) 400 pp. $12.95

Bus Touring: Charter Vacations, U.S.A., Stuart Warren with Douglas Bloch (28-95-8) 168 pp. $9.95

Catholic America: Self-Renewal Centers and Retreats, Patricia Christian-Meyer (65-20-3) 325 pp. $13.95

Complete Guide to Bed & Breakfasts, Inns & Guesthouses, Pamela Lanier (65-43-2) 512 pp. $15.95

Costa Rica: A Natural Destination, Ree Sheck (65-51-3) 280 pp. $15.95

Elderhostels: The Students' Choice, Mildred Hyman (65-28-9) 224 pp. $12.95

Europe 101: History & Art for the Traveler, Rick Steves and Gene Openshaw (28-78-8) 372 pp. $12.95

Europe Through the Back Door, Rick Steves (65-42-4) 432 pp. $16.95

Floating Vacations: River, Lake, and Ocean Adventures, Michael White (65-32-7) 256 pp. $17.95

Gypsying After 40: A Guide to Adventure and Self-Discovery, Bob Harris (28-71-0) 264 pp. $12.95

The Heart of Jerusalem, Arlynn Nellhaus (28-79-6) 312 pp. $12.95

Indian America: A Traveler's Companion, Eagle/Walking Turtle (65-29-7) 424 pp. $16.95

Mona Winks: Self-Guided Tours of Europe's Top Museums, Rick Steves (28-85-0) 450 pp. $14.95

The On and Off the Road Cookbook, Carl Franz (28-27-3) 272 pp. $8.50

The People's Guide to Mexico, Carl Franz (28-99-0) 608 pp. $15.95

The People's Guide to RV Camping in Mexico, Carl Franz with Steve Rogers (28-91-5) 256 pp. $13.95

Preconception: A Woman's Guide to Preparing for Pregnancy and Parenthood, Brenda Aikey-Keller (65-44-0) 236 pp. $14.95

Ranch Vacations: The Complete Guide to Guest and Resort, Fly-Fishing, and Cross-Country Skiing Ranches, Eugene Kilgore (65-30-0) 392 pp. $18.95

The Shopper's Guide to Mexico, Steve Rogers and Tina Rosa (28-90-7) 224 pp. $9.95

Ski Tech's Guide to Equipment, Skiwear, and Accessories, edited by Bill Tanler (65-45-9) 144 pp. $11.95

Ski Tech's Guide to Maintenance and Repair, edited by Bill Tanler (65-46-7) 144 pp. $11.95

A Traveler's Guide to Asian Culture, Kevin Chambers (65-14-9) 224 pp. $13.95

Traveler's Guide to Healing Centers and Retreats in North America, Martine Rudee and Jonathan Blease (65-15-7) 240 pp. $11.95

Undiscovered Islands of the Caribbean, Burl Willes (28-80-X) 216 pp. $12.95

22 Days Series
These pocket-size itineraries are a refreshing departure from ordinary guidebooks. Each author has an in-depth knowledge of the region covered and offers 22 tested daily itineraries through their favorite destinations. Included are not only "must see" attractions but also little-known villages and hidden "jewels" as well as valuable general information.

22 Days Around the World by R. Rapoport and B. Willes (65-31-9)
22 Days in Alaska by Pamela Lanier (28-68-0)
22 Days in the American Southwest by R. Harris (28-88-5)
22 Days in Asia by R. Rapoport and B. Willes (65-17-3)
22 Days in Australia by John Gottberg (65-40-8)
22 Days in California by Roger Rapoport (28-93-1)
22 Days in China by Gaylon Duke and Zenia Victor (28-72-9)
22 Days in Dixie by Richard Polese (65-18-1)
22 Days in Europe by Rick Steves (65-63-7)
22 Days in Florida by Richard Harris (65-27-0)
22 Days in France by Rick Steves (65-07-6)
22 Days in Germany, Austria & Switzerland by Rick Steves (65-39-4)

22 Days in Great Britain by Rick Steves (65-38-6)
22 Days in Hawaii by Arnold Schuchter (65-50-5)
22 Days in India by Anurag Mathur (28-87-7)
22 Days in Japan by David Old (28-73-7)
22 Days in Mexico by S. Rogers and T. Rosa (65-41-6)
22 Days in New England by Anne Wright (28-96-6)
22 Days in New Zealand by Arnold Schuchter (28-86-9)
22 Days in Norway, Denmark & Sweden by R. Steves (28-83-4)
22 Days in the Pacific Northwest by R. Harris (28-97-4)
22 Days in Spain & Portugal by Rick Steves (65-06-8)
22 Days in the West Indies by C. & S. Morreale (28-74-5)

All 22 Days titles are 128 to 152 pages and $7.95 each, except *22 Days Around the World* and *22 Days in Europe*, which are 192 pages and $9.95.

"Kidding Around"
Travel Guides for Children
Written for kids eight years of age and older. Generously illustrated in two colors with imaginative characters and images. An adventure to read and a treasure to keep.

Kidding Around Atlanta, Anne Pedersen (65-35-1) 64 pp. $9.95
Kidding Around Boston, Helen Byers (65-36-X) 64 pp. $9.95
Kidding Around the Hawaiian Islands, Sarah Lovett (65-37-8) 64 pp. $9.95
Kidding Around London, Sarah Lovett (65-24-6) 64 pp. $9.95
Kidding Around Los Angeles, Judy Cash (65-34-3) 64 pp. $9.95

Kidding Around New York City, Sarah Lovett (65-33-5) 64 pp. $9.95
Kidding Around San Francisco, Rosemary Zibart (65-23-8) 64 pp. $9.95
Kidding Around Washington, D.C., Anne Pedersen (65-25-4) 64 pp. $9.95

Automotive Books

The Greaseless Guide to Car Care Confidence: Take the Terror Out of Talking to Your Mechanic, Mary Jackson (65-19-X) 224 pp. $14.95
How to Keep Your VW Alive (65-12-2) 424 pp. $19.95
How to Keep Your Subaru Alive (65-11-4) 480 pp. $19.95
How to Keep Your Toyota Pickup Alive (28-89-3) 392 pp. $19.95
How to Keep Your Datsun/Nissan Alive (28-65-6) 544 pp. $19.95
Off-Road Emergency Repair & Survival, James Ristow (65-26-2) 160 pp. $9.95
Road & Track's Used Car Classics, edited by Peter Bohr (28-69-9) 272 pp. $12.95

Ordering Information
If you cannot find our books in your local bookstore, you can order directly from us. Your books will be sent to you via UPS (for U.S. destinations), and you will receive them approximately 10 days from the time that we receive your order. Include $2.75 for the first item ordered and $.50 for each additional item to cover shipping and handling costs. UPS will not deliver to a P.O. Box; please give us a street address. For airmail within the U.S., enclose $4.00 per book for shipping and handling. All foreign orders will be shipped surface rate; please enclose $3.00 for the first item and $1.00 for each additional item. Please inquire about foreign airmail rates.

Method of Payment
Your order may be paid by check, money order, or credit card. We cannot be responsible for cash sent through the mail. All payments must be made in U.S. dollars drawn on a U.S. bank. Canadian postal money orders in U.S. dollars are also acceptable. For VISA, MasterCard, or American Express orders, include your card number, expiration date, and your signature, or call (505)982-4078. Books ordered on American Express cards can be shipped only to the billing address of the cardholder. Sorry, no C.O.D.'s. Residents of sunny New Mexico, add 5.625% tax to the total.

Address all orders and inquiries to:
John Muir Publications
P.O. Box 613
Santa Fe, NM 87504
(505) 982-4078
(505) 988-1680 FAX